JOH FOR PM

PAUL DAVEY is a former journalist and was National Party federal director for nearly ten years – including during the Joh for PM campaign – and the New South Wales party's general secretary for more than three. He also worked as a senior staffer for party ministers in Canberra and Sydney. He is the author of: *The Nationals: The Progressive, Country and National Party in New South Wales 1919 to 2006*; *Politics in the Blood: The Anthonys of Richmond*; *Ninety Not Out: The Nationals 1920–2010*; and *The Country Party Prime Ministers: Their Trials and Tribulations*.

JOH FOR PM

THE INSIDE STORY OF AN EXTRAORDINARY POLITICAL DRAMA

PAUL DAVEY

NEWSOUTH

A **NewSouth** book

Published by
NewSouth Publishing
University of New South Wales Press Ltd
University of New South Wales
Sydney NSW 2052
AUSTRALIA
newsouthpublishing.com

© Paul Davey 2015
First published 2015

10 9 8 7 6 5 4 3 2 1

This book is copyright. Apart from any fair dealing for the purpose of private study, research, criticism or review, as permitted under the Copyright Act, no part of this book may be reproduced by any process without written permission. Inquiries should be addressed to the publisher.

National Library of Australia Cataloguing-in-Publication entry
Creator: Davey, Paul, author.
Title: Joh for PM: the inside story of an extraordinary political drama/Paul Davey.
ISBN: 9781742234335 (paperback)
 9781742247298 (ebook: pdf)
 9781742242002 (ebook: epub)
Subjects: Bjelke-Petersen, Joh, Sir, 1911–2005.
 National Party of Australia – Queensland.
 Political leadership – Queensland.
 Political leadership – Australia.
 Queensland – Politics and government.
 Australia – Politics and government.
Dewey Number: 324.2943

Design Josephine Pajor-Markus
Cover design Xou Creative
Cover image Fairfax Syndication
Printer Griffin

All reasonable efforts were taken to obtain permission to use copyright material reproduced in this book, but in some cases copyright could not be traced. The author welcomes information in this regard.

This book is printed on paper using fibre supplied from plantation or sustainably managed forests.

CONTENTS

Prologue		1
1	Prelude to conflict	7
2	Not always plain sailing	19
3	The Joh campaign hits the road	31
4	Turning a skirmish into a war	45
5	Tactics and numbers	57
6	A Queensland backdown?	71
7	Confusion	88
8	The Coalition breaks	101
9	The indiscretions of Ian Cameron	118
10	An early election looms	127
11	Two memorable events	142
12	Sinclair delivers the policy	155
13	The irritation of Joh Independents	168
14	The recriminations fly	174
15	Back towards Coalition	185
16	A Queensland no show	190

17	The Coalition re-forms	196
18	Once more unto the breach …	210
19	Flames flare in Queensland	216
20	Let's have a committee!	227
21	The eye of the storm	239
22	Joh's last campaign	252
23	Nixon does his job	265

Epilogue	273
Acknowledgements	278
Page Research Centre Limited	280
Notes	281
Select bibliography and further reading	293
Index	296

PROLOGUE

> The reason I'm standing for federal parliament is because I'm standing to be the next prime minister of Australia.
>
> Clive Palmer, ABC Television *Lateline*, 26 April 2013

Australians went to the polls on 7 September 2013 and comprehensively rejected the incumbent federal Labor government, delivering 90 House of Representatives seats to the Coalition and only 55 to Labor. The Liberal Party's Tony Abbott and the National Party's Warren Truss became prime minister and deputy prime minister respectively.

The election ended six years of Labor administration under Kevin Rudd, Julia Gillard and then Rudd again. It was a messy time for Labor and not only because of leadership tensions and changes. Labor had held office since the 2010 election, thanks only to the support of a clutch of Independents in the lower house and the Greens in the Senate.

There was a sting in the 2013 result for the new Abbott–Truss government. Despite its comprehensive majority in the House of Representatives, it was unable to win a majority in the Senate, thanks in part to a Queensland businessman, Clive Palmer. Palmer declared in April 2013 that he was forming a political party and would become prime minister. It brought back jarring memories of events 26 years earlier – Joh for PM, when the then Queensland National Party Premier, Joh Bjelke-Petersen, embarked on a similar crusade.

Palmer formed the Palmer United Party (PUP) and, in terms of winning parliamentary representation, was more successful than Bjelke-Petersen. No Joh candidates won seats, whereas Palmer marginally won the Queensland seat of Fairfax and three PUP senators were elected, one in each of Queensland, Tasmania and Western Australia. For a short time from 1 July 2014, when the new Senate was sworn in, until 24 November 2014, when the Tasmanian senator, Jacqui Lambie, quit the PUP to sit as an Independent, Palmer's party held the balance of power. Its harmony further crumbled when its Senate leader, the former National Rugby League star, Glenn Lazarus, from Queensland, announced he was also leaving the party to sit as an Independent from 13 March 2015.

I had been the federal director of the National Party of Australia, also referred to as the Nationals and formerly the National Country Party of Australia and Australian Country Party, throughout the turbulent time of the 1987 Joh campaign, undoubtedly the most difficult period in the party's history. It deeply divided the party at all state and federal levels, and it caused a brief end to the federal Coalition in Opposition between the National and Liberal parties in Canberra. It still reverberated in my mind as the hardest time of my professional association with the party, which spanned more than 20 years.

The Joh campaign was made harder because the National Party truly is a 'family'. Everyone knows everyone. There is a strong sense of camaraderie and unity of purpose. I had known the Queensland premier and the party's state president, Robert Sparkes, since I was the ABC's Brisbane reporter for its *AM* and *PM* radio current affairs programs between 1974 and 1977. When I was transferred to the Canberra press gallery, Bjelke-Petersen presented me with a velvet-lined cufflink box, made from Queensland cedar with the state Coat of Arms, in pewter, on the lid. I still remember the premier quipping: 'I don't know why anyone would want to go down there!' I still have the box.

As director of the party's federal secretariat in Canberra, a position I took over early in 1984, I was deeply involved in meetings at the highest levels of the party – the ruling body, federal council, and its executive, federal management committee. I was not a voting delegate to these meetings, but attended them all. I drafted agendas, in consultation with the party's federal president and the parliamentary leader. I provided any necessary background briefing papers, speaking notes and other advice as required, notably on issues relating to the federal party constitution.

There was no question in my mind as to where my responsibilities lay. A former leader, deputy prime minister and prime minister, John McEwen, instigated the establishment of the federal secretariat in the mid-1960s, and it was opened by the Prime Minister, John Gorton, on 4 November 1968. McEwen's rationale was that such a facility could provide additional research, advice and support to the federal leader and the parliamentary party, independent of the Liberal Party, especially in times of Opposition, when unrestricted access to the Commonwealth public service was heavily curtailed. The secretariat could similarly support the activities of the party's federal president, organise meetings of federal council and the federal management committee, and develop advertising and other strategies for the federal leader's election campaigns.

My job was therefore to work with the federal leader and the federal president. If conflict arose between the federal organisation and any of the independent state party organisations, which was generally infrequent and not of a very serious nature, I would provide advice on finding solutions that would preserve the integrity of the federal parliamentary party and organisation. This remained the case when the Joh for PM campaign was unveiled, and it strained some long-standing relationships.

There were some similarities between the Bjelke-Petersen and Palmer campaigns. Palmer had been a strong supporter of the Queensland National Party, almost a fellow traveller with Bjelke-Petersen. Neither Joh nor Palmer was a member of the Commonwealth parliament when they made their bid to become prime minister. Joh, however, was a parliamentarian and, as Premier of Queensland, was the stand-out non-Labor leader in Australia in the early to mid-1980s. Palmer, not a member of any parliament, enjoyed a relatively high public profile, especially in Queensland, as a result of his business interests, his stated wealth and his sometimes quirky ambitions, for instance, to build a replica of the RMS *Titanic*. Joh was also able to think big. In the mid-1970s, he and the Western Australian mining magnate, Lang Hancock, dreamed of building a northern Australia railway linking the West's iron ore mines with Queensland's northern coal fields and establishing twin steel mills in both states.[1]

Joh and Palmer were both disillusioned with the Labor government of the day in Canberra and with the Coalition Opposition. Palmer was also disillusioned with the Liberal National Party (LNP) government of Campbell Newman in Queensland. The LNP had been formed by a merger of the Queensland National and Liberal parties on 26 July 2008. Palmer had fallen out with Newman and the party to the extent where he returned his life membership in November 2012 and quit the party. Previously, he had been arguably its biggest financial supporter.

Joh and Palmer were also not averse to publicity – 'feeding the chooks' of the media, as Bjelke-Petersen described it. They both adhered to the philosophy that there's no such thing as bad publicity.

Beyond these similarities, however, there were fundamental differences. The core strategy of the Joh campaign was to tackle Canberra from within the existing political party framework.

Using the federal and state National Party organisations as his spearhead, Joh intended to drag sitting federal National and Liberal parliamentarians into his campaign, thereby, together with other endorsed candidates supporting his cause, smashing the traditional non-Labor parties and effectively setting up a new conservative movement. Palmer ignored the party status quo and set up his own political organisation. Therefore, while the Joh campaign seriously fractured the National Party, the Palmer campaign ran independently.

The Joh and Palmer campaigns were acts of audacious brinkmanship. The National Party has not been averse to such tactics since its inception as a federal party in January 1920. As the smaller non-Labor party in national politics, it has sometimes had to flex its muscles to reinforce its relevance and reason for being.

One Country Party leader, Earle Page, forced the resignation of the then Nationalist leader, Billy Hughes, in 1922, enabling him to negotiate a Coalition government with Hughes's successor, Stanley Bruce. Page was not so successful in his second attempt to influence the senior Coalition party's leadership. After the death of the Prime Minister, Joe Lyons, in 1939, he warned the then United Australia Party (UAP) that he would withdraw the Country Party from the government if it replaced Lyons with Robert Menzies. The UAP ignored him. In taking the Country Party out of Coalition, Page questioned Menzies' suitability to lead the country when the world was again on the brink of war, noting that Menzies had not served in the Australian Imperial Force in World War I. The attack split the parliamentary Country Party and ultimately ended Page's leadership.

Another Country Party leader, John McEwen, was more successful 28 years later when he told the UAP's successor, the Liberal Party, that he would not serve in a continuing Coalition government if the Liberals chose Bill McMahon to replace the

Prime Minister, Harold Holt, who had disappeared in the surf off Cheviot Beach, Victoria, in December 1967. The Liberals heeded the warning and selected John Gorton instead, and the Coalition was maintained.

The big difference between these acts of brinkmanship and that of Joh for PM was that they were all contained within the federal parliamentary parties concerned. Moreover, on each of the three occasions, the parliamentary Country Party supported the tactical position of its leader, even though some were appalled by Page's attack on Menzies. The Joh campaign, on the other hand, came from outside – from a nationally recognised state political leader on the federal conservative parties that he would ordinarily be expected to support. Palmer's brinkmanship was based on thumbing his nose at the established parties and setting up his own organisation.

From the federal National Party leadership point of view, at both parliamentary and organisational levels, the Joh campaign was utterly unsupportable. It was a direct attack on the autonomy of the federal parliamentary party, and it threatened to usurp the right of the state National parties, which operated under their own constitutions, to preselect their candidates, with Joh saying that, where necessary, he would install his candidates in electorates across Australia, including those held by the National Party. To all intents and purposes, the Queensland Premier and many in the hierarchy of the Queensland National Party, as well as anyone else supporting the Joh campaign, became direct political opponents of the federal party establishment and those who supported it, notably the National Party in New South Wales. The scene was set for a bitter trench warfare, the ramifications of which would last the best part of a decade.

1
PRELUDE TO CONFLICT

> They'll [Coalition leaders] work with the policies I set or
> I will work against them, and I've told them that.
>
> Joh Bjelke-Petersen, *The Australian*, 3 November 1986

There had long been competitive tension between the Queensland and federal National parties, but they took a new direction following the election of the Malcolm Fraser – Doug Anthony Coalition government in December 1975.

The Queensland Premier, Joh Bjelke-Petersen, had been a prime mover in getting rid of the Whitlam Labor government. He campaigned long and hard across Australia, warning of the perils of socialism and the way Whitlam had been wrecking the nation since his election in 1972. He used every tactic in the book to undermine Whitlam, the most memorable being to send Albert Field to the Senate to replace Bertie Milliner, the Australian Labor Party (ALP) Queensland senator who died on 30 June 1975, creating a casual Senate vacancy.

Under normal convention in such circumstances, the vacancy would be filled by a member of the same political party, nominated by that party and accepted by the state parliament concerned. On this occasion Bjelke-Petersen refused to accept

Labor's nomination, Mal Colston. Initially, he insisted the Labor Party put forward three names, from which the state parliament would select one. Labor refused. Out of the blue, Joh produced Field, a French-polisher, member of the ALP for more than 30 years, and Queensland president of the Federated Furnishing Trade Society of Australasia. More important, Field was disillusioned with Whitlam, something that was vital to the Coalition in a Senate where the numbers were finely balanced. It put a whole new perspective on the prospect of blocking supply – budget bills that were essential to the government being able to pay its public service.

When Bjelke-Petersen announced Field's nomination to the Queensland parliament on 3 September 1975, there was pandemonium. Labor leader, Tom Burns, declared that any person nominated as a Labor alternative would cease to be a member of the ALP, and branded Field a renegade and impostor. It made no difference: Joh's National Party–dominated Coalition had the numbers in the single-house parliament – there is no Legislative Council in Queensland – to ensure the result. Field took up his Senate seat, formally holding it as an Independent until 11 November 1975, despite a High Court challenge to his right to do so.[1]

The affair was seen as a monumental dirty trick by Bjelke-Petersen – one that went against convention, protocol and decency. Nonetheless, the premier pulled it off and gave Fraser the opportunity he needed to force an election. The incident demonstrated the lengths to which Bjelke-Petersen was prepared to go in playing the political game.

He did not stop with Field. He dabbled in the Khemlani loans affair – a dubious attempt by federal Labor to use a self-proclaimed international financier, Tirath Khemlani, to raise billions in Middle Eastern petrodollars to finance the development of Australia's resource industry infrastructure. Bjelke-

Petersen enlisted the services of an American, Wiley Fancher, who lived on the Atherton Tablelands in far north Queensland, as a trouble-shooter charged with getting to the bottom of the affair. Fancher never achieved that aim, but he, and more particularly Bjelke-Petersen, did help keep the pressure on a rapidly waning Whitlam administration.

It was these efforts as much as anything else that made Bjelke-Petersen believe he would have significant influence on the policy implementation of a future federal Coalition government. After the Coalition's resounding victory on 13 December 1975, at which Labor was reduced from 66 to 36 seats in the 127-seat House of Representatives, he was confident relations with Canberra would rapidly improve. After all, Fraser and Anthony had been elected with a massive majority, including control of the Senate, on a platform full of policies to wash away the socialism Whitlam had imposed on the country in three short years. Not the least of their commitments were those to crack down on trade unions and irresponsible strikes, especially in the export industries, and get off the backs of the states by handing back to them greater responsibility, power and independence.

Bjelke-Petersen believed Fraser and Anthony never implemented those, or many other commitments. To his horror, he found the federal government meddling even more in his own state's affairs. It intervened to block sand mining on Fraser Island, and it interfered with Queensland's administration of Aboriginal and Torres Strait Island lands, notably at Aurukun on Cape York in 1978–79. Far from improving relations, Fraser and Anthony were an interfering nuisance.[2] On top of this, the prime minister began supporting such 'trendy' ideas as human rights and equal opportunity, industrial democracy and freedom of information. And he brought in retrospective tax laws.

§

Bjelke-Petersen shed few tears when the Fraser–Anthony government was beaten by Labor under Bob Hawke at the polls on 5 March 1983, and he remained unimpressed with the Coalition Opposition, led by Fraser's Industry minister, Andrew Peacock, and Doug Anthony, until the latter's resignation from parliament in January 1984. Anthony's successor as National Party leader was his former deputy and Fraser minister, Ian Sinclair. Joh saw the Opposition as still being under the control of men from the failed Fraser era. He was not alone in this view. A senior member of the Queensland National Party executive and future state party president and federal president, David Russell, a Queen's Counsel, in recordings in December 2011 for the *Queensland Speaks* project of the Centre for the Government of Queensland, said there was an 'enormous sense' in the Queensland party organisation that the Fraser government 'had been a catastrophe'. Moreover, Russell said the Queensland party 'had no respect whatever for Ian Sinclair' for various reasons. One was that neither he nor the other major state National parties, New South Wales and Victoria, had any interest in being anything *other* than a junior country party, while the Queensland Nationals had no interest in being *just* a country party: 'The Queensland Nationals were so totally different from the rest of the Nats, it just wasn't funny.'[3]

Interestingly, given events that unfolded over the coming three years, no-one from the Queensland National Party had anything to say when Anthony retired from parliament after a career of more than 26 years, 13 of which were as the party's federal leader: 'When I resigned from parliament, I never heard one word from the Queensland organisation. I never got one note of recognition from them. New South Wales, Victoria, even Western Australia, sent messages of best wishes and sorry to see me go, but nothing from Queensland.'[4]

Joh used the advent of the new Hawke Labor government

Prelude to conflict

to his political advantage, berating it at every opportunity and strengthening for himself a strong anti-socialist profile that he would use to achieve what he had long desired – a National Party government in its own right in Queensland.

He achieved the goal by default at the 22 October 1983 state election. The Nationals won 41 of the 83 seats in the parliament. The Liberals won only eight. Their embarrassment was heightened by the defection to the Nationals of two members, Don Lane and Brian Austin. The Liberals were depleted to just six, while the Nationals had 43, enough to form their own government.

This was good for Bjelke-Petersen, but not totally sweet. Too many people noted that had it not been for the Liberal defections, he would not have been in such a fortunate position. He had to build on the 1983 success. This he did, much to the surprise of just about everybody and contrary to most opinion polls, at the next state election on 1 November 1986. Bjelke-Petersen – now Sir Joh after being knighted in 1984 – increased the number of National MPs to 49, giving himself a workable majority in the Assembly, which by then had been increased to 89 members.[5] Joh was the stand-out, superstar leader of state and federal non-Labor parties.

The extraordinary electoral performance placed not only Joh but also the Queensland National Party on a political 'high'. It crystalised the premier's political thinking and also that of several seemingly influential supporters. His attention focused more squarely on getting rid of the Hawke socialists in Canberra. Predicting that the Queensland election result would have repercussions right across Australia, Bjelke-Petersen declared: 'What I can say to Bob Hawke is enjoy the time that you are there, because you are not going to be there much longer. ... Our assault on Canberra begins tonight.'[6] But, unlike 1975, he would make sure the Hawke administration was replaced with a conservative government that did what he wanted. No more Frasers for Joh Bjelke-Petersen:

> I definitely intend to have a big input in relation to [federal] policies, because I've had the bitter experience of giving 18 years of work for the two federal parties and received nothing for it other than bitterness and disappointment with Fraser and John Howard and his retrospective tax, land rights, a stack of things that Whitlam left. I had many arguments and talks trying to change their direction, but this time I won't be working through them. They'll work with the policies I set or I will work against them, and I've told them that.[7]

Sinclair and Howard were certainly apprehensive about these comments. The last thing they needed was a wild card Bjelke-Petersen disrupting Coalition unity. Few others in Canberra took much notice. It was just Joh blowing his trumpet after a stunning victory. The parliamentary session was drawing to a close and Christmas was around the corner. Even Sinclair and Howard could not have foreseen the enormity of what was about to be launched from Queensland.

Perhaps the original shots had been fired much earlier – by the powerful Queensland National Party president, Robert (Bob) Sparkes, in his report to the July 1986 annual conference on the Gold Coast. A principal concentration of the conference was the campaign for the state election to be held towards the end of the year. Sparkes stressed the imperative of achieving a strong National Party result and the impact it could have on federal politics:

> No doubt the offensive to remove the Hawke Government will have to be spearheaded from here. If we don't achieve

a good result at the State election our capacity to spearhead the offensive next year will be greatly impaired, and that would be a tragedy for the nation.[8]

Suggestions of spearheading the offensive from Queensland were hardly a ringing endorsement of the federal Opposition.

§

In the wake of his election victory, Joh was finding support – even admiration – from the growing hard-line conservative movement in Australia, echoed mainly through the so-called New Right. He was actively encouraged to transfer to Canberra and become prime minister, and the bait was sweetened with pledges of substantial financial backing.

By early 1987, it was widely reported that at least $25 million had been pledged to support such a campaign. The media suggested that much of the support was potentially coming from the 'white shoe brigade' – an apparent group of wealthy Gold Coast developers, entrepreneurs and businessmen. The Labor Party was happy to fuel the speculation, as evidenced by its Minister for Foreign Affairs, Bill Hayden: 'A secret club of land developers and their mates have put up $20 million so that he [Bjelke-Petersen] can run around Australia peddling snake oil.'[9] The president, Sparkes, who had been re-elected annually since first winning the position in 1970, scoffed at reports of multi-million dollar donations:

> No, we never have plenty of money … But I'm confident the people of Australia are so concerned about our future as a nation, they're concerned that we're going down the hill rapidly, and they'll contribute sufficient funds to enable us to secure our political objectives to save this country.[10]

Finances aside, if Joh was to succeed in making sure a future conservative government in Canberra implemented the policies he wanted, he had to achieve influential control. He probably did not give much detailed thought to this; his style, once he had made up his mind to do something, was to simply do it. But if he was to achieve his ambition, he would need to gain majority support among National Party organisations, at all state and federal levels.

A major irritant between the Queensland and other state and federal National parties was the long-held belief by the Queenslanders – reinforced by their successes in winning metropolitan seats at the state level, particularly in 1983 and 1986 – that the other parties should have been more ambitious to become the dominant partner in Coalition with the Liberals, rather than content to be the junior partner. This ignored some fundamental facts. While the National Party in Queensland had long been the dominant non-Labor party at state level, National parties in other states were not. Further, the Queensland Nationals were not as dominant federally, indicating a difference in voting trends between state and federal elections. For instance, in the December 1984 federal election, none of the party's 11 candidates in seats in and around Brisbane, or in the two Gold Coast seats of McPherson and Moncrieff, had made it to Canberra.[11] The party had contested all 24 House of Representatives seats in the state, winning eight, all of which were rural or regional constituencies.[12]

The results had been worse in other states. The Victorian party had stood 14 candidates in and around Melbourne.[13] In every seat, the National candidate had failed to get the required four per cent of the primary vote, and had lost his or her deposit. In South Australia, the party had contested five seats in and around Adelaide, with all candidates losing their deposits.[14]

The New South Wales National Party had for many years

refrained from contesting metropolitan seats. Its relations with the Liberal Party were generally strong and the two parties had stood joint tickets for New South Wales Legislative Council and Senate elections. In the 1984 federal election, the New South Wales party had contested 16 rural and regional seats, winning ten, an increase of two on its 1983 election result.[15]

In short, the 1984 federal election proved the National Party was not acceptable to metropolitan voters, especially in Melbourne and Adelaide. It showed the core strength of National appeal remained in country and regional areas. Bjelke-Petersen and the Queensland Nationals thought otherwise. Spurred on by their 1986 state election result, they believed the party could ultimately dominate the Coalition in Canberra. As the New South Wales senator since December 1984, and state party chairman from 1983 to 1986, David Brownhill, concluded from his own research of electoral statistics, the Queenslanders began pursuing an 'impossible dream'.[16] The scene was set for the running difference of opinion between the Queensland and federal National parties to blow wide open. Joh was going to dictate to Canberra and Canberra could like it or lump it. His immediate objective was to break the federal Coalition.

§

Joh knew this objective would be difficult to achieve. His prime opponent in 1987 was the Nationals' federal parliamentary leader, Sinclair – a man who the juggernaut of the ALP had tried and failed to kill off politically for over a decade. In Sinclair, Joh was faced with a man who was a coalitionist; highly adept at political argument; with ministerial and shadow ministerial experience and 24 years as a member of the federal parliament, preceded by two and a half years in the New South Wales Legislative Council; and who had grown up with the long-held traditions and beliefs of the National Party and its predecessors, the Australian Country Party and the National Country Party of Australia.[17] Sinclair, groomed as he had been by one of Australia's toughest politicians, John McEwen, knew the game. Known affectionately as Sinkers, he was politically as hard as nails.

It should have helped Joh to know his adversary. He knew Sinclair's attitude to National Party convention, his belief, backed by experience and the history of the party, that the federal parliamentary party had the right to ultimately determine federal party policy, including whether or not to be in Coalition, and not be dictated to by any other element of the party, not even its top organisational body, the federal council. Joh knew all this, so he should have been able to predict how Sinclair would react to the campaign he was about to unleash.

He knew, too, that breaking the Coalition, particularly with Sinclair heading the parliamentary party, would be no easy task. After all, it had continued unbroken since 1949, with the single exception of 18 months between December 1972 and June 1974 when the Whitlam Labor government was in power. On that occasion both the Liberal and then Australian Country Party leaders, Billy Snedden and Doug Anthony, had agreed to co-operate but not coalesce in Opposition. This time was different. Sinclair and John Howard were convinced Opposition unity was essential and the only way back to government was by retaining Coalition in Opposition. Their attitudes were based on what they saw as the failure of the 1972–74 experiment of independence in Opposition, which had allowed Whitlam to exploit policy differences between the parties in the May 1974 double dissolution election. Anthony and Snedden had reached the same conclusion after that poll and had restored the Coalition in Opposition from 14 June 1974.

Joh had one significant point in his favour: the National Party broadly liked, respected and wanted him, whereas there were some doubts about Sinclair's electoral appeal. Sinclair had been forced to stand down temporarily from the Fraser ministry on 27 September 1979, following allegations contained in an inquiry established by the New South Wales Labor government of Neville Wran that he had forged his father's signature on corporate returns relating to a group of companies that he had inherited some years earlier on the death of his father. He was subsequently cleared on charges resulting from the inquiry and returned to the Fraser cabinet on 19 August 1980. But the episode, which Sinclair was convinced had been deliberately motivated by Wran and his Attorney-General, Frank Walker, damaged him politically.[18]

Joh, or at least his strategists, had to consider – and where necessary try to change – the views of the various state organisations. The attitude of the parties around Australia would be vital when it came to votes at the federal council, which would next meet in Canberra between 27 and 29 March 1987. Each affiliated state had six delegates to the council, with those states which had federal parliamentary representation having an additional delegate. Queensland, New South Wales and Victoria would each have seven delegates, while South Australia and Western Australia would have six. The Northern Territory Country Liberal Party (CLP) would also send delegates, but, because it was associated rather than affiliated with the National Party, they could only vote on issues relative to the Territory.[19]

In addition, the council had an executive, known as the federal management committee, of nine. For the 1987 meeting, this consisted of the federal president, Shirley McKerrow, from Victoria; the secretary, David Thomson, a former Queenslander and Fraser government minister; the treasurer, Hugh Rogers, a Melbourne businessman; the immediate past president, Tom Drake-Brockman, from Western Australia, a minister in the Gorton and McMahon governments; the federal leader, Sinclair, and deputy leader, Ralph Hunt, both from New South Wales; the leader in the Senate, Stan Collard, from Queensland; the president of the women's federal council, Jean McIntyre, from Queensland; and the president of the Young National Party of Australia, Julian Anderson, also from Queensland. The total voting strength of federal council at this stage in early 1987 was assumed to be forty-two. Those votes would become crucial to the future of the party.

The Queensland organisation, and particularly its president, Sparkes, had long held the view that policy resolutions of federal council should be binding on the federal parliamentary party, in much the same way as the platform of the ALP's biennial national conference was supposed to be binding on the parliamentary Labor caucus.

Convention in the National Party had been that the parliamentary party took note of and guidance from the resolutions of council, but was not bound to adopt them. If Joh was to ensure his policies were to become policies of the parliamentary party, he would have to get this changed – and the only way to do that was by winning majority support on federal council.

Compounding the challenge was the fact that in the seven months up to and including January 1987, the Coalition Opposition had consistently been ahead of the government in the opinion polls. *The Bulletin* magazine's first Morgan Gallup poll for 1987 put the Coalition's primary vote at 49 per cent to Labor's 46 per cent. Why risk upsetting the apple cart when the Coalition was so consistently in a leading position?

2
NOT ALWAYS PLAIN SAILING

> That this Conference recommend to the Federal Parliamentary
> Party that it withdraw from the Coalition in Opposition ...
>
> Motion to Queensland National Party annual conference,
> Gold Coast, 16–20 July 1986 – defeated

The question of Coalition has historically been controversial and at times divisive for the National Party, particularly for the state parties.

The first group of so-called 'country' members elected to federal parliament went in after the election on 13 December 1919 – the first conducted with preferential voting. There were 15 of them. They were members of various existing political parties of the time, or endorsed by farm organisations, and had campaigned and won election on the basis that the interests of non-metropolitan Australians needed greater attention in the national parliament. They had supported an objective of the Australian Farmers' Federal Organisation:

> To watch over and guard the interests of primary producers;
> to prevent duplication of taxation and the overlapping of
> State and Federal administration; to obviate conflict between

Commonwealth and State industrial laws and awards; to encourage scientific agricultural education and cooperative trading in the interests of primary producers.[1]

On 22 January 1920, nine of the 15 members met at Parliament House in Melbourne and unanimously agreed to form an independent political party: 'That the Party shall be known as the Australian Country Party and shall act independently of all other political organisations.' A further meeting on 24 February saw two more members join the party, giving it a parliamentary strength of eleven.[2] The party elected the Tasmanian Member for Franklin, William McWilliams, as its leader. On 10 March, McWilliams outlined his party's objectives to parliament, highlighting that it would be a crossbench party:

> I may say at the outset that the Country Party is an independent body quite separate from the Nationalists or the Labour Party. ... We occupy our own party rooms, we have appointed our own Leader and other officers. We take no part in the deliberations of the Ministerialists or of the Opposition. We intend to support measures of which we approve and hold ourselves absolutely free to criticize or reject proposals with which we do not agree. Having put our hands to the wheel, we set the course of our voyage. ... We have not entered upon this course without the most grave consideration. ... We have recognised ... that drastic action was necessary to secure closer attention to the requirements of primary producers of Australia than they have hitherto received.[3]

McWilliams remained leader until 5 April 1921, when it was agreed the party should review all its positions. He did not stand for re-election and was succeeded by Earle Page, the Member for

Cowper in New South Wales, who won unanimous support.⁴

After the federal election on 16 December 1922, the Country Party held 14 seats in a House of Representatives of 75 members. On 19 February 1923, Page entered a Coalition with the Nationalist Party of Stanley Bruce – Bruce being prime minister and Page, treasurer and effectively deputy prime minister. Only two other Coalition governments had preceded this one since 1901: the Free Trade – Protectionist Coalition of George Reid and Allen McLean in 1904–05, and the Protectionist–Free Trade–Tariff Reform Coalition under Alfred Deakin in 1909–10.⁵

The Bruce–Page government held office to 22 October 1929, when it was defeated by the Labor Party under Jim Scullin. Scullin was defeated at the 6 January 1932 election, and the then United Australia Party (UAP) of Joseph Lyons governed in its own right until 9 November 1934, when Lyons and Page re-formed a Coalition government that lasted until Lyons' death in office on 7 April 1939.

Page took over as prime minister for 19 days, forming his own Coalition ministry, pending the election of a new UAP leader. The UAP elected Robert Menzies, whom Page both disliked and distrusted. Page refused to work with him, taking the Country Party out of Coalition and leaving Menzies with a minority government.

With the outbreak of World War II, the conservative parties recognised the need for maximum co-operation. A new Coalition was needed. Page would still not work with Menzies, and Menzies in turn made it plain that Page would not be welcome in a Coalition cabinet. Page solved the problem by resigning as Country Party leader on 8 September 1939 – five days after the outbreak of war. The party elected Archie Cameron, the Liberal Country League (LCL) Member for Barker in South Australia, its new leader and the Coalition was restored from 14 March 1940.

The UAP–Country Party Coalition was just able to hold office following the 21 September 1940 election. Cameron enjoyed little support in his party room. As a result he did not contest the leadership, which was traditionally declared vacant after each election. He resigned from the party and joined Menzies' UAP, which he was entitled to do under the LCL's rules.

Page and the Victorian Member for Echuca, John McEwen, tied in the subsequent leadership tussle. To break the deadlock, the party room agreed to appoint Queenslander, Arthur Fadden, the Member for Darling Downs, acting leader for the time being. The party formalised Fadden as its leader on 12 March 1941. He held the job for the next 17 years, standing down on 26 March 1958 and retiring from politics on 14 October 1958, just before the general election. Fadden was succeeded by McEwen, who held the position until retiring in February 1971, to be succeeded by Doug Anthony, the Member for Richmond in New South Wales.

Soon after the September 1940 election, the Menzies administration ran into difficulty. The Coalition was able to govern only with the support of two Victorian Independents – one of whom, Alexander Wilson, was a member of the Victorian United Country Party and a staunch supporter of its anti-Coalition stance. Moreover, Menzies was losing support within his own party. He ultimately stood down as prime minister in August 1941. A meeting of the joint UAP–Country parties on 23 August elected Fadden unopposed as prime minister.

It was a short-lived administration. The two Independents joined Labor in voting to amend Fadden's budget on 1 October 1941, effectively a motion of no confidence, thereby ousting the government after what Fadden described as 'forty days and forty nights' in office. With Fadden as Opposition leader, the UAP and Country Party remained in Coalition in Opposition until the election on 21 August 1943, again won by Labor. After this, the two parties agreed to co-operate outside any formal Coalition arrangement.

The Labor Party, successively under John Curtin, Frank Forde and Ben Chifley, held office until the election on 10 December 1949, following which a new conservative force, Robert Menzies' Liberal Party of Australia and the Country Party, formed a Coalition government. The two parties continued in Coalition and in government up to the election of the Whitlam Labor administration on 2 December 1972.

Following that election, Billy Snedden succeeded the former prime minister, Bill McMahon, as Liberal leader. He and Doug Anthony agreed their parties would act independently in Opposition but maintain co-operation where possible. They reviewed their position after losing the 18 May 1974 double dissolution election, during which Whitlam exploited the differing policy positions of the non-Labor parties, and agreed to establish a Coalition in Opposition.

Anthony was convinced the reunited Coalition was a major reason behind the Opposition's success in destroying the credibility of the Whitlam government in 1975, leading to its dismissal by the Governor-General on 11 November and its crushing defeat at the polls a month later, on 13 December. It was with the benefit of his experience in non-Coalition that Anthony readily agreed to maintain a Coalition Opposition after the Fraser government's defeat by Bob Hawke on 5 March 1983.

Anthony announced his retirement from politics at the end of December 1983 and was succeeded on 17 January 1984 by Ian Sinclair. Sinclair, also a key player in the 1972–74 non-Coalition years, was happy to continue the Coalition, first with Andrew Peacock and then with John Howard, who defeated Peacock in a Liberal leadership spill in September 1985.[6]

§

When Bruce and Page established their Coalition in 1923, the forerunner of the Country Party of New South Wales, the Progressive Party, was split over Coalition at the state level.[7] The Progressive Party was established by the state's Farmers and Settlers' Association and the Graziers' Association in October 1919. The parliamentary party split on 15 December 1921 over whether to be part of a Coalition with the Nationalists under George Fuller. Seven of the party's 15 parliamentarians, led by Mick Bruxner, from Tenterfield, defected to sit on the cross benches, refusing to be part of a formal Coalition. This non-Coalition position of the Bruxner Progressives, who had become known as the 'True Blues', persisted until after the state election on 8 October 1927, when the Lang Labor government was soundly defeated. Bruxner, who had handed the leadership to Ernest Buttenshaw, the Member for Clarence, saw the success of the federal Country Party in getting policies on the statute books by being a part of a composite government. He realised the party in New South Wales could best achieve similar outcomes by negotiating a Coalition agreement with the Nationalists.[8] The founding Coalition government for the Country Party in New South Wales took office from 8 October 1927, and Coalition in government, although not always in Opposition, has continued to the present day, despite spats from time to time with the Nationalists, United Australia Party and Liberal Party over three-cornered electoral contests and amalgamation.

In 1919, the Victorian party, then known as the Victorian Farmers' Union (VFU), imposed a pledge requiring that none of its parliamentarians join a composite government unless the party held a majority of the portfolios.[9] John McEwen was famously expelled from the then Victorian United Country Party in November 1937 for accepting a ministry in the federal

Coalition government of Joe Lyons and Earle Page, resulting in a breakaway Liberal–Country Party being formed in the state.

The Country Party in South Australia split in the late 1920s over a proposed 'closer union' with the Liberal Federation. Three of the Country Party's state parliamentarians quit the party to join the Liberals. In Western Australia, the issue of supporting other parties simmered on and off for decades after the Country Party's inception in March 1913. The party split seriously in 1978 over Coalition and was not reunited until October 1984.[10]

In Queensland, however, there was a history of amalgamation and Coalition in Opposition, even though by the early 1980s, Joh and the Nationals were going all out to achieve power in their own right. In May 1925, the Nationalists, by then rebadged as the United Party, and the Country Party united to form the Country Progressive Party, and from December that year, the Country and Progressive National Party (CPNP). The amalgamated party survived for almost 12 years and held government in Queensland from 1929 to 1932. Arthur Fadden had been a CPNP member of the Queensland parliament from 1932–35, during which time he became shadow treasury spokesman. An independent Country Party re-emerged in 1936, largely because control of the CPNP 'was mainly by city representatives'.[11] For the next 20 years the non-Labor parties battled unsuccessfully to break the ALP's stranglehold on the state government. In 1956, they contested the state election as a Coalition Opposition and, while not winning, significantly improved their percentage of the vote, so that on 3 August 1957 they were able to win office, with the Country Party's Francis Nicklin as premier, thereby ending Labor's supremacy in Queensland politics.

§

The question of how the federal Coalition was ended and re-established in the 1970s became relevant in 1987 when the Queensland National Party claimed the party's federal council had the power to direct the parliamentary party on whether or not to be in Coalition.

Up to then, Coalition arrangements so far as the Country Party, and subsequent National Country Party and National Party, was concerned were a matter for the parliamentary leader to negotiate with his conservative counterpart and then ratify with his party room.

In 1972, Anthony and Snedden had agreed to end the Coalition. Anthony then received the unanimous support of his party room. The matter was never referred to the federal council for ratification or endorsement. Similarly, the Coalition had been re-established in June 1974 by agreement between the leaders, with Anthony receiving unanimous endorsement from his party room. Again, there was no reference to federal council. It was accepted by party organisations at federal and state levels that Coalition was a matter for the federal parliamentary party.[12]

The federal constitution of the party as it existed in 1987 was specific (albeit in a strange way) about what powers the federal council had to direct the parliamentary party in the area of Coalition. Clause 18 stated: 'Unless the Federal Council has decided to the contrary, portfolios in a composite Government may be accepted by the National Party.' The council could therefore only direct the parliamentary party when in government, not in Opposition. Further, the council had no power to direct the party *not* to enter into a Coalition in government. It could only stipulate the party *not* hold portfolios in such government. This was ridiculous. It was unthinkable that either the parliamentary party or the federal council would accept being part of a Coalition government and then refuse the opportunity of holding portfolios in that government.

There was a view in the party at the time that while clause 18 referred to government, by extension it also applied to Opposition. But the clause was specific in its reference only to a 'composite Government'. Even if it was applied to Opposition, the same conditions of interpretation would have to apply; namely, federal council could direct the parliamentary party not to hold shadow portfolios in a composite Opposition, but it had no power to direct the party not to enter a Coalition in Opposition, or to quit a Coalition in Opposition. The latter scenario was what the Queensland National Party ultimately instructed its federal members and senators to do. While interpretation of clause 18 became an issue in the lead-up to the 27–29 March 1987 federal council, it was never put to the test during the council meeting.

Since the election of the Hawke government in March 1983, there had been closer questioning of the wisdom of Coalition in Opposition among the broad membership of the National Party. The issue was widely canvassed by branches, electorate councils, state executives and conferences. By March 1987, the attitudes of the various states were finely balanced.

At its annual conference on the Gold Coast towards the end of July 1986, the Queensland Party debated the following motion:

> That this Conference recommend to the Federal
> Parliamentary Party that it withdraw from the Coalition
> in Opposition and that the question of Coalition and the
> conditions of such Coalition be negotiated between the
> respective Party organisations, if it is necessary that such a
> Government be formed.[13]

The motion was lost, in no small part due to the intervention of Sparkes, who, as state president, presided over the conference. While acknowledging that he had been opposed to resuming the federal Coalition in Opposition after the December 1984 federal election, Sparkes said that withdrawal in 1986 would be detrimental: 'The nation is faced with a potential economic disaster. If we were to pull out of the coalition [now] I am sure the nation, the anti-socialist section, would say we were acting irresponsibly at a time of national peril.'[14] Sparkes' views invariably carried considerable weight among conference delegates. The motion went down.

The New South Wales party, because of its generally co-operative arrangements with the Liberal Party at the state level, had always been more inclined to support a continuing federal Coalition, even in Opposition. Moreover, it had agreements with the Liberals to stand joint candidate tickets for Legislative Council and Senate elections, and, since the introduction of public funding in 1984, to share monies resulting from those elections. No state conference of the New South Wales party in recent years had directly questioned federal Coalition arrangements, although, at its conference in Armidale in June 1981 (when the conservatives were in government in Canberra), it did carry a motion calling on the party to emphasise its 'distinct and separate role and policies'.[15] Joh's electoral successes in Queensland also impressed the then New South Wales parliamentary leader, Leon Punch, and prompted the state party to invite the premier to be its guest speaker at a fundraising luncheon at The Regent Hotel in Sydney in November 1983.

Relations soured after Joh embarked on his Canberra campaign in January 1987, with the New South Wales central executive on 6 March unanimously carrying a motion supporting the continuation of the federal Coalition and the leadership of Ian Sinclair. The resolution was endorsed by a meeting of the

New South Wales central council on 10 April 1987.[16] Nonetheless, more than a few of the party's membership, and several in its Young National Party, were Joh supporters. The Young Nationals' state chairman from June 1986 to June 1987, Philip Black, declared in February 1987 that he had been waiting for Joh to become prime minister 'for years', and stood unsuccessfully as a Joh Independent candidate against the Treasurer, Paul Keating, in his Sydney seat of Blaxland.[17]

John Anderson, who would succeed Ralph Hunt in his northern New South Wales electorate of Gwydir at a by-election in April 1989 and later become federal leader and deputy prime minister, was a 30-year-old newly elected Gwydir electorate council chairman in 1987. He remembered a meeting in Narrabri early in the Joh campaign that he and Hunt attended with about 18 party members, including farmers Bevan O'Regan and John Uebergang:

> Ralph was told very seriously 'the future of the country is in your hands. You alone can save this nation', to which he replied 'Oh, and how might that be?' Uebergang said 'go over to that phone and ring Sinclair and tell him to stand aside and you'll take over the leadership temporarily until Joh gets to Canberra'. I remember thinking this is bizarre. Ralph refused. He said 'don't be silly and anyway it's not my gift to do that – the party room decides the leadership'. Ralph was deeply upset by it all. He wanted to retire and yet here was Sinclair, a man to whom Ralph was unquestionably loyal, in the gun with people saying he had to go.[18]

In Victoria, the state's central council on 27 February 1987 reaffirmed an earlier resolution supporting the continuation of the federal Coalition and Sinclair's leadership. At its annual conference at Wangaratta on 10 April 1987, it considered a motion to 'endorse the move by Sir Joh Bjelke-Petersen to remove the National Party from the Federal Coalition'. The motion was lost by 139 votes to seventy.[19]

The affiliated National parties in Western Australia and South Australia were against Coalition in Opposition. The Western Australian party's conference in August 1986 had a motion on the agenda calling on the National Party not to enter into an agreement of Coalition in Opposition. The motion was not considered because of time constraints. On the authority of the conference, it was referred to the party's state council, which adopted it at a meeting a month later and forwarded it for inclusion on the agenda for the next federal council meeting, which would be that held in March 1987. The South Australian party, at its annual conference in August 1986, adopted a position calling on the federal and state National parties to break Coalition in Opposition and only consider Coalition while in government. This position was altered by the state's central council on 5 March 1987, as a result of which the following motion was sent forward to the federal council agenda:

> That this Council supports the principle of the National Party being a separate entity whilst in Opposition. The final decision and timing as to whether and when the National Party withdraws from the Coalition shall be left to the Federal Parliamentary National Party.

The real crunch to the future of the federal Coalition, and the action that precipitated serious reconsideration of the issue by other state executives, would come from a Queensland central council meeting at Hervey Bay on 27–28 February 1987 (discussed at length in chapter 4). In the meantime, Joh Bjelke-Petersen was running his own race.

3
THE JOH CAMPAIGN HITS THE ROAD

January to February 1987

It's like the old bumble bee – he's not supposed to fly, but he still flies. I've done it, it's launched, it's on the way.

Joh Bjelke-Petersen, Perth, 3 February 1987

Joh wanted an end to the Coalition Opposition in Canberra. Knowing as he did that Sinclair and Howard were both strongly pro-Coalition, he had to find a policy issue of national significance that would have wide community appeal and that would drive a wedge between the National and Liberal parties. The issue he chose was tax.

His launch pad was Wagga Wagga in the southern New South Wales Hume electorate of Liberal front bencher, Wal Fife. Here, on 31 January 1987, he thundered out his ideas and demands to an enthusiastic crowd, estimated at 2000, which gathered at the city's Weissel Oval. The rally had been organised by Wagga's Grassroots 2000 movement, part of a growing organisation known as the Small Business People's movement that claimed 35 branches across New South Wales.[1]

People wanted lower taxes, Joh said, and he had the policy

that everyone would support – a 25 cents in the dollar single rate of tax, with no offsetting broad-based indirect or consumption taxes. People paying less than 25 cents in the dollar income tax would stay where they were, while those above that level would come down to it. It was simple.

Joh had a number of advantages in pushing this line. The National Party had supported the flat or single rate tax philosophy for many years. Doug Anthony had first floated it in 1977.[2] The New South Wales party's annual conference in Sydney in June 1985 had called for 'the progressive introduction of a flat rate of tax'. Joh himself had presented a flat tax concept to a national tax summit in Canberra in July 1985.[3] He knew it appealed to a large section of the party membership and the broader community, even though it was generally derided by economists. He also knew the Liberal Party believed any move towards a single rate of tax would have to be progressive and accompanied by some form of broadened indirect tax, such as a consumption or value added tax. Joh could argue that under his policy Australians would have lower taxes, while under the Liberals (and, so long as they remained in Coalition, the Nationals) they would have new and, therefore, higher taxes.

The simplicity of his presentation and the lack of detail as to how it might work caused a headache for conservative politicians in Canberra – especially as Joh told the Wagga rally that unless sitting federal National and Liberal Party members and senators adopted his policies, one of his own conservative candidates would stand against them for election. He was flagging a new conservative force in national politics: 'The circumstances absolutely demand we've got to go beyond the two party policy, with new ideas and concepts, new policies, with candidates in every seat. ... I want to free this country from the policies of the last three governments.'[4] Shirley McKerrow and I were astounded. How could a state premier endorse candidates for a federal election, especially beyond his own state? Who and where were these candidates? What was the detail of this mysterious tax policy? It made no sense.

Adding to the intrigue, Joh was promoting something in clear contravention of the written economic affairs policy and the published platform of his own Queensland National Party. The policy, which at the time was being revised but which had not actually been replaced, supported a single rate tax system (without specifying any level) and also stated in clause 2.3: 'The National Party favours increased reliance upon indirect (consumption-based) taxation.' The Queensland party platform, which had been revised as recently as just prior to the November 1986 state election, similarly supported an unspecified single rate of tax, and said in clause 7 that 'there should be increased reliance upon indirect, rather than direct taxation'.

Howard and Sinclair decided Joh could no longer be allowed to go unchallenged. After the first meeting for 1987 of the joint National and Liberal parties in Canberra, on 2 February, Howard called on Joh to either be supportive of the Coalition or keep out of the federal scene.[5] The following day, Sinclair called a news conference and warned Joh to work within the National Party system and not undermine the federal Coalition, declaring: 'We have taken a decision to stand as a Coalition with the Liberal Party at the next federal election and we will be standing with the Liberal Party, and no individual premier or leader of any other state parliamentary party will have a direct role in determining any other course.'[6] The New South Wales party organisation also warned Joh not to meddle with its candidate preselection process, with the state chairman, Doug Moppett, saying that the premier 'will be on a collision course with the NSW National Party if he persists with his proposal to intervene in the process of selection of candidates in NSW'.[7]

Sinclair's comments played into Joh's hands. The premier

could now link him with the Liberals and their alleged support for new indirect taxes. At a news conference in Perth, Joh said he was not interested in Howard or Sinclair or the federal National Party — only in implementing his 'good policies for the people of Australia'. In direct response to Sinclair's comments, he came out with classic 'Joh-speak': 'It's like the old bumble bee — he's not supposed to fly, but he still flies. I've done it, it's launched, it's on the way.'[8] Anything Sinclair said was immaterial.

Joh was happy to let the confusion build, as was clear from an interview he gave to ABC Radio two days later:

Q: How do you expect to stay part of the Nationals?

A: I am not interested in staying part of the National Party and I am only interested in doing what the people of Australia are interested in.

Q: Are you going to resign from the National Party?

A: I am not going to resign.

Q: You just said you were not interested in staying.

A: I can't stay. What I am saying I am interested in is doing something for the people of Australia.

Q: If the National Party in Canberra won't do what you want will you leave it?

A: Lead it, I will lead it.

Q: I said leave it.

A: Don't be stupid. Don't be so stupid otherwise I will not talk to you. You know I'm not one of those that run away. I am Sir Joh Bjelke-Petersen, a National Party Member of Parliament for 40 years and Premier. What I am doing in Queensland I am now going to do for Australia.

Q: When are we going to meet your candidates?

A: They grow up like mushrooms.

Q: You said you have met four or five during your trip to Melbourne. A lot of people are interested in meeting them.

A: Don't you worry. You write your little story.[9]

The significance of this interview was that, for the first time, the premier had indicated the possibility of seeking election to the federal parliament so that he could lead the National Party.

§

Running in tandem with Joh's personal campaign was the emergence of a new political party, calling itself the National Party of Australia – Northern Territory, or NT Nationals, which was formed in December 1986. It was modelled on the Queensland National Party and supported its policies. Joh and the Queensland organisation were giving the NT Nationals moral support, and were pushing for their affiliation with the National Party of Australia.

The problem for the federal party was that it was already associated with the Northern Territory Country Liberal Party (CLP), a conservative party which was in government in the Territory and which the federal Country Party, on the instigation of its then leader, John McEwen, had helped to establish as the Australian Country Party – Northern Territory in 1966. The CLP, formed in 1974 through a merger of Country and Liberal Party interests in the Territory, had originally maintained its affiliation with the federal Country/National Country Party. But it decided to change its relationship to one of 'association' in early 1979 so that it could be associated with both the Country and Liberal parties in Canberra.[10] When it had two federal parliamentarians, they generally divided themselves so that one sat with each party in parliament. At this stage in 1987, however, the CLP's two federal parliamentarians, Paul Everingham (Northern Territory) and Senator Bernie Kilgariff, were both sitting with the Liberals – a fact not lost on Robert Sparkes and the Queenslanders. While the CLP had been going through a rocky period in the previous year, by early 1987 it was largely back on track, with the election of a new chief minister, Steve Hatton, to replace Ian Tuxworth, who resigned and joined the NT Nationals, and the election of a new president, Grant Heaslip.

The CLP had also endorsed Grant Tambling as its Senate candidate to replace Kilgariff, who was retiring at the next election. Tambling had sat in the House of Representatives with the National Country Party from October 1980 until his defeat in March 1983, and could be expected to again sit with the National Party if elected to the Senate. But that would not be the case if the federal Nationals supported the NT Nationals, who were gearing up to fight a Territory election against the CLP. Joh threw his weight behind the new party because it was potentially valuable to him in his push for greater power over the federal National Party organisation.

A Northern Territory election took place on 7 March 1987, after a rapid three-week campaign. Hatton called the snap poll to nip the NT Nationals in the bud. The rebels stood candidates in all 25 Territory electorates. They won nearly 18 per cent of the vote, but only got one member into the Assembly, Tuxworth. The result for the fledgling party, barely three months old, was not bad – 18 per cent of the vote was a significant inroad. But it was not good enough for the Queensland campaign, which needed at least four or five seats to fall to the NT Nationals. Had that occurred, it would have been difficult for the federal party to justify rejecting an application for affiliation. The NT Nationals could have argued they had significantly damaged the CLP hold on government as a result of policies espoused by Joh and the Queensland National Party, and therefore had a strong claim for affiliation with the National Party of Australia.

More important was the prospect that, with a fully affiliated NT National Party, Queensland could count on six or seven additional votes on any motions it put to federal council – votes that would be vital on such issues as Coalition and the election of the federal president.

At the beginning of February 1987, all of this was for the future. No Northern Territory election had been announced. Public interest in the growing disunity in conservative politics was still centred on the aftermath of the Wagga Wagga rally and Joh's pledge to stand candidates in seats around Australia.

§

It was against this background that the federal management committee of the National Party met in Sydney on 5 February 1987. Given the tensions of the past month, it was a remarkably relaxed and convivial meeting. The Joh push was discussed at length and at the end of the meeting, Sinclair, the federal president, Shirley McKerrow, and Sparkes held a joint news conference to assert the committee's view that any attempt by Joh to enter federal politics would be welcome, but that the various state party constitutions were supreme – in other words, Joh must work within the rules – and the rules enabled the federal parliamentary party to make decisions on Coalition, and forbad any state party from endorsing candidates in other states where an affiliated National Party existed.

During the management meeting, Sparkes revealed an interesting attitude to the Joh campaign. He did not think Joh had his intentions clearly formulated and he had not had much contact with the premier recently – the last time had been some weeks earlier in general discussions about the possibility of Joh becoming the party's federal president. It was well known within the party that McKerrow, who had held the position since March 1981, would not seek re-election. The federal president's position was declared vacant at each annual federal council. Joh had told Sparkes he was not interested in the president's job. Uppermost in his mind was a deep concern about future conservative policy implementation and a firm belief that the National Party in the Fraser administration had failed.[11] According to David Russell in his December 2011 reflections for *Queensland Speaks*, Sparkes was 'tremendously worried' that if Joh made the move to Canberra and the Queensland organisation did not support him, it would split the party in the state, something that had to be avoided at all costs. He said Sparkes' view was that by supporting and managing Joh, there might be a chance of positively changing the direction of conservative politics federally, adding that Sparkes was not overly concerned at any potential damage it might cause in Canberra, because 'there was nothing down there that was really worth saving'.[12]

The question of affiliation of the NT Nationals came before the meeting. A telex letter from the convener of the NT Nationals, James Petrich, was received at the National Party federal secretariat in Canberra on the morning of 5 February and forwarded by facsimile to Sydney. Addressed simply to the 'Party

President', the letter began: 'Dear Sir, I am writing to formally seek your support for the Northern Territory Nationals to be admitted to the National Party of Australia's Federal body.' Under the National Party's federal constitution, applications for affiliation had to be supported by three 'reputable citizens', confirm that the applying organisation generally subscribed to the federal policy of the party, and be accompanied by a set of draft regulations.[13] Also relevant was clause 9, which said that for the purpose of the constitution, the Northern Territory 'is deemed to be a State'.

The Petrich letter was not signed by three people and not accompanied by draft regulations. Federal management had no option but to advise Petrich that it was not possible to consider the proposal. No-one on the committee disagreed – indeed the motion to that effect was moved by the senior federal vice-president and Queensland vice-president, Charles Holm. Sparkes, however, made it clear that Queensland would continue to press for the affiliation of the NT party. He said he was bound by his state executive, which at a meeting on 30 January had unanimously resolved to support the establishment of the NT National Party and required the Queensland delegation to put a recommendation to that effect to federal council. The feeling in Queensland was that wherever there was an opportunity to promote and expand the National Party, it should be seized. For the time being, though, the issue was on the backburner and unlikely to arise again until the next meeting of management, set down for the morning of 27 March in Canberra, immediately prior to the opening of federal council.

§

The next critical events for Sinclair were the start of the new parliamentary year on 17 February and a parliamentary National

Party meeting he had called for the morning of 16 February.

Sinclair needed a demonstration from the meeting of support for his leadership and for the Coalition. He needed it because the war of words between himself and Joh had reached a critical level. For example, *The Sydney Morning Herald* on 9 February had quoted Joh saying: 'We will ... bypass them [Howard and Sinclair]. We will annihilate them and they cannot expect to keep their positions.' For his part, Sinclair had been taunting Joh about the possibility of him coming to Canberra, suggesting that if he was serious, he should stand against the Minister for Foreign Affairs, Bill Hayden, in his outer Brisbane seat of Oxley. In a press statement on 8 February, in a direct slap at Joh, Sinclair had declared that 'grandstanding outside of Parliament alone has rarely achieved anything'. On the morning of the party meeting, *The Sydney Morning Herald* reported: 'For the past two weeks, Sir Joh has been insisting the first Federal National Party meeting of the year would see a challenge to Mr. Sinclair's leadership and possibly an end to the Coalition. He said it would be D-Day for Mr. Sinclair.'

The party meeting backfired on Sinclair – and it was largely his fault. Before it began, he scheduled a news conference for later in the morning. Several members were angry when they learned that Sinclair was potentially going to truncate discussion on issues of fundamental importance – the Joh push and the Coalition – and seek a definitive party room position so he could meet a media deadline that he had set himself. The result was a resolution that raised more questions than it answered. It failed to support Sinclair's leadership and it failed to support the Coalition:

> That this Party, recognising the crisis in the Australian economy and the need to defeat the Hawke Labor Government, states its accord with the thrust of that which the Premier of Queensland seeks to achieve and supports

his general philosophy. This Party proposes that the benefits which the Premier would bring to such a united effort be harnessed by requesting the Premier to become fully involved with the Federal National Party in the campaign to remove the Hawke Government from office and thereby gain the maximum benefit of the electoral support the Premier of Queensland has within Australia.[14]

Sinclair had received his first indication that the 12 Queensland senators and members in the 26-strong party room were not going to dump Joh.

At his press conference, he argued there was no need for any party room re-endorsement of either his leadership or the Coalition, because these were not at issue.[15] Rather, the party room was offering Joh an olive branch to work with the federal party. It sounded pretty thin, which was how – aided by the response from Bjelke-Petersen – it was interpreted by the media. For example, reporter Heather Ewart commented on the ABC Radio *AM* program on 17 February: 'Senior members of the Liberal Party and indeed some in the National Party had expected a clear public statement of support for Ian Sinclair from the meeting. Instead there was a resolution supporting the thrust of Sir Joh's philosophy and suggesting he become fully involved in the federal National Party's campaign to remove the Hawke government from office.' Joh flatly rejected the 'olive branch' offer, claiming the party room resolution was a 100 per cent endorsement of his campaign and policies and that Sinclair and Howard were 'liabilities'. 'All Sinclair's MPs for me: Sir Joh' was *The Canberra Times* front-page banner headline.[16]

The situation worried Howard. He needed National Party support for the Coalition to placate those in the Liberal Party who were now questioning why the Liberals should maintain Coalition with a party that was deeply divided.

Parliamentary National Party meetings were normally held each Tuesday morning during parliamentary sitting weeks and preceded a meeting of the joint Liberal and National parties, which began at about 10.30am. Despite the meeting on 16 February, a Monday, the normal meeting remained scheduled for the next day. Here, Sinclair managed to regain some ground. He won majority party room support for continuing the Coalition, as a result of which a short, joint press statement with Howard was issued after the joint party meeting:

> At today's Joint Party Meeting Mr. Sinclair informed the meeting of the desire of the National Party to continue the existing Coalition with the Liberal Party. The Joint Party Meeting reaffirmed the desire of both Parties to maintain that Coalition and its belief that the maintenance of that Coalition is the most effective instrument to destroy the Hawke Government.

While that settled Howard's immediate problem, Sinclair was faced with the fact that his party room had still not provided a vote of confidence in his leadership. He stuck with the line that it was not in question. Others, however, were not so generous, suggesting that had the leadership been put to a vote, he might not have had the numbers. Sinclair could have been unsure himself, which would explain why he did not push more directly for the endorsement he needed. Had he got support for his leadership as well as the Coalition, subsequent events may well have been different. Instead, a running sore had been opened, which festered in the ensuing weeks.

Joh was having a field day. *The Sydney Morning Herald* on 18 February quoted him saying Sinclair was 'history' and 'he's got no power at all. ... Nobody supports Sinclair'.

Opinion polls were showing that Joh had strong support. For

instance, *The Australian*'s Newspoll, published on 17 February, indicated the existing Coalition would win 47 per cent support to Labor's 43 per cent. With Joh as the National Party leader, Coalition support increased to 52 per cent, while that for Labor fell to 41 per cent. Added to this, Sinclair had given Joh the bonus of being seen to have bungled his party room meetings; and the Northern Territory Chief Minister, Hatton, on 16 February, had called his snap election for 7 March. Joh was confident the NT Nationals would justify his claims that he had the people and the policies Australians wanted. The premier had barnstormed the Territory earlier in the month, helping to get the NT Nationals established and ready for the election. He had addressed rallies in Alice Springs and Darwin and proclaimed the eyes of Australia and the world would be on the Territory election.

The eyes of Australia certainly were. As the campaign unfolded, it became apparent that the NT Nationals were not going to do as well as Joh would have liked. He walked away from them. He did not return to the Territory for the rest of the campaign, although his wife, Lady Flo, did campaign on their behalf for two days in the last week. After the result, with the NT Nationals only winning one of 25 seats, Joh said the election had been a local one, fought on local issues – 'it had nothing to do with me,' he said. While it was a setback, it was of minor consequence, because media attention had focused on the implications of the tumultuous decisions taken by the Queensland central council at Hervey Bay the previous weekend, 27–28 February.

§

A growing number of people already realised the crisis had gone too far and was seriously damaging the National Party. A compromise had to be found. In early February 1987, the

Queensland party vice-president, Charles Holm, invited Sinclair to a meeting. The idea was fleshed out a few days later, when David Russell saw Sinclair in Canberra. The meeting was set for 13 February – ominous as it was a Black Friday. It was held at the Brisbane home of the Queensland party's treasurer, Bill Allen. Present were Holm, Allen, Sinclair and Joh. It got nowhere. Joh insisted that Sinclair accept his demands, saying he was happy for Sinclair to remain as caretaker leader. Unsurprisingly, Sinclair refused.[17] He returned to Canberra and issued a two-line statement, saying the meeting had been to discuss relations between the Queensland Premier and the National Party and that all details would be kept confidential.[18]

4
TURNING A SKIRMISH INTO A WAR

27–28 February 1987

> ... all members of the National Party in this State, both
> Parliamentary and Organisational, are fully committed
> to this cause which can be appropriately styled –
> 'JOH FOR P.M. FOR AUSTRALIA'S SAKE'.
>
> Central council resolution, Queensland National Party,
> 28 February 1987

The state National parties, while autonomous and operating under their own constitutions, generally had, and still have, similar organisational structures.

Each party's governing body is the central council, made up of delegates from all of the party's state and federal electorate councils, as well as the Young Nationals and the women's organisation, where these are established. Central council meetings are usually held at least four times a year. To manage the party's affairs in the intervening periods, central council elects from among its number at each annual meeting a smaller management committee, or state executive. If a potentially controversial issue is to be considered by a central council meeting, it is not uncommon for the matter to be approved first by the management committee. In this way, the issue can be presented to central council as a recommendation from the executive, enhancing its chances of being approved.

It was being tipped in the last week of February that the Queensland central council meeting at Hervey Bay would carry a resolution supporting an end to the federal Coalition. Joh was confidently predicting that it was 'within days of collapse'.[1] However, the extent of the Hervey Bay resolutions had not been anticipated – not even by most of the 250 delegates present.

Sparkes was the mastermind of the resolutions.[2] Virtually no-one else was privy to them. The party's Senate leader at the time, Queenslander Stan Collard, said the resolutions were developed 'without any consultation with the Feds [Queensland federal parliamentarians], not a phone call to Ray Braithwaite [Member for Dawson] or myself'.[3] Sparkes was confident he could get them approved, first by his state management committee, which would meet on the morning of 27 February, and then by central council later in the day. Sparkes commanded strong support and respect throughout the Queensland organisation, having been the state president since 1970 and unopposed for the position every year until 1986, when he was returned with 509 votes to forty-eight.[4]

Sparkes was in a dilemma. He was sympathetic to the premier's ambition of influencing conservative policy, especially in key areas such as tax and industrial relations. He knew the Queensland party organisation would have to become involved. It could either support the premier or walk away from him. Given Joh's enormous popularity in the state, enhanced by his election victory three months earlier, the party would split disastrously if it did not get behind Bjelke-Petersen; simple as that.

Moreover, if the organisation did not support him, Joh would ignore it and carry on anyway. The premier had the results of nation-wide polling, involving a sample of 2000 people in each state, which showed that while Howard and Sinclair could not win an election, if Joh spearheaded a federal campaign, he would lift the National Party vote by four per cent – sufficient to change the government.[5] On the other hand, Sparkes knew that backing Joh would set the Queensland party on a collision course with the federal Opposition, with Sinclair, and with the National Party organisations in New South Wales and Victoria. At the end of the day, as president of the Queensland party, preserving its unity was paramount to Sparkes.

That decided, the next problem was that the Joh campaign, to this point somewhat erratic, unpredictable and lacking direction, was in danger of flying off the rails if it was not professionally planned and managed. Even though the relationship between Sparkes and Joh had frequently been testy, Sparkes believed he could devise a means by which he could effectively manage the premier without antagonising him. His resolutions basically achieved this, but they also turned what up to now had been largely a cold war between Sinclair and Joh into a fully-fledged battle campaign. The Hervey Bay resolutions were:

> That the National Party of Australia (Qld) fully supports the move by Sir Joh Bjelke-Petersen to attain the Prime Ministership so that he can put in place an anti-socialist Federal Government equipped with appropriate policies, and the will to implement those policies, which are so patently necessary to save this Nation from the economic and political ruin into which the Hawke Socialist Government is plunging us. Accordingly, as a consequence of this decision, all members of the National Party in this State, both Parliamentary and Organisational, are fully committed to

this cause which can be appropriately styled – 'JOH FOR P.M. FOR AUSTRALIA'S SAKE'.

That with a view to facilitating the realisation of the Premier's vitally important goal, this Council makes the following recommendations and/or observations:-

1. Recognising that no great battle can be won by great and charismatic generalship alone and hence that a vital prerequisite for the success of the Joh for P.M. campaign is adequate efficient organisational structure, we strongly recommend that wherever practicable existing National Party structure be used because –

    (A) time does not permit the establishment of adequate alternative structure right across the nation; and

    (B) attempted operation outside existing National Party structure and probably in conflict with it, could have serious adverse repercussions on our State National Party – something that must be avoided at all times.

2. As the instrument for overall control and co-ordination of the Joh for P.M. campaign, we recommend the establishment of the National Joh for P.M. Committee, appointed jointly by the Premier and the State President, and with the power to co-opt. The chairman of this committee would be the Premier and the deputy chairman, the State President. It is envisaged that the committee would utilise the

existing National Party Headquarters and facilities at Bjelke-Petersen House [in Brisbane] supplemented by additional staff and equipment as required.

3. Whilst it is envisaged that the National Joh for P.M. committee should have unrestricted discretionary authority in determining all aspects of the campaign, it is suggested that the committee consider the following structural blue print:-

   (A) appoint sub-committees to handle such matters as strategy, structure, policies, finance, publicity;

   (B) appoint a small sub-committee for each State other than Queensland;

   (C) appoint a National co-ordinator;

   (D) appoint a co-ordinator in each State whose principal functions would be to set up Joh for P.M. committees where no adequate National Party structure exists and to co-ordinate with existing National Party organisation.

This Council asserts that it is the right of Party Organisation to determine whether or not its Parliamentary representatives enter into or remain in any coalition arrangement or other form of association with any other political entity. Accordingly to give the people of this nation clear cut policy choices – something they are so obviously seeking:-

1. We request that the National Party Federal Parliamentary Leader, Mr Sinclair, to [sic] immediately withdraw the National Party from the Federal Opposition Coalition because of basic differences in taxation and other philosophies and policies;

2. Failing that we request the Queensland delegation to the next National Party Federal Council meeting to [sic] put forward a motion to the effect that the Federal Opposition Coalition be terminated immediately;

3. and failing that, we request that our Queensland National Party Federal Shadow Ministers to [sic] immediately withdraw from the Federal Shadow Ministry and all Queensland National Party Federal Parliamentarians who are members of joint policy committees to [sic] withdraw from those committees.[6]

These were momentous decisions. It was now formal: with the full backing of the Queensland organisation, Joh Bjelke-Petersen would contest the next federal election with the aim of becoming prime minister and implicitly toppling not only Sinclair but also John Howard; Joh for PM sub-committees would be set up in states beyond Queensland; and a mechanism had been spelled out to smash the federal Coalition. A line had been drawn in the sand. The Queensland and federal parties were at loggerheads.

Up to this point, there had been regular and ongoing discussions between variously Sinclair, his principal private secretary, Liam Bathgate, his press secretary, Geoff Mort, the deputy leader, Ralph Hunt, the federal president, Shirley McKerrow, and myself, on Joh's campaign. From now on there would be a constant flow of discussions, formal and informal meetings, phone calls and exchanges of facsimiles as potential strategies and countermeasures were considered, put in place, or shelved. Bathgate, Mort and I would spend hours going over scenarios, with Bathgate puffing on his pipe, Mort on a cheroot and me chain smoking cigarettes. There would be increased communication with the New South Wales and Victorian party leaders and executive officers. There would be little time for sleep.

Tom McVeigh, the Member for Groom, a former Fraser government minister, a strong Joh supporter and a delegate to both the management committee and the central council at Hervey Bay, said the atmosphere of the central council meeting was 'one of total support for what Joh was trying to do, because people were cranky at the way the federal Coalition and its leadership were seen to be so weak'. He disputed media reports at the time that debate on the resolutions had stretched into the small hours of 28 February before being overwhelmingly carried. 'It wasn't a big debate. It went on intermittently as part of a long session of central council, which included the preselection of candidates for our Senate team.'[7]

Not everyone was compliant. The Member for Dawson, Ray Braithwaite, a shadow minister in the federal Coalition, told the meeting the resolutions were 'a load of crap'. He was warned that acceptance of them was a condition of his continued endorsement, and recalled that a motion was carried requiring all Queensland members and senators to pledge their support 'otherwise their endorsements would not be approved'.[8] Despite this, he and his Dawson electorate delegates voted against the resolutions – just about the only people to do so. Ultimately, Braithwaite fell into line, realising that he would 'never have held Dawson as an Independent candidate'.[9] Queensland Senator Ron Boswell made an impassioned plea not to force an end of the federal Coalition, while his colleague and party Senate leader, Stan Collard, was also deeply concerned, but held his silence for the time being.

Reactions to the Hervey Bay resolutions were swift. Sinclair, attending the annual meeting of his New England electorate council in Inverell, said they were tantamount to 'a bid to hijack the federal [National Party] organisation'. He won a unanimous vote of confidence from the electorate council for his leadership, and an 89 to 11 vote favouring a continuation of the Coalition in Opposition.[10] Howard said Joh was embarking on a wrecking course, and described the premier as 'a standover man gratifying a selfish drive for power'.[11] The former National Party federal leader and deputy prime minister, Doug Anthony, said the idea of Joh becoming prime minister was 'absurd'.[12] The New South Wales party chairman, Doug Moppett, described the Hervey Bay resolutions as 'notorious'. The intention to establish Joh for PM sub-committees and co-ordinators in all states beyond Queensland, and to potentially endorse candidates in other states, was, according to Moppett, 'in flagrant breach of the Party's Federal Constitution'.[13]

Federally, the resolutions raised a number of issues. First was the sheer arrogance of them: there was no recognition of the fact that the parliamentary party was made up of members from other autonomous state National parties, which might not agree with the Queensland thrust. Therefore, could Joh set up Joh for PM sub-committees in states outside Queensland under the federal constitution of the party, let alone state party constitutions? What would happen if he campaigned on policies that conflicted with those of the federal party? Did the Queensland party have the right or the power to instruct its federal parliamentarians to withdraw from the Coalition? Were the actions of the Queensland party such as to warrant disaffiliating it from the federal organisation?

Serious consideration of these questions had to be given urgently, especially with federal council coming up in four weeks' time. McKerrow agreed that party constitutional implications should be thoroughly studied and that independent legal advice should be sought.

The advice confirmed that the Queensland party could not pursue policies that were inconsistent with those of the federal party, so long as it remained affiliated with the federal body. Any attempt by Queensland to endorse candidates in states where an affiliated National Party organisation existed would be unconstitutional and such candidates would not be able to run as candidates of the National Party of Australia, or National Party, which were the party names registered under the *Commonwealth Electoral Act*. And further: 'Any candidate for election to Federal Parliament who runs for election on policies of the Queensland Party which are inconsistent with the policies of the National Party of Australia, if elected, would not be a member of the Federal Parliamentary National Party.'[14] Therefore, existing MPs and candidates who contravened the parliamentary party policy to remain in Coalition could potentially be expelled or excluded from the parliamentary party – something that would only have deepened the rift.

Similarly, moving to disaffiliate the Queensland party, while tempting in theory, in all probability would have led to the complete destruction of the federal organisation. Interestingly, the party federal constitution made no provision for disaffiliation. It could be argued that if it provided for affiliation, which it did, by extension it provided for disaffiliation. But there was no written provision – an indication that the party's founding fathers, when they drafted the first federal constitution in March 1926, never foresaw the prospect of relations deteriorating to the point where such action would be contemplated.[15]

The New South Wales party was determined to maintain

a hard line on its constitutional right to endorse candidates. Moppett told his central council that at a meeting with Sinclair and Hunt 'I undertook to dissociate ourselves from candidates who did not have our endorsement, but who purported to be National Party, and to do everything possible to deny them use of our name'. He said any attempt at 'what I would call the fraudulent use of our name in NSW is a matter of the deepest concern and has far-reaching ramifications'.[16]

A close examination of whether the Queensland party had the right to instruct its federal senators and members to withdraw from the Coalition, and what obligations rested on those parliamentarians under the federal constitution, indicated that it was on shaky ground.

After the Hervey Bay meeting, Sparkes appeared on the ABC TV's *7.30 Report* on 2 March. Referring to the decisions aimed at ending the Coalition and the consequent obligations on Queensland federal politicians, he said: 'We've taken a major policy decision here and they're obliged to follow it, it's as simple as that.' Was it as simple as that? Sparkes used the word 'policy'. Under the Queensland party constitution, 'policy' decisions could only emanate from annual state or special state conferences.[17]

The Hervey Bay resolutions did not come from such conferences. Moreover, they completely reversed the resolution of the July 1986 Queensland state conference, which rejected a motion to recommend to the federal parliamentary party that it withdraw from Coalition in Opposition. Despite this, Queensland federal politicians believed they were bound by Hervey Bay. Their general view was that they had given an undertaking at Hervey Bay to abide by the resolutions, and that that undertaking overrode all other considerations – including obligations placed on them by party constitutions.

Clause 30 of the federal constitution made it clear that state central councils endorsed candidates for federal elections on behalf of the National Party of Australia and 'subject to this [federal] Constitution'. Clause 17 provided that 'National Party candidates shall contest elections on policy acceptable to the National Party' – that is, to the *federal* National Party. Once elected, those members sat in the federal parliament as members of the National Party of Australia, not the Queensland National Party, or any other state party, and were obliged to support federal party policy. Federal policy at the time was to support continuing the Coalition with the Liberal Party. The policy had been reaffirmed by the party room as recently as 17 February and made public the same day in the joint Howard–Sinclair statement. There was no change in the federal parliamentary party's majority support to continue Coalition between 17 February and the Hervey Bay meeting less than two weeks later.

The Queensland federal parliamentarians also had to consider three clauses in their state constitution, which specifically related to federal politicians. The first was clause 107: 'Members of the Party elected to the Commonwealth Parliament shall govern their affairs in accordance with their own rules or in accordance with the rules of such Party as the Party is affiliated with in accordance to the provisions hereof.' 'In accordance with their own rules' meant the rules of the federal parliamentary party room. In accordance with the 'rules of such Party as the Party is affiliated with' meant the federal National Party of Australia and its constitution. In short, Queensland federal politicians were required by their state constitution to uphold obligations imposed on them by the federal parliamentary party and the federal constitution.

Clause 108 of the Queensland constitution stated: 'It shall be the responsibility of members of the Party elected to the Commonwealth Parliament to implement the Party platform as far as possible.' In this case, 'the Party platform' meant the platform of the Queensland National Party. This should have caused Queensland federal politicians no heartache, as there was at this time no major conflict between the policy objectives and philosophies in the Queensland platform – which was revised in 1986 shortly before the state election – and the federal platform. Despite Joh's insistence that his tax policy was for a single rate of 25 per cent with no new indirect taxes, the Queensland platform specifically recommended that 'there should be increased reliance upon indirect taxation, rather than direct taxation'. This was consistent with the then federal platform, published in November 1984, which said the tax system should be simplified and take account of 'the necessity to broaden the tax base …'.

Clause 109 of the Queensland constitution required its federal MPs to 'advise the [state] Management Committee of action taken by them in respect of policy decisions of Central Council or State Conference …'. The inclusion of central council in this clause appeared to contradict the clauses stipulating that policy could only emanate from annual state or special state conferences. Even so, it should not have been difficult to comply with this, even if it meant reporting that while they had supported a Queensland 'policy' position on an issue in the party room, the majority view of that meeting had endorsed a different course.

Despite these facts – technical and constitutional though they were – the Queensland federal politicians still believed the Hervey Bay undertakings were final. Some, like Braithwaite, Collard and Boswell, had serious reservations about them, but any attempt to dispute them would likely lead to immediate loss of endorsement. Hervey Bay was gospel and would be implemented, irrespective of the damage it would do to Sinclair, the split it would cause to the party and the Coalition, and whether it was right or wrong, either morally or constitutionally.

5
TACTICS AND NUMBERS

March 1987

For the Queensland organisation to direct and threaten elected Members of Parliament smacks of those features of the Labor Party we've always deplored.

Doug Anthony, speech to Sydney Rotary Club, 2 March 1987

The month of March 1987 was highlighted by deepening confusion within the National Party. Joh jetted out of Brisbane for Tokyo on 1 March for a week's visit promoting trade and investment between Queensland and Japan. On the eve of leaving, he declared that 'now in the Federal Parliament there will be no Coalition. ... If Ian Sinclair doesn't want to go that way that's his decision'. Sparkes denied the Queenslanders were trying to hijack the federal party, saying he and the premier were trying to save the nation.[1] Nonetheless, the Queensland party was now determined that the overall National Party would do what Queensland wanted.

The next regular meeting of the federal parliamentary National Party was due to be held on 17 March, the day federal parliament would resume. There was speculation that Sinclair would move for a secret ballot on whether or not the party supported the Coalition, the rationale being that in a secret ballot, those Queenslanders who might want to support the Coalition could do so with anonymity. The danger was that any southern members who wanted to vote against Coalition could also do so in secrecy. Could Sinclair guarantee he had the numbers?

Sparkes was agitated at the prospect of a secret ballot: 'I think if there's any suggestion that that should happen our Queensland members of course would probably withdraw from the party room and abstain from voting.'[2] By just floating the idea, Sparkes was seen as trying to tell the Queensland federal politicians what to do in the privacy of the party room. It added weight to allegations that the Queensland organisation was using stand-over tactics to ensure the Queensland members upheld the Hervey Bay resolutions. Doug Anthony raised the point in a speech in Sydney on 2 March:

> Whatever the divine inspiration that motivates my Queensland colleagues, I cannot stomach the intimidatory action against sitting Members of Parliament. By threatening them with their pre-selection if they don't obey the organisation, is political blackmail. It is also galling to see them humiliating the Party's elected Leader, Ian Sinclair, a distinguished Leader, a Federal Minister for 16 years, Leader of a Party that offers no suitable, experienced, replacement. For 60 years, the Party was proud of its Parliamentary freedom and goodwill. For the Queensland organisation to direct and threaten elected Members of Parliament smacks of those features of the Labor Party we've always deplored.[3]

Sparkes, interviewed by Quentin Dempster on the *7.30 Report* that evening, denied the federal Queensland parliamentarians had been blackmailed:

Q: But you have blackmailed those 12 National Party members from Queensland, haven't you, by threatening their endorsement?

A: Blackmail is a very emotive term, it's completely not applicable in this situation. All we've done is indicate to our federal parliamentarians that we believe very, very strongly in the premier's thrust for the prime ministership and I think it's not unreasonable to expect them, as our representatives, or the representatives of the Queensland National Party, to support the premier in that thrust.

Q: So they have to toe the line though, don't they?

A: Well, they're our representatives and if they're not prepared to do what the party believes is in the interest, not only of this state, but the whole of the Australian nation, I think it's not unreasonable that we should say to them that you've got to observe the decisions that were taken at Hervey Bay last weekend.

Q: Well that's tantamount to a direction, Sir Robert.

A: No, when members of parliament are endorsed by whatever party, they undertake to carry out the constitution and platform and policies of the party and we've taken a major policy decision here and they're obliged to follow it, it's as simple as that.

It was questionable whether Sparkes was getting close to breaching parliamentary privilege, as defined by the parliamentary bible, *House of Representatives Practice*. This stated that '… to attempt by any means to influence a Member in his conduct as a Member, is a breach of privilege. So too, is any conduct having a tendency to impair a Member's independence in the future performance of his duty'.[4] Had Sparkes' comments and the clause of the Hervey Bay resolutions calling on Sinclair to end the Coalition been brought before the House, it is possible they could have been referred to the Privileges Committee. Sinclair considered the idea. Melbourne's *The Age* newspaper on 7 March reported him repeatedly raising the spectre of the Queensland Nationals, including Sparkes, facing possible action for breaching parliamentary privilege. The problem was that if he did, he would split the party further. The matter was not pursued.

Sinclair's exasperation at the actions and statements of the Queenslanders was no doubt fuelled by the Morgan Gallup poll in *The Bulletin* of 3 March. It showed that a Joh-led National Party would gain 27 per cent primary support, compared to one led by Sinclair gaining only three per cent. It also showed that Labor support had increased by five per cent to 47 per cent over the previous poll, while Coalition support had dropped from 48 to 45 per cent. ALP support was higher than before the Queensland Premier began his Canberra crusade, confirming the Howard–Sinclair fear that the Joh campaign was helping Labor at the expense of the Coalition. Reacting to the poll, Sparkes could barely contain his view about what Sinclair should do: 'I would say that what Ian Sinclair has to do is recognise the writing is on the wall – I suppose one should more accurately say the Gallup poll speaks for itself – and adjust his tactics accordingly. If I was Ian Sinclair, I would accept the inevitable.'[5]

Sinclair would have had this poll result in mind when he attended a meeting of the New South Wales party's central executive in Sydney on 6 March 1987. While acknowledging Joh's popularity, he warned that 'the path he [Joh] had taken could demolish the whole National Party organisation', and stressed that the federal parliamentary party's autonomy 'must be protected'.[6] The executive was keen to establish a public position that supported Sinclair and the Coalition in light of the 17 March federal party meeting and the forthcoming federal council. A motion was suggested that the central executive 'authorise the State Chairman [Doug Moppett] to continue to request the NSW Federal Members to remain in Coalition irrespective of any resolution of the Federal Council'. This was dropped in favour of another set of words that 'should Federal Council refuse to support the continuation of the Coalition, the NSW organisation continue in Coalition'. This was carried. After further discussion, another motion was carried unanimously and issued to the media:

> That the Central Executive of the National Party of Australia – NSW reaffirm its total confidence in The Rt Hon Ian Sinclair as Federal Leader, its support for the Coalition with the Liberal Party and uphold the autonomy of the Federal Parliamentary Party.[7]

By mid-March, the media was reporting that the Joh for PM campaign was losing impetus and some of the Queensland federal politicians were wavering in their support for the Hervey Bay resolutions. The latter point must have concerned the Queensland organisation, because all 12 of the state's federal MPs were summoned to a meeting in Brisbane on 16 March – the day before the federal parliamentary party meeting.

On the eve of the Brisbane meeting, Queensland solidarity cracked: Stan Collard declared his support for the Coalition, saying it would go on. Asked if he thought the Joh campaign was losing support, he replied: 'Did it ever have much?' In response, Joh declared: 'Stan's day of reckoning will come one of these days, you can count on that.'[8] Joh and Sparkes emerged from the meeting with the parliamentarians declaring that each and every one of them was rock solid behind Hervey Bay, including Collard.

In the party room the following day there was no further vote on the Coalition, because one had been taken a month earlier. There was also no vote on Sinclair's leadership. There was, however, criticism of some of Sinclair's recent comments – notably his suggestion that Sparkes might have breached parliamentary privilege.

The Member for Groom, Tom McVeigh, chose this meeting to formally implement the Hervey Bay resolutions for himself and unilaterally withdrew from the Coalition. McVeigh told Sinclair that while there was no challenge to him, he should resign anyway. For the time being, McVeigh was on his own; the remaining 11 Queenslanders opted to stay with the Coalition pending the outcome of federal council.

McVeigh had been variously Minister for Housing and Construction, assisting the Minister for Trade and Resources, and Minister for Home Affairs and the Environment in the Fraser–Anthony government. After the March 1983 election, Anthony appointed him shadow Minister for Primary Industry. He was moved to shadow Minister for Trade by Sinclair in December 1984. Then, with the reshuffle that followed Howard's succession from Peacock in September 1985, Sinclair dropped him from the shadow ministry altogether.

Following Hervey Bay, McVeigh became openly critical of Sinclair and Hunt, predicting that they could be disposed of and interim leaders appointed, pending the arrival of Joh.[9] He said the fact that he was out of the Coalition on his own did not matter as his colleagues would be with him in a couple of weeks: 'I believe it's inappropriate for someone who has indicated along with his Queensland colleagues that he's not going to be part of the Coalition after certain steps are taken in two or three weeks' time, in the meantime to take part in joint policy developments and views on legislation.'[10]

A further worry for Sinclair was that two of his New South Wales colleagues, Ian Robinson (Page) and Bruce Cowan (Lyne) appeared to be wobbling.

Robinson said there was a 'silver lining' to the Joh campaign in that it had created a groundswell of support for the party in his electorate.[11] He had bitter exchanges with his parliamentary colleagues, some of whom accused him of being a traitor, which he strenuously denied:

> My view was that we had to do all we could to accommodate the groundswell that had been created, to find ways of utilising it to our advantage. That is very different from saying that I was totally in support of the proposition that Joh could go to Canberra and become leader of the party, or the Coalition for that matter.[12]

Cowan, who was identified by the media as a Joh supporter, denied that he had supported the campaign, but acknowledged sympathy for what Joh was doing: 'I admired him for the great things he achieved for Queensland. I was sympathetic to Joh as a great politician. And there were tensions in the [federal] Coalition, so there was some sympathy for what Joh was trying to do.'[13]

In the meantime, Sparkes was changing the thrust of the Joh campaign. No longer was it Joh for PM, but Joh for Canberra. This change of emphasis first emerged in an interview he gave to the ABC Radio *PM* program on the evening of 16 March. When asked if his message was that Joh was still bound for The Lodge, Sparkes replied:

> Yes, I think perhaps there's been too much emphasis placed on personal political aspirations and aggrandisement.

I want to stress and stress very strongly that as far as the National Party in this State is concerned our objective is not to promote the premier, our objective is not to promote the power of the National Party, but to ensure that we have in place in Canberra after the election a conservative government with the right policies and the guts to implement them.

Q: Yes, but what does Joh for PM mean, doesn't it mean just that, Joh for PM?

A: Well, yes, but what I'm stressing is that we're not particularly concerned about Joh achieving the prime ministership except in the sense that it will enable us of course to put into place the sort of policies that we believe are necessary.

Sparkes also made a significant admission on Channel 9's *Willesee* program on 16 March. Interviewer Mike Willesee asked what Sparkes would say if the price of internal fighting meant further success for the Labor Party. Sparkes replied: 'If the price is further success for Labor then we've made a very serious mistake. We've gambled and the gamble has not come off.' By this stage it was too late to call off the gamble, but the change in emphasis of the campaign indicated a mellowing of the way it was now being played, at least so far as Sparkes was concerned.

Joh, however, was not letting up one iota. On 21 March, he hit the southern New South Wales town of Albury, in the Farrer electorate of federal National MP and shadow Minister for Veterans' Affairs, Tim Fischer. Introducing the premier, Fischer said he was 'at one with [Joh on] the need to defeat the Hawke government', but disagreed with the premier's methodology. The premier was unperturbed, telling the crowd of around 1000 people at the Albury racecourse that if the Liberal and National parties stayed together, they would 'hang together'. Claiming that Howard and Sinclair had let the nation down, he said he was 'not prepared to trust the future to these ridiculous people' and added that his anti-Coalition candidates would be known as Joh National candidates.[14]

Fischer, who would be the federal party leader for nine years from 1990 and deputy prime minister for more than three years from March 1996, remembered the Albury rally clearly: 'It went okay, but I realised I would have to get off the fence a bit; that Joh was not the silver bullet that some people thought he was. There were a number of local party members pressuring me to support Joh, but the majority were more with the federal Coalition per se.'[15]

Joh had preceded his Albury statements by predicting on ABC Radio *AM* on 16 March that Sinclair had no hope of winning the election – 'he lost the last election' – referring to the poll of 1 December 1984 at which, under Sinclair's leadership, the National Party won 21 House of Representatives seats – an increase of four and the largest number the party had held since 1975, when it had twenty-three. True, the increase was as much a result of the increase in the size of the parliament from 125 to 148 members as anything Sinclair did, but bums on seats were all that ultimately mattered and Sinclair, as leader, had got them there.

By 23 March, *The Northern Daily Leader* in Tamworth, the heart of Sinclair's New England electorate, reported Joh saying he had the people to stand against Sinclair and Hunt.

§

As the federal council grew closer, lobbying among delegates became more intense. So, too, did the development of tactics, both for the council and the preceding meeting of the federal management committee. Numbers were crucial. If the Queensland party won the votes in management and council, it would effectively win control of the entire federal party organisation, including the federal secretariat and other assets and resources. It would move quickly to bring about fundamental constitutional changes. The Queenslanders could be expected to get written into the federal party constitution a provision categorically requiring the parliamentary party to implement the policies of federal council; to have clearly defined the authority of the council to dictate to the parliamentary party whether or not to enter into a Coalition, either in or out of government; and to change the representational structure of each state delegation on the council so that those with more federal parliamentarians had more votes than those with fewer or none.

The numbers for the forthcoming federal council, to be held at Canberra's Lakeside International hotel, stacked up precariously when it came to predicting the vote on issues such as Coalition and the federal presidency. Adding to the problem was the question of just who out of the 42 delegates was actually entitled to vote. The constitution was not specifically clear. McKerrow called for a legal opinion, which was that the treasurer and secretary were not entitled to any vote on any issue, while the president was entitled to a casting vote only. All other delegates, other than those from the associated Northern Territory CLP, had deliberative voting rights, providing they were financial members of their respective state parties. In light of this, McKerrow would rule in her report to council that the immediate past president, Tom Drake-Brockman, from Western Australia, was not entitled to vote. Drake-Brockman was a life member of the National Country Party of Western Australia, which became defunct in October 1984 when it and the breakaway National Party of Western Australia reunited under the single National Party of Australia (WA) banner. However, he never formally joined a branch of the united party. It is a matter for speculation whether his vote would have made any difference to the outcome of the major council decisions, but it is unlikely.

Some consideration was given by McKerrow to trying to revamp the Tasmanian National Party, so it could send six delegates to council. The party in Tasmania had been affiliated, but had been defunct since 1975. Any attempt to resurrect it now would have been seen as a blatant attempt to rig votes. The idea was dropped. Another alternative, which appeared to have more credibility, was whether or not the South Australian delegation, which would be likely to support Queensland initiatives in federal council, could participate, given that the state had not paid affiliation fees for several years, due to financial difficulties. The problem with this was twofold. First, despite its non-payment of fees, South Australia had previously been allowed to take its place on council and vote, and it would therefore be seen, again, as an attempt to rig the numbers to bar them now. Second, the federal constitution made no provision for banning state parties from council meetings for non-payment of fees. This idea was also dropped.

A third alternative arose by accident because of the continued attempt by the NT Nationals to be affiliated with the federal body. The NT Nationals had resubmitted an application for affiliation, which this time complied with the requirements of the federal constitution. McKerrow, well aware of the controversial nature of the forthcoming management and council meetings – both of which she would chair – was determined they be run strictly according to the constitution. She did her homework thoroughly. In preliminary consideration of the NT Nationals' application she wondered how to handle the CLP if the NT Nationals were to become affiliated. The two parties had been fighting each other barely a month earlier in the Northern Territory election. McKerrow was worried about the embarrassment it would cause the CLP if, as a result of management's decisions, the NT Nationals were able to take seats in council and have full voting rights, while the CLP delegates could only participate on matters relating to the Territory – if at all. Could the Territory have an affiliated party and an associated one simultaneously represented on federal council? Probably not. While the constitution made no provision for a status of association, it did specify that an organisation in a state (or territory) wherein there is no affiliated organisation may apply to be admitted to the party.[16] This implied that if the NT Nationals became affiliated, they would be the only Territory organisation eligible to be represented on federal council. The CLP would have to be dumped.

On the Monday before federal council, McKerrow came to Canberra so that she would have ample time to study and be fully briefed on the council and management agendas. She called for an investigation of the records of previous council and executive meetings to see whether any specific provisions existed for the associated CLP.[17] No-one was in any doubt that the CLP was only an associate; that had been decided in February 1979 when the CLP agreed that its relations with the non-Labor parties in Canberra should be equal. The search turned up the startling fact that, while it had been the clear intention of the CLP to disaffiliate from the federal National Country Party, the disaffiliation had not formally been carried out. Urgent clarification was sought from the Darwin office of the CLP. Its records similarly showed disaffiliation had not formally taken place.

The Australian Country Party – Northern Territory was first affiliated with the then Australian Country Party on 19 April 1971. After its formation into the CLP in July 1974, the Territory party remained affiliated with the Australian Country Party and subsequent National Country Party of Australia (NCP). It was still affiliated with the NCP during the first half of 1978. This was borne out by an undated press release issued by the then NCP federal president, Adrian Solomons, from New South Wales, in which he said: 'The Country Liberal Party is affiliated with and a constituent part of the National Country Party of Australia.' On 17 August 1978, Solomons wrote a report for the federal management committee, in which he indicated that, following discussions with the Liberal Party and the CLP, a proposal was likely to emerge that would involve the CLP disaffiliating with all southern political parties for the time being.

On 4 November 1978, the central council of the CLP met at Nhulunbuy in the Northern Territory and carried a motion authorising its chairman to confer with the NCP and Liberal Party to achieve final agreement on a proposal for association without affiliation with the two parties. The next meeting of the CLP's central council, on 2 February 1979, carried a motion recommending to the next conference that the CLP relinquish affiliation with the NCP and adopt a position of association with the Liberal and National Country parties. The question was whether or not this motion was ever ratified by a conference of the CLP – logically, its next annual conference. The CLP's Darwin office, after a search of its records, came back with advice that the motion had not, in fact, been put before a conference.

This was confirmed to McKerrow in a facsimile letter from the CLP general secretary in Darwin, John Hare, on 25 March 1987. Hare asked McKerrow to pass the information on to his president, Grant Heaslip, who was on his way to Canberra as part of the CLP delegation to federal council. McKerrow showed Heaslip the letter the following day. Heaslip wrote her a further letter: 'I can also confirm that our records show we have never formally disaffiliated from the National Party of Australia, since first being affiliated by your Federal Executive on April 19, 1971.'

This had enormous implications. First, if the CLP wanted to maintain its affiliated status, it would be liable to pay affiliation fees backdated to 1978. Second, irrespective of affiliation fees, it meant the application for affiliation from the NT Nationals could not be considered by the federal management committee. The constitution provided for the affiliation of only one organisation from each state or territory.

Of greater immediate significance was the question of voting rights for CLP delegates to council. If the CLP's continuing affiliated status was upheld, the party would be entitled to six, and possibly seven, delegates to council with full voting rights – and those delegates would be almost guaranteed to vote in favour of the federal Coalition, given their party's close relationship with both the federal National and Liberal parties.[18] There was scope to crush any attempt by Queensland to end it.

§

Sinclair was able to take heart from the Morgan Gallup poll in *The Bulletin* on 24 March. In answer to the question 'If you're a National Party voter, would you prefer Sir Joh Bjelke-Petersen or Ian Sinclair?', 57 per cent of the nearly 2000 people polled Australia-wide preferred Sinclair to 33 per cent for Joh. Responding to this, Joh wrote it off, preferring to cite Sinclair's three per cent rating from the Morgan poll of 3 March:

> Now how can a man go from three per cent to 57 per cent? I wouldn't know. Three per cent has been his rating for many, many months – never above nine per cent. Now, all of a sudden, he's 57 per cent. It sort of makes you sometimes wonder how these polls are put together or what area they're put together in.[19]

6
A QUEENSLAND BACKDOWN?

27 to 29 March 1987

… there is no intention on our part to run candidates against sitting National Party Members anywhere – it's unfortunate Joh's been saying otherwise.

Robert Sparkes, federal management committee,
Canberra, 27 March 1987

Shirley McKerrow was an astute political operator who did her homework thoroughly. A member of the Victorian party, she had been its president for four years from 1976 before taking on the federal presidency in 1981. In both roles, she was the first woman to hold such positions in Australian political history.

The federal management committee delegates began assembling in a conference room at the Lakeside International shortly after eight o'clock in the morning of Friday 27 March. Tea, coffee and light refreshments were available. Given the turn of events resulting from the Hervey Bay resolutions, the atmosphere was noticeably tense, but polite.

McKerrow held the information on the CLP affiliation closely. On the Wednesday before federal council, she mentioned it in confidence to Sinclair at a private meeting in his Parliament House office, but to no-one else.

After opening the federal management meeting at 8.30am, McKerrow suggested the committee should first turn its attention to the federal council meeting, and in particular the program. She explained that it had been structured so the most controversial issues, notably Coalition, would be dealt with last, on the Sunday morning, 29 March, to minimise the spectacle of a disunited organisation over the weekend. The Lakeside was crawling with media from far and wide. Almost the entire contingent of political reporters from Brisbane, including TV commentators and crews, had come to town to supplement the force of the Canberra press gallery. Never before had a federal council of the National Party attracted such attention. Damage control was an important consideration.

By suggesting discussion on the program structure, McKerrow was able to get some insight into the tactics of the Queensland delegation. She wanted to find this out, if possible, in the privacy of management, rather than be taken by surprise in the public arena of council.

Sparkes put forward changes the Queenslanders wanted. While he respected the rationale behind the structuring of the agenda, he thought it was unrealistic to defer consideration of the Coalition until Sunday. He suggested it be brought forward for discussion on Saturday. Also, he wanted Joh to be given the same time as Sinclair to address the council immediately after Sinclair had spoken that afternoon. He said this would enable Joh to put his case and then return to Brisbane. Joh was due to arrive in Canberra at about midday that day.

After considerable discussion, during which Sinclair objected to the idea of Joh speaking on the same day as himself, as it would simply pit the views of one against the other, management agreed to alter the program to allow Joh to address the council first thing on Saturday morning and open debate on the economy and taxation. No support was given to the proposal that Coalition motions be brought forward to Saturday morning, although this would not preclude a motion from the floor at any time to suspend standing orders and bring them on. Sparkes had received a minor setback in not winning support for Joh to speak that afternoon.

Sparkes gave the committee a run-down on the Joh campaign. He said as a result of the Hervey Bay meeting, the Queensland organisation had assumed control of the exercise: 'We will be having the last say, not Joh, in terms of who runs where. If he doesn't accept that, he goes his own way.'[1] He said Joh remained obsessed that Fraser had failed and he was now vitally concerned that Howard and Sinclair would similarly fail. Joh had never had any personal animosity towards Sinclair or Hunt, but research had been done, and was continuing, that supported Joh's concern and his actions and showed there must be a change in federal Opposition leadership and policy. Sparkes said he was worried about the mudslinging that had gone on in the media:

> But, if the mudslinging continues, then Joh will get tougher and stand against Hunt and Sinclair. We [Queensland party organisation] would say that that's not on. I'm strongly of the view that we can harness the scene, whereby Joh shuts up about Ian and vice-versa. There is no intention on our part to run candidates against sitting National Party Members anywhere – it's unfortunate Joh's been saying otherwise.

The last statement was a key issue, as it went to the heart of the independence and autonomy of the respective state National parties and their exclusive right to preselect candidates – something that the New South Wales chairman, Doug Moppett, was quick to pick up and emphasise to the meeting. Sparkes reiterated the point nearly three weeks later, ruling out running Joh National candidates against sitting National Party MPs 'anywhere in Australia. We won't be running against them'.[2] But he was contradicting himself. In his presidential report in the March 1987 issue of the Queensland National Party magazine, *National Outlook*, which must have been written after the Hervey Bay resolutions and before the March meeting of federal management and federal council, he said:

> It is my intention to work closely with the Premier to ensure that every Federal Division in Australia is contested by a candidate loyal to our cause. I anticipate that these candidates will be endorsed National Party candidates and that we can work through the National Party organisations in other states. If this proves impossible in any area, the 'Joh for P.M.' Committee will seek out and endorse candidates.[3]

When the management committee moved on to correspondence, the affiliation application of the NT Nationals came forward and was supported by a written resolution from the Queensland management committee, recommending that 'the National Party Federal Council officially recognises the Northern Territory National Party'.

At this point, McKerrow carefully detailed what she had discovered about the CLP and its affiliation status. She had told no-one about it up to now, except Sinclair. She concluded that under the circumstances, in her view, federal management could hardly consider the application. Her revelation shocked delegates.

Sparkes' reaction was immediate. He described it as an 'intolerable argument', saying the CLP, if not expressly disaffiliated, was technically so. He said the real test of the bona fides of the CLP was where their politicians sat in the federal parliament, noting that at the time both were sitting with the Liberal Party.

Sinclair did not support the president's position either. He said the NT application had to be rejected because, with a federal election possibly only weeks away (speculation was rife an election could be held as early as 9 May), the federal party had to maintain its links with the CLP to ensure Northern Territory representation in the federal parliament was retained by the conservatives. He did not want to see any action taken that would change the status of CLP representation and participation at federal council.

In the end, management carried a motion that 'the NT Nationals be requested to defer their application for 12 months'. While McKerrow did not achieve what she wanted, the Queensland attempt to have the NT Nationals affiliated, and therefore able to take up voting places at council, was thwarted. The NT Nationals had their delegates in Canberra – in fact at the Lakeside – ready to take their places as soon as they got the nod. It never came.

The management committee's discussions were remarkably restrained throughout the meeting. There was no shouting, swearing or slamming of fists on the table. Delegates made their points forthrightly and politely. Its business concluded, the committee adjourned so that its members could grab a quick sandwich before the opening of federal council at 2pm.

§

Ultimately, it was just as well the McKerrow initiative failed. While she and the CLP president, Heaslip, were confident their information and conclusions were correct, it was discovered about six weeks later that the CLP had, in fact, formally disaffiliated from the National Country Party in 1979. John Hare advised on 11 May 1987 that he had discovered the CLP central council, which had met on 2 February 1979 and recommended disaffiliation, had been followed the next day by a special conference of the party in Darwin. The conference had endorsed the council recommendation to relinquish affiliation with the NCP and 'adopt a position of association with the Liberal Party of Australia and the National Country Party'.[4] Disaffiliation had been formalised from 3 February 1979. Hare's discovery prompted Heaslip to convene a meeting of the CLP management committee on 12 May 1987, following which a clarifying letter was forwarded to the National Party for its records.

§

Joh Bjelke-Petersen, who had never made much secret of his belief that federal council was a waste of time and achieved little if anything, arrived in Canberra shortly before the meeting began. He was briefed by Sparkes on the outcome of the management committee and told he could not address the council until the following morning. He went to his suite in the Lakeside and did not emerge until his scheduled speaking time at nine o'clock on Saturday.

Sinclair's speech was the first major event of the afternoon. It was awaited with considerable anticipation and interest by all delegates, who listened attentively. There were no interruptions. Sinclair made a strong plea for unity and maintaining the Coalition, especially given the threat of an early election. He conceded that the Coalition was not a sacred cow to be worshipped at all costs, but continued:

> Its benefits, for those we represent, and for Australia, are such that it should only be broken when there is a

fundamental difference between the two Parties. In the current political hothouse, with an election inevitable and a double dissolution imminent, changes in our effective working relationship without valid reason will only weaken public support for the National Party and help the Hawke socialists.[5]

Partly to offset the impact Joh was having with his policy initiatives, Sinclair used the occasion to release his own lengthy discussion paper on federal National Party policy objectives. It highlighted, he said, the party's ability to put forward its own policy priorities, while at the same time remaining in Coalition – something which Joh and Sparkes argued could not be done.

During Sinclair's address the Queensland Premier's press secretary, Ken Crooke, appeared in the hotel foyer and began casually talking to journalists. Word spread that Crooke had news from the Queensland camp and a major press briefing developed. Crooke said Queensland would be supporting the thrust of the South Australian motion to council, which supported the principle of not being in Coalition in Opposition, but which also left the decision on whether or when to break the Coalition in the hands of the federal parliamentary party. It was a bombshell and looked like a huge capitulation. Crooke claimed there was no backdown, but rather, with the prospect of an election being called within weeks, there was sense in not implementing the Hervey Bay resolutions immediately.

Sinclair was jubilant, telling an impromptu media briefing after his speech: 'I think all the battle's behind us and let's get on with beating Hawke. ... We now have a cohesive basis on which we can provide the alternative to the government.' Howard was equally excited, sending Sinclair a message: 'I told them to put their money on Sinkers. Great news.'[6]

But, as was so often the case with Joh, it was dangerous to

count chickens. While the Queenslanders were apparently prepared not to try to force a vote to immediately break the Coalition, there was still a lot of confusion as to what they did intend. Joh kept the confusion going on Saturday when he started his address to federal council. He began with a conciliatory line: 'You are part and parcel of a very important organisation that has played, and will play, I am sure, an even greater part in the history of this nation in the years to come.'[7] Then he thrust both arms high in the air and declared:

> I have some very, very good news for you today – the Coalition is finished. I told you that quite a long time ago and I remind you of it again today. And anyone who thinks otherwise, of course, has got his head in the sand. And, you know, if you keep your head in the sand you're likely to get some of the feathers in your tail pulled out.

He chided the party federally and at state levels, other than Queensland, for not being more politically aggressive:

> But you have stayed in the shadow whether you like it or not. Any tree or anything that stays in the shadow doesn't grow the way it ought to grow. You've got to come out into the sunshine, you've got to get the heat and the warmth, you've got to take responsibility – no good always being co-pilot.

He told the gathering he thought federal council was 'futile' and he would take no notice of its decisions:

> The decisions you make here are the decisions you have a right to make and a responsibility to make; whatever, you make them, that's your responsibility and so on. But I tell

you it won't make one iota of difference, as I've said in the media so often, to what I do in the interests of Australia.

As though emphasising the point, he returned to Brisbane almost immediately after his speech. His attitude was now very publicly in contrast with the position of the Queensland party, which was that resolutions of federal council should be binding on the party, even its federal parliamentary wing. In the lead-up to the meeting, Sparkes had even been arguing that the council had the power to direct the parliamentary party to leave the Coalition. While Sparkes was emphasising the importance of council decisions, his premier was writing them off as irrelevant, prompting *The Canberra Times* to suggest: 'Sir Joh has proved to be, beyond doubt, Mr Hawke's best ally.'[8]

§

Immediately after Joh's address, Sparkes moved suspension of standing orders to bring on an urgency motion:

> That this Council, recognising that Australia's critical economic condition requires resolute action to promote national recovery which can only come from sound policies and the total commitment of outstanding Australians, welcomes the announcement by the Premier of Queensland that he will promote such policies and seek a Federal seat in the forthcoming election.[9]

After lengthy debate, the motion was carried with three amendments — two moved by New South Wales — that required Joh to 'promote National Party policies and work within the State and Federal Constitutions of the National Party wherever there is a State organisation and seek a federal seat in the forthcoming election'. In other words, according to federal council, Joh would have to promote federal party policies and could not stand candidates in seats against endorsed National Party candidates, or in states where affiliated National Party organisations existed, unless those organisations agreed to let him do so.

The council then brought forward the two Coalition motions that were on the agenda. The first, proposed by South Australia, which the Queenslanders had indicated they would support, was:

> That this Council supports the principle of the National Party being a separate identity whilst in Opposition. The final decision and timing as to whether and when the National Party withdraws from the Coalition shall be left to the Federal Parliamentary National Party.

Queensland tried to have it amended, with Sparkes unsuccessfully moving that the second sentence be deleted. It was ultimately carried, with a New South Wales amendment which extended the first sentence by adding the words 'but recognises there are problems in an election year' and placed the word 'Therefore' at the start of the second sentence.

With this resolution, McKerrow ruled that the second motion, which read 'That the National Party does not enter into an agreement of Coalition in Opposition', had become irrelevant. She was overruled and the motion was carried without alteration. It was moved by Western Australia, with the state parliamentary leader, Hendy Cowan, leading the debate. In his summing up, he made it clear the motion was meant for the future, not the present:

> Can I point out that the purpose of this particular motion is that at the moment we have an agreement to be in Coalition

in Opposition. This particular motion does not address when that agreement is to be broken. It does not address that question. It talks about not entering into any further agreement. Perhaps we should have said further agreements, but we didn't. But the fact of the matter is that we are addressing a future position. We are not addressing the question of what pertains at the moment. I want that made very, very clear.

Despite this clarification, the motion's meaning was later twisted. Joh, for example, despite claiming the decisions of federal council were of no interest to him, would claim that Sinclair was in breach of the wishes of the council by maintaining the party in Coalition.

Because the Queenslanders had decided to change tactics and support the thrust of the South Australian motion, there was no move to have the council vote to immediately end the Coalition.

Sparkes, as architect of the Hervey Bay resolutions, had been insisting they were binding on Queensland federal MPs. Hervey Bay specifically required the Queensland delegation to federal council to 'put forward a motion to the effect that the Federal Coalition be terminated immediately', if the federal leader had not withdrawn the party from Coalition by the time of council. Sinclair had not done this. It was therefore presumably incumbent upon Sparkes, as leader of the Queensland delegation, to put such a motion to council. He did not do so, obviously because of the change of tactics. But if the masterminds of Hervey Bay believed those resolutions were binding on the politicians, they should arguably also have accepted they were binding on themselves.

§

There was another significant motion carried by council. It was moved by Queensland and required 'that this Council request the Parliamentary wing to present its policies as National Party policies only'. Sinclair was not concerned about it as it only requested the parliamentary wing. Also, while the party was involved in the presentation of Coalition policies, it was not precluded from developing its own objectives – he had just released an updated version of these to council as part of his address. Sinclair's argument was that being in Coalition did not stop the National Party promoting its own ideas and highlighting its differences from the Liberal Party. National Party policies, or objectives, could be put forward in addition to those of the Coalition, so the electorate could see the emphasis the Nationals wanted incorporated by a future Coalition government.

The Queenslanders did not see it this way. To them the motion meant the party should not be associated with Coalition policies – full stop. The motion did not say that, but Queensland was later able to use it to press its claim for the implementation as policy of two other significant motions at council, both of which were carried, one supporting a 25 cents in the dollar flat tax with no accompanying consumption taxes, and the other calling for a stringent toughening of Australia's industrial laws.

Taxation and industrial reform had become the two major federal policy planks for the Queensland National Party. By getting these motions carried, it now had the weight of federal council approval for such policy approaches. By also having carried the motion that the parliamentary wing be requested to present its policies as National Party policies only, it had added clout to try to impose Queensland-oriented directions on the federal parliamentary party.

The federal constitution at the time was not so cut and dried on these matters. Indeed, it was complex and cumbersome. It required that a motion for consideration as party policy be considered by a joint meeting of the federal council and the members of the federal parliamentary party 'before ratification by Federal Council'. All those present at such meetings would have the right to speak, but only members of federal council could vote on policy motions. Motions adopted by a simple majority 'of Federal Council members present at such Joint Meetings shall be adopted as Policy of the Federal National Party'.[10] The current meeting was a federal council only. Strictly speaking, the Queensland policy motions – and any others from other states – should be put to a joint meeting before becoming policy. From that point, it would be debatable whether they were binding on the parliamentary party, or, as had been the convention, be taken into consideration in its development of policies. In any event, the joint meeting provisions were not brought up by any delegates and so were not put to the test.

§

As with any political conference, federal council saw intense and constant behind the scenes lobbying and negotiation – last-minute attempts to shore up votes, especially on the important Coalition issues, and on the federal presidency, the vote for which would be taken on the Sunday morning.

Not widely known was a decision by McKerrow to bring in the former minister and National Party heavyweight, Peter Nixon, as a peace negotiator. He came secretly from Melbourne to Canberra and the Lakeside on Friday afternoon for a last-ditch attempt to reach a compromise between Sinclair and Joh. Nixon had been the Member for Gippsland in Victoria from 1961 and a minister in Coalition governments from December 1966 until his retirement in March 1983. He was well respected throughout the National Party and had a reasonable relationship with the Queensland Premier, often being called on by Malcolm Fraser to negotiate with Joh during the term of the Fraser–Anthony government. Nixon said his Lakeside expedition was a tense time:

> I sneaked into the hotel and then ran into Hendy Cowan in the lift! He said 'What are you doing here?' and I said 'I'm just a guest'. I was the only one Joh would talk to. I tried to reason with him, explain to him that he could never become prime minister unless he was a Liberal, and that there was no guarantee that he would even become leader of the National Party.[11]

Apart from his one-on-one meeting with Joh, Nixon also met with the Queensland president and vice-president, Sparkes and Holm, trying to explain that the Joh campaign was unworkable. Then he, Sinclair, Sparkes, Holm and McKerrow met late into Friday night in McKerrow's hotel suite. They developed a set of objectives aimed at achieving the defeat of the Hawke government, the maintenance of the National Party as one party, the presentation of a united view to the electorate, the use of the Joh factor to help defeat Hawke, and the acceptance or recognition of each state organisation's rights and powers.

Early the next morning Nixon drafted a form of words based on the night's discussions. Sinclair and Sparkes each received a typewritten copy for consideration, and, if acceptable, signature. Both signed the document. Nixon kept the signed original and returned to Melbourne on a breakfast flight believing he had 'got within an ace' of reaching peace with Bjelke-Petersen. But events rapidly overtook the Nixon plan.

§

A Queensland backdown?

The last major business of federal council was the election of the federal president. The position became vacant, along with those of the treasurer, secretary and vice-presidents (six of whom could be appointed, generally each state's president or chairman, and the longest serving of whom became the senior federal vice-president), each annual federal council.

McKerrow had been re-elected each year since taking on the presidency in March 1981. Early in 1987, she made it known she would not seek re-election. The senior vice-president, Holm, a close supporter of Joh and Sparkes, put himself forward as a candidate. So, too, did the immediate past president of the Victorian National Party and a former Victorian parliamentarian, Stuart McDonald. Both men lobbied heavily for the job and before the council the media was generally tipping that, while it would be close, Holm was likely to win. McDonald, like McKerrow, was from Victoria and it was good to share the presidency around the affiliated states if possible. Moreover, Holm was the senior vice-president.

Early in the New Year and before relations turned nasty, Sinclair had been happy to support Holm. He had believed it was logical and proper to support the nomination of the man who had been the senior vice-president for many years. His attitude changed as the gap between him and the Queenslanders widened. Holm would not have received Sinclair's vote in the ballot on 29 March. It was taken secretly, as was always the case. McDonald was declared the winner, with a decisive majority of ten votes. It was a blow to the Queenslanders. Having one of theirs as the federal president would have been an enormous help to their strategy. Holm did, however, retain the senior vice-presidency.

By the end of federal council, it was evident the Queenslanders had not fared well. They had not managed to get the Northern Territory Nationals affiliated; they had backed down on immediately ending the Coalition; their urgency motion had been watered down to confine Joh's activities within the rules and constitutions of the state and federal parties; the Queensland federal members and senators, with the exception of McVeigh, were still in the Coalition; and they had not managed to get their candidate up as president.

Sinclair was exuberant – too much so. As he was leaving the Lakeside he confidently told newsmen the Queensland federal politicians had 'confirmed to me that they will not be withdrawing from the Coalition'. When told of this, Sparkes described it as 'grossly inaccurate'.[12] He said if the Labor Party did not call an early election, the full impact of Hervey Bay would be brought to bear and the overall situation reviewed at the next Queensland state executive meeting, in Brisbane on 10 April.

While Sparkes regained some initiative after three days of losses, the stoush with Sinclair ensured negative headlines the next day, including 'Sinclair trumped', 'Nationals in turmoil as leaders brawl', 'Nationals threat to split Coalition', 'Sparkes, Sinclair clash', and 'Nationals in bitter clash on Coalition'.[13] The party had spent a lot of time, money and effort bringing delegates from all over Australia for a three-day conference under the spotlight of the national media – and had resolved nothing.

§

The social agenda of federal council meetings traditionally involved a senators and members cocktail party on the first evening, in this case Friday 27 March.

During the event, I got into a conversation with the president of the women's federal council, Jean McIntyre, and fellow Queenslander, Mendy Campbell. McIntyre and I had generally enjoyed a good relationship. She was a commercial Devon cattle breeder, while I ran Devons on my small farm near

A Queensland backdown?

Mudgee in New South Wales. We had something in common.

During the conversation, one of the ladies asked me what I thought of 'our wonderful premier'. I replied with injudicious words to the effect that I thought he should be strung up. Needless to say, this was reported to the new federal president, McDonald, with a demand that, at the very least, I be severely reprimanded, if not sacked.

When McDonald came to the federal secretariat on the Monday morning after federal council, he sat me down and said my comments had been 'pretty bloody stupid', with which I agreed. He then said 'consider yourself severely reprimanded'.

7
CONFUSION

April 1987

We suddenly find that we're in a situation where we return to Canberra not knowing whether we remain a part of the great National Party of Australia, or whether we're going to be a different identity, or what the hell we're going to be.

Bob Katter senior, ABC Radio, *AM*, 13 April 1987

The federal parliamentary party gathered for its regular meeting on Tuesday 31 March. It was a peaceful event. Everyone, it seemed, was too wrung out from the weekend's federal council to rock more boats.

The following day, only one relevant story appeared in the national press: a report in *The Sydney Morning Herald* saying the party room had discussed a paper on tax options presented by Queenslander, Ray Braithwaite. According to the *Herald*, the party room expressed strong support for a single rate tax of 25 per cent and no further indirect taxes, highlighting the difficulties for the National and Liberal parties in presenting a unified Coalition tax policy. The story might have perturbed Howard, but no-one in the National Party was particularly concerned. After all, the parliamentary party was acting on a key policy resolution of the federal council.

Confusion

Of more interest to Sinclair were the results of some new opinion polls. One, in *The Australian* on 1 April, showed support for Joh was on the slide and Sinclair was the most preferred person to lead the National Party. Another was material prepared by the ALP's pollster, Rod Cameron, which, according to the media, would determine whether or not Hawke would go for a 9 May election. It showed the government and Opposition closely matched, with concern in the electorate focused on tax, the family and the economy. Hawke decided to bide his time, quite likely in the hope of further disunity in the non-Labor parties. On that day, 1 April, April Fools' Day, he released a statement in which he said: 'I have decided, however, that the election will be held towards the end of this year, or early next year.' On the strength of this, Sparkes said the Queensland party's management committee on 10 April would endorse the withdrawal of Queensland federal politicians from the Coalition: 'I don't want to be seen to be pre-empting the decision of the meeting on April 10, but I would expect they will withdraw.'[1]

When the Queensland management committee met in Brisbane, the Victorian party's annual state conference was underway at Wangaratta, with Sinclair due to arrive shortly after lunch. The Queensland meeting confirmed the appointment of Fred Maybury, the party's advertising consultant and campaign director for the 1986 state election, as the national co-ordinator of the Joh for Canberra committee. Then, at about one o'clock in the afternoon, news reached Wangaratta that the management committee had ordered its remaining 11 federal parliamentarians to quit the Coalition forthwith. Sparkes said the decision meant the Queensland members and senators 'won't be participating in any Coalition activities whatsoever'.[2] Sinclair's reaction was bitter. I have rarely, if ever, seen him so agitated. He told journalists: 'It's a very sad day for democracy when federal senators and members find themselves in a position where they have no choice but to accept the dictates of their organisation.' He said the Queensland action had destroyed the National Party 'family', but insisted that the Coalition would continue: 'There will be a Coalition. How many will be in it may well be another question. ... The position remains that we are in Coalition with the Liberal Party.'[3]

According to media reports, ten of the 12 Queensland MPs attended the Brisbane management committee meeting and, although some argued against breaking the Coalition, Joh and Sparkes won a unanimous decision for the walkout. Sparkes said the result did not split the National Party. He asserted that MPs from the southern states would come to accept that the Queensland action was right. Joh declared the decision to be 'a big, big step forward to get rid of Hawke', adding that Sinclair should now resign as federal leader. Senior Liberals began openly suggesting the Coalition should be ended. Andrew Peacock, sacked by Howard as the Opposition's foreign affairs spokesman on 23 March because of a much-publicised private telephone conversation with the then Victorian Liberal Opposition leader, Jeff Kennett, in which Peacock was seen to be disloyal to Howard, called for a break: 'I am unable to see the logic of continuing to coalesce with part of a party. It would therefore be preferable for the Liberal Party to go its own way.'[4] Hawke's intuition of further chaos among the conservatives was proving right.

Sinclair's anger was still evident when he addressed the Victorian conference the next morning, Saturday 11 April: 'The Queensland Party's moves threaten our Party in the same way as the split in the Labor Party in the fifties almost destroyed it. For 23 years, that Party remained in Opposition. Is that the course the Queensland Party wants to take?'[5] He was able to take small comfort from a conference decision taken just before his address. A motion calling on the conference to 'endorse the move by Sir Joh Bjelke-Petersen to remove the National Party from the Federal Coalition' was defeated by 139 votes to 70. Victoria and New South Wales were still with Sinclair and the Coalition.

The same day, Joh was again on the attack, this time at a 'Go for Australia' rally in the northern New South Wales town of Narrabri, in the Gwydir electorate of the deputy federal leader, Ralph Hunt. On this occasion, it was Joh's turn to make a tactical error. He announced that he had formed a new political party, to be known as the New Nationals.[6]

A number of federal Queensland MPs, notably Bob Katter senior, the Member for Kennedy, expressed dismay.[7] They argued that Joh, by forming a new party, was doing precisely what they had desperately been trying to avoid; namely, split the National Party.

Sinclair, back in Sydney from the Victorian party conference, was in the midst of negotiations with Howard to work out how and if the Coalition could be saved. Joh's talk of a new party gave him ammunition, which he used on the Channel 9 *Sunday* program, then hosted by Jim Waley. He was able to argue that if the Queensland MPs were supporting Joh, whose intention was to form a new party and therefore run against the National Party, those rebels could not attend parliamentary meetings of the National Party in Canberra:

> … they are forming a new party – they are not members of the National Party, that's what it's all about. The National Party is in Coalition. If they're in some other element they're not in the National Party. … You either belong to us or you don't. … If they come into the party room they are members of the Coalition and if they don't wish to be part of the Coalition, then it means they vacate the National Party room.[8]

Sparkes realised the potential damage. By the Sunday afternoon he had tried to kill the story, saying that all Joh meant to do was differentiate between candidates sponsored by the Queensland National Party and those supporting the Sinclair-led party. He had to work hard to settle things down. He sent a circular to all Queensland National Party politicians, officials and branches stressing that no new party was being formed. He also counselled Joh to clarify his position. The premier did not help his president when he told ABC Radio's *AM* program on Monday 13 April that the name New Nationals was one he had 'thrown into the ring in connection with the new members, and there'll be many of them right across Australia, so people can discern between the old Nationals under Sinclair and those under me'.[9] Sparkes, on the same program, tried to further clarify what was meant:

> The fact of the matter is that we're not proposing to set up any new National Party. The National Party of Australia – Queensland, will continue to function as is and our 12 federal members [and senators] will of course continue to be an integral part under the Constitution of the federal party, of the federal parliamentary wing.
>
> Q: Well did Sir Joh Bjelke-Petersen make a mistake when he referred publicly to the formation of a new party?
>
> A: I'm not aware as to precisely what comments he made, but I am aware that he has since made it very plain that what he was proposing was that candidates sponsored by us, by the Joh for Canberra Committee, would be identified as New Nationals and they of course will be running in areas where there are no sitting National Party members. There was no suggestion on his part that there should be a separate structure set up. ...

Q: So does that mean that existing Queensland National Party members of parliament will be going to the next election under the National Party banner, whereas people who are not already in parliament but are candidates endorsed by you will be calling themselves New Nationals?

A: This would be the case in those areas where there is no existing National Party structure. In Queensland they'll be just the Nationals. It would be basically in places like Sydney and Melbourne and Adelaide and Perth, where the party has no present representation or structure at all.

Bob Katter remained unconvinced and exasperated, saying on the same program: 'We suddenly find that we're in a situation where we return to Canberra not knowing whether we remain a part of the great National Party of Australia, or whether we're going to be a different identity, or what the hell we're going to be.' Katter's concern was that the prospect of a new party had suddenly been introduced, which he as a Queenslander might be expected to support, without any consultation with him. His apprehension was allayed to some degree by the clarifications, but he remained bitter that Queensland federal politicians had not been consulted or asked for their opinions. He set about the unusual course of organising a meeting of the 12 Queensland members and senators, so they could discuss the affair. It was to take place in Brisbane on 23 April.

§

In the meantime, Howard and Sinclair continued their efforts to thrash out a Coalition arrangement to accommodate the new Queensland position. In the existing Coalition Opposition, seven National Party parliamentarians were shadow ministers – two of them, Braithwaite and Collard, from Queensland. Other Queensland members and senators were on Coalition committees and all were at some stage or other involved in the development of Coalition policies and tactics. Given Sparkes' declaration that the Queensland politicians 'won't be participating in any Coalition activities whatsoever', if a Coalition system was to survive, an accommodation had to be developed to take that into account. From Sinclair's point of view, while the Queenslanders had to be – indeed they wanted to be – excluded from Coalition, they must still remain in the National Party. For Howard, a guarantee of total isolation of the Queenslanders from all Coalition activity was the minimum he could accept. He insisted that a continuing Coalition had to be 'honourable'.

The Sinclair–Howard negotiations had begun over the weekend of 11–12 April and continued for a further two days. The shadow ministry met at Lilydale, near Melbourne, on 14 April, where the outline of an agreement was put forward and accepted. Howard and Sinclair announced that the details would be revealed the following day. They released the two-page agreement at a joint press conference in Sydney. It was a unique document in the history of non-Labor coalitions formed since 1923. None before or since have been like it. The key clauses were:

(i) The Coalition shall comprise 73 Liberals and a minimum of 14 members of the National Party.

(ii) Representation in the Shadow Ministry will reflect the numerical inputs to the Coalition from the two Parties.

(iii) There will be Coalition policies for the forthcoming election. All members of the Coalition are bound to support those policies in the normal way.

Confusion

(iv) Arrangements regarding endorsements, three cornered contests, etc., will continue to be entirely a matter for the respective State organisations of the two Parties as in the past.

(v) Joint Party meetings will continue as in the past with Liberals and Coalition Nationals only attending those meetings.

(vi) Separate meetings of the Liberal Party will be held as in the past.

(vii) Regular meetings of the Coalition Nationals will replace normal meetings of the full Parliamentary National Party.

(viii) Full meetings of the Parliamentary National Party will only be held in special cases, eg: internal Party ballots.

(ix) There will be no joint policy development between Coalition and non-Coalition Nationals.

(x) Non-Coalition Nationals will be welcome to rejoin the joint Party room on the basis of their supporting the Coalition and Coalition policies.

Sinclair had to fight hard to get the agreement. The pressure within the Liberal Party to dump the Nationals was immense. Howard wanted to maintain the Coalition, or at least some form of it. At the same time, he had to be careful not to be seen by his Liberal colleagues as letting the Nationals get away with setting Coalition ground rules. It was a different matter for Sinclair. He knew that two and possibly three of the agreement's clauses could prove unacceptable to a majority of his party room because they curtailed National Party meeting processes.

Howard took some time following the 15 April announcement before detailing the new front bench. He had to have a reshuffle anyway. He had replaced Peacock in foreign affairs with his deputy leader, Neil Brown (Menzies, Victoria). His shadow Minister for Community Services and Women's Affairs, Senator Peter Baume (New South Wales), had quit the shadow ministry on 26 March because he disagreed with Liberal policy on equal opportunity.[10] Now, Howard would have to take account of the Queensland Nationals, Braithwaite and Collard, who were out of the Coalition.

Howard worked on the shadow ministry over the Easter weekend and announced it on 21 April. It was a calculated gamble to announce the front bench only days *before* the new Coalition agreement was to be discussed by the entire parliamentary National Party, on 28 April. But there was little choice. If Howard held off making the announcement, he would implicitly have been admitting his own lack of confidence in the future of the arrangement.

He made adjustments to the Liberal line-up, including replacing his former shadow Minister for Communications, Ian Macphee, a man who had served 10 years on the Liberal front bench, seven of them as a minister in the Fraser government, with the Victorian Member for Bruce, Julian Beale. Dealing with the National Party was not too hard. He replaced Braithwaite and Collard with Liberals, which was understandable given that in the new Coalition there would be only 14 Nationals, including senators, meaning the party's front bench representation should be reduced accordingly. Sinclair, as leader, had the right to choose his preferred portfolio. He decided to move from defence to trade, which was previously held by Braithwaite. Politically, this was a good but belated move. Trade was more significant for the

National Party than defence and was traditionally the National Party leader's job. Sinclair's predecessors, John McEwen and Doug Anthony, had both held the portfolio. Many people had tried to persuade Sinclair in this direction since he took over the leadership in 1984. Up to now he had refused and left himself open to accusations of being indifferent to the party's stated major interests, export industries, and especially primary industry.

The other National Party shadow ministers retained their previous portfolios – Ralph Hunt, primary industry; Bruce Lloyd, transport and aviation; Charles Blunt, social security; and Tim Fischer, veterans' affairs.

§

The clauses of the 15 April Coalition agreement that most upset Sinclair's party critics were those that stipulated that 'regular meetings of the Coalition Nationals will replace normal meetings of the full Parliamentary National Party', and 'full meetings of the Parliamentary National Party will only be held in special cases, eg: internal Party ballots'. There was also confusion over the clause stipulating that 'there will be no joint policy development between Coalition and non-Coalition Nationals'. Some believed that this meant the whole National Party could not meet as one, even to develop specific National Party policy, although the intention was that there should be no meetings of the entire National Party to discuss joint Liberal–National policy development.

Critics claimed these clauses proved Sinclair had agreed to split the National Party and had put Coalition above the independence and integrity of the party as a whole. Joh again suggested Sinclair should resign as he was nothing more than a closet Liberal. The Queensland Member for Wide Bay, Clarrie Millar, said Sinclair was reducing the party to 'a position of mediocrity'.[11]

By the morning of the Katter-organised meeting of Queensland members and senators in Brisbane, 23 April, Millar had hardened his attitude: 'I can only say that if I were in his [Sinclair's] position and the party room was of an opinion so contrary to that which he had elected virtually on his own initiative to adopt, that I would resign, and I should imagine that – I would hope that – he would have sufficient sensitivity to do so.'[12] In reply, Sinclair said the Queensland organisation was to blame:

> Responsibility for the current position, and for the reduced shadow cabinet influence which flows from it, rests fair and square with the Queensland organisation. It is tragic that they should promote division by pressing on with this power play when farmers, small business people and those the party represents are facing their gravest economic crisis. The new Coalition arrangements mean Queensland members and senators remain full, normal members of the parliamentary party, despite their organisation's decision.[13]

The Katter meeting went ahead. Only one person did not attend – Flo Bjelke-Petersen, who said she did not need to because she knew what she was doing anyway, namely standing by her husband. The meeting agreed to put a motion to the party meeting in Canberra on 28 April:

> That this Federal National Party Room rejects the Agreement which has been entered into by the Federal Leader. That the Party Room agrees with the resolutions passed at Federal Council
>
> (1) that the National Party promote National Party policies only.

> (2) the principle of the National Party being a separate identity whilst in Opposition be supported.
>
> Further undertakes to extend co-operation and consultation to the Liberal Party where mutual benefit may result in addressing the defeat of the Hawke Government.

The final part of the motion indicated that not all the Queensland politicians were happy with the prospect of bailing completely out of the Coalition. Overall, the motion made it look as though the Queenslanders were trying to have two bob each way – they wanted the party room to reject the new Coalition agreement, which arguably now had nothing to do with them, and they still wanted to keep the door open to co-operate with the Liberals.

Sinclair interpreted the Queensland MPs' position another way, saying it demonstrated they were prepared to accept that a majority decision of the party room would be binding on them, even on Coalition:

> If the majority decision of the Parliamentary Party Room prevails, and not the Queensland Party's Hervey Bay resolution, the amended Coalition Agreement will be totally unnecessary. The Agreement was put in place only to accommodate the Queensland Party's direction to its Federal Parliamentary Party members.[14]

He was clearly hoping the 14 southern members of the parliamentary party would support the new Coalition arrangements, and therefore give him the opportunity of criticising the Queenslanders for not accepting a democratic majority decision if they still chose to go their own way. McVeigh, on the other hand, saw the outcome of the Katter meeting as the end of the road for his leader:

Well there's no purpose in a challenge [to Sinclair]. Sir Joh Bjelke-Petersen is the real leader of the National Party in federal politics in Australia at the present time … . We've got to have a leader in the meantime awaiting his arrival as leader of the party in Canberra after the next election. We might as well stick with Ian Sinclair because few people take him seriously – no-one seems to follow him any more – and to replace him at this stage wouldn't serve any real purpose, given those circumstances.[15]

8
THE COALITION BREAKS

April to May 1987

Mr. Sinclair and I reached an agreement which was an honourable agreement. But because a few Queensland National Party Members did not have the guts to stand up to the maverick Premier of Queensland, the National Party has broken that Agreement and thus the National Party has brought an end to the Coalition.

John Howard media release, 28 April 1987

Sinclair, as he had feared, found there were doubts among some southern parliamentary colleagues as to the viability of the new Coalition agreement. They questioned why the party should accept any arrangement in which the Liberals dictated when the Nationals could meet as a party in their own right. Bruce Cowan, Ian Robinson and the Victorian Member for Mallee, Peter Fisher, were among members who were deeply concerned. Sinclair only had to lose the support of one of the southern members and the party room vote would be tied at 13 all. As leader and chairman of the meeting, he would have a casting vote, but if the vote was going to be that close, any hope of the arrangement lasting even a couple of weeks would be doomed.

Sinclair decided to call the southern politicians together to shore up support. He believed he could do this by reassuring them the wording of the agreement was sufficiently broad to allow flexibility. Telegrams were sent out on Friday evening, 24 April, by the party whip, Noel Hicks, the Member for Riverina-Darling in New South Wales, advising the New South Wales and Victorian parliamentarians that a special meeting would be held in the party room on Monday evening. The fact that the meeting had been called leaked and it was all over the newspapers by Monday morning.

The meeting went ahead, lasting more than two hours. Sinclair could not get agreement to have the Katter meeting resolution overturned. But he did not come away empty-handed. The southern members agreed to support a strategy whereby, when the Queensland motion was brought on, a member from one of the other states would move that it not be considered. That would have been carried by 14 votes to twelve.

The strategy was never put to the test. Howard, who had read press reports of the growing concern among southern Nationals, saw Sinclair briefly, just before 9am on Tuesday morning, 28 April. He told Sinclair that he could not maintain a Coalition if the National Party tried to change the arrangements in any way. By this stage, many people were convinced the Coalition was beyond salvage.

The parliamentary National Party meeting got underway at its normal time of 9.30am. Given the gravity of the impending debate – whether or not to accept the new Howard–Sinclair Coalition arrangements – it began, unusually, with an impromptu prayer. The whip, Noel Hicks, a self-confessed not very religious person, observed that the meeting needed 'some divine intervention' to help it through its dilemma:

The Coalition breaks

A few of the members looked a bit askance, as if to say 'Is this bloke for real?' But they all went along with the idea. I said a few off-the-cuff words, something like 'Please guide us in our deliberations and give us a helping hand', and they all said 'Amen'.[1]

The meeting did not end in time for the joint Liberal and Coalition National Party meeting at 10.30am; in fact, it continued until shortly after 1.30pm. It was a hard meeting for Sinclair. He could not get his colleagues to accept the Coalition agreement, which had been struck just 13 days earlier. By consensus, the party room agreed to the following position, masterminded by McVeigh:

1. We acknowledge the Agreement between Leaders of the Liberal Party and the National Party.

2. We retain the separate identity and integrity of the National Party.

3. With regard to Clause 8 of the Agreement, regular meetings of the Parliamentary National Party will be held where Coalition policies will not be discussed.

4. We promote and develop National Party policy objectives in the normal way.

5. After discussion, the Queensland [Katter meeting] resolution was withdrawn by the Queensland Senators and Members.

Sinclair must have known at this point that the Coalition would not survive the day. The new set of words would be unacceptable to Howard.

The party room had refused to accept the clause stipulating that full meetings of the parliamentary National Party could 'only be held in special cases, eg: internal Party ballots'. Howard had insisted that this clause be included, as it ensured the greatest possible isolation of the Queensland Nationals. Sinclair was unable to get him to budge on it. He had tried, arguing to Howard that the clause should not be included, as it had nothing to do with Coalition but specifically impinged on the independent rights of the National Party. He had hoped, given Howard's intransigence, that he would get the southern Nationals to understand his predicament. He failed – some of them agreed with McVeigh's view that the clause threatened the independence, integrity and unity of the parliamentary National Party.

The party room similarly agreed that another clause, stipulating that regular meetings of the Coalition Nationals would replace normal meetings of the full parliamentary National Party, fell into the same category: here was a further attempt by the Liberals to dictate what the Nationals could and could not do. This, too, was unacceptable. Driving the wedge further, the party room instructed Sinclair to tell Howard the party would 'promote and develop National Party policy objectives in the normal way'. To Howard, these demands meant an 'honourable' Coalition could not be maintained.

Sinclair told Howard of his party room's wishes at the start of the parliamentary question time at 2pm. They were unacceptable. The two agreed to meet after question time to see if any compromise could be reached, even though they both knew the chances were getting slimmer by the second. They met off and on throughout the afternoon and into the evening, on their

The Coalition breaks

own and with senior colleagues. A scheduled dinner meeting at the Commonwealth Club of the Opposition leaders' group – made up of the parliamentary leaders and deputies of both parties, the Liberal Senate leader and deputy, and each party's federal director, and held regularly during parliamentary sitting weeks – was cancelled. These meetings customarily discussed Coalition strategy and parliamentary tactics. In the present circumstances, there was nothing to discuss. Besides, there was neither the time nor the inclination for dinner.

As the situation deteriorated, Howard received endorsement, first from his shadow ministers and later from the parliamentary Liberal Party, to end the Coalition. By this stage, just about everyone in Parliament House knew it was finished. It was only a matter of waiting for the formal announcement.

Sinclair called his party room together. As well as advising members that the Liberals would not accept any changes and therefore the Coalition was over, he received endorsement as leader.

At 8.30pm, Howard called a press conference to formally declare that the Coalition was over. It was an historic announcement. With the exception of 18 months from late December 1972 to mid-June 1974, Australia's conservative parties had been in continuous Coalition federally since 1949. Even the decision in 1972 had none of the drama or agony of this event, as on that occasion both parties had agreed to go it alone. In a written statement, Howard said the agreement struck between himself and Sinclair at Lilydale had been broken by the National Party 'because a few Queensland National Party Members did not have the guts to stand up to the maverick Premier of Queensland'. He was disappointed that some sections of the National Party had decided to 'hitch their wagon to the fading star of the Queensland Premier', adding that Bjelke-Petersen would 'clearly go down in history as the Coalition wrecker and he has no chance of ever becoming Prime Minister'.[2]

Sinclair's statement was simpler, expressing 'deep regret' that the Coalition had ended. He believed the points he had taken to Howard 'were right for both Parties to be able to operate as individual identities'.[3]

An era in Australia's political history was over. A Coalition that had lasted the best part of 38 years was finished. This latest agreement had survived only 13 days and the joint shadow ministry just seven. It was the shortest Coalition arrangement in federal political history.[4] Moreover, it had never been consummated, as the National Party room never accepted it. An arrangement that had taken hours of painful negotiation to develop was killed off almost in the blink of an eye. The National Party Member for Gilmore in New South Wales, John Sharp, was in Sinclair's office when Howard came round just after 8pm to tell Sinclair the Coalition had to break. Sharp recalled that the conversation 'took less than two minutes'.[5]

For the National Party, the real battle was about to begin. The Coalition had merely been the first shot in the Queensland gun to win control. The second was aimed directly at Sinclair. As long as he remained leader, he was the major stumbling block to the Queensland campaign. Its efforts to politically discredit him were about to escalate.

§

There were mounting tensions within the parliamentary National Party. Back in their electorates, members got on with the job of representing their communities, attending local functions and bringing representations to Canberra. But as a group, the party room was divided and leaking like a sieve, undermining confidence and trust. The party had always been respected by the press gallery and envied by the Liberal and Labor parties for its ability to maintain confidentiality of its party room affairs, but not any more.

Noel Hicks said his role as whip became 'almost impossible' as leaks 'were reported almost verbatim in the next day's newspapers'. He became so concerned that he suggested to Sinclair that the party room should be swept for listening devices:

> Ian, very reluctantly, agreed and suggested I speak quietly to the relevant authorities within the parliament to have the search carried out. He added that if the information leaked that we were doing this, as a party we could be somewhat embarrassed. I was unaware that, for the job to be done, more than a few people within the parliament had to be consulted. Not surprisingly, next morning in the press was a headline along the lines 'National Party Room searched for listening devices'![6]

As Joh's wife and a National Party senator, Flo Bjelke-Petersen was in a particularly difficult position. She backed her husband, although she was not convinced he should switch to federal politics: 'I always believed he should have stayed in Queensland where he'd won the state election so well, but he was being pushed all the time.' Nonetheless, she supported the thrust of what Joh was trying to achieve and found her parliamentary colleagues generally understanding: 'I worked my way through it alright. Ian Sinclair treated me alright, although he and John Howard didn't like it at all.'[7]

§

The day after the Coalition ended, there was renewed speculation around Parliament House of an imminent challenge to Sinclair's leadership, even though it had been re-endorsed by the party room less than 24 hours earlier. Joh gave the issue a stir, saying he would put forward National Party policies for the next election and the party would stand candidates in every federal seat. Of Sinclair, he said: 'He's there at the moment, but that's immaterial. We've changed the direction of the National Party. I will be putting forward the policies and those are the ones which will be on the front pages across the whole nation.'[8] *The Age* in Melbourne reported him the same day saying it would be appropriate for him to deliver the election policy speech without being leader 'because Federal politics needs these policies. I will launch these policies and they will be mine. I will deliver that policy speech. I will draft it. I am delivering policies all the time'.

The comments prompted a sharp response from Sinclair: 'The only person who will deliver the policy speech for the next election will be the Federal Parliamentary Leader.'[9] He also vented his anger at the Queensland party over the Coalition split: 'If its objective is to lose the next election, then it may be that it is succeeding in what he [Bjelke-Petersen] is doing. At the moment, I believe most of the actions of the Queensland organisation – and I am not too sure who calls the shots up there – have been destructive, rather than constructive.' His fears were echoed by political analyst Malcolm Mackerras, who foreshadowed that Labor would win the next election:

> Before the break-up of the Liberal–National Coalition, it seemed to me that the chances for the forthcoming Federal election were about 50–50. The destruction of the Coalition means, in my judgment, that the chances are now about 80 percent for a Labor win and 20 percent for a non-Labor win. ... There is no way that Labor will be defeated if the Liberals and Nationals go into the election fighting each other as well as Labor.[10]

The Coalition breaks

Sinclair made a tactical mistake when he appeared on the ABC Radio *PM* program on 29 April. He told the truth about the obvious problems that were going to arise between the National and Liberal parties working outside Coalition:

> The Coalition gave us an opportunity to go into government and make sure the right policies were in place to take effect as of day one. Now it will be necessary to go into the election campaign with our separate policies and then, after the election, to enter negotiations with the Liberal Party for a Coalition, and then work out which of the policies that have been presented to the people are going, in fact, to be put in place.

Hawke seized the opportunity to capitalise on the comments in question time the next day. Answering a Dorothy Dix question about consumption tax, he read Sinclair's comments from the *PM* transcript, and continued:

> Have Honourable Members ever heard anything more pathetic? We have now revealed the ludicrous nature of what has emerged on the Opposition side. The Leader of the National Party, in one of his rare moments of lucidity and absolute straightforwardness with the Australian electorate, said 'this is what will happen. John Howard will go and give you one set of policies and I will go and give you another set of policies. Sir Joh will give you yet another set of policies. It does not matter what we have said in the election campaign. If, after that, you were silly enough to vote for us, we would then sit down and work out which of the policies we would put into place.' The fact is that the leaders of these two parties – Mr. Howard and Mr. Sinclair – have no status and nor do their policies. They present the people of Australia with an alternative of chaos.[11]

Hawke was highlighting the potential confusion in conservative policies in precisely the same way that Whitlam had done successfully in 1974.

§

At 8.30 on the morning of 29 April, the time when the previous Coalition tactics committee would meet daily to plan its strategy when parliament was sitting, Sinclair summoned the National Party executive to his office. The executive under the Coalition regime had consisted of himself and his shadow ministers – Hunt, Blunt and Fischer from New South Wales, Braithwaite and Collard from Queensland, and Lloyd from Victoria; the party whip, Hicks; and Queenslander, Ian Cameron, whom Sinclair had appointed as his parliamentary secretary.

When this group met, Sinclair already had an outline of how the new non-Coalition arrangements would work. He would retain the executive, making each of the previous shadow ministers a chairman of a committee of members and senators responsible for a group of portfolio areas. Each committee would have to oversee government legislation and develop National Party strategy to it; monitor all government statements in its area of responsibility; plan counter-statements and questions for parliament; and develop National Party policy.

The plan meant that all of the 26 National parliamentarians would have several specific jobs and areas of responsibility. There was no other way the party could hope to monitor the activities of 28 government ministers. The five National Party senators would have to monitor all government portfolios and activities in the Senate and keep their House of Representatives colleagues up to date on all developments. It was going to be an enormous task. Sinclair persisted with his plan. So far as he was concerned, the action of the Queensland organisation and

The Coalition breaks

the capitulation to it by the Queensland members and senators meant an enormous added workload for all in the party room: let the Queenslanders be held responsible. He took the plan to the party room with his executive's endorsement. On Thursday 30 April he announced his complex set of arrangements.

The executive remained the same as it had been in Coalition, but with two additional members – Victorian, Peter McGauran, and Queenslander, Bob Katter senior – making a total of eleven. The committee structures were:

COMMITTEE CHAIRMAN	Portfolios	Member	Senator
FOREIGN RELATIONS, DEFENCE, LEGAL			
SINCLAIR McGauran to assist	Trade, Resources & Energy	SINCLAIR	(Brownhill)
	Defence & Northern Development	KATTER	(Collard)
	Foreign Affairs	HICKS	(Collard)
	Attorney-General	MCGAURAN	(Brownhill)
RURAL AFFAIRS, HEALTH			
HUNT Cameron to assist	Primary Industry	HUNT	(Brownhill)
	Health	NEHL	(Sheil)
	Housing & Construction	CAMERON	(Bjelke-Petersen)
INDUSTRY POLICY			
BRAITHWAITE	Industry, Technology & Commerce	BRAITHWAITE	(Boswell)
	Employment & Industrial Relations	COWAN	(Sheil)
	Small Business	(Conquest)	BOSWELL
	Science	SLIPPER	(Bjelke-Petersen)

111

COMMITTEE CHAIRMAN	Portfolios	Member	Senator
TRANSPORT & COMMUNICATIONS			
LLOYD	Transport & Aviation	LLOYD	(Collard)
	Communications & Roads	SHARP	(Brownhill)
	Local Government & Administrative Services	MILLAR	(Boswell)
HUMAN RESOURCES			
COLLARD	Arts, Heritage & Environment	(Fisher)	COLLARD
	Education & Family	(McVeigh)	BJELKE-PETERSEN
	Sport, Recreation & Tourism	FISHER	(Collard)
	Women & Youth Affairs	CONQUEST	(Bjelke-Petersen)
ECONOMY & WELFARE			
BLUNT	Social Security & Electoral Affairs	BLUNT	(Sheil)
	Community Services	(Cowan)	SHEIL
	Treasury	COBB	(Brownhill)
	Finance	(Cobb)	BROWNHILL
	Special Minister of State	ROBINSON	(Boswell)
VETERANS, IMMIGRATION, ABORIGINES			
FISCHER	Veterans' Affairs	FISCHER	(Sheil)
	Immigration & Ethnic Affairs	ADERMANN	(Bjelke-Petersen)
	Aboriginal Affairs	MCVEIGH	(Boswell)

NOTE Names in capitals denote prime portfolio responsibility. Names in brackets denote assisting portfolio responsibility in the alternative chamber.[12]

The Coalition breaks

Even though the Coalition was formally over, Howard and Sinclair developed co-operative and consultative arrangements to avoid policy conflicts between the parties. Howard had flagged that this would be the case in his 28 April statement announcing the end of the Coalition: 'My Party and I will be seeking a sound basis for ongoing co-operation in Opposition with the National Party so we can continue our common objective of ridding Australia of the Hawke–Keating Government.' Howard denied that this meant the Coalition would continue in everything but name: 'No, you can't say that, but there will certainly be a sensible working arrangement where that is possible.'[13] Reflecting on this many years later, Sinclair said it had been 'an absolute necessity to maintain lines of communication' while at the same time recognising the non-Coalition status of the two parties.[14] He said he and Howard were in fairly regular contact throughout the 1987 election campaign.

They also encouraged the maintenance and development of more co-operative arrangements between the National and Liberal party organisations in New South Wales. Sinclair, strongly backed by his New South Wales party chairman, Doug Moppett, and state parliamentary leader, Wal Murray, wanted to barricade the state as much as possible from the Joh campaign. Howard agreed. Negotiations began in mid-May and were concluded by the beginning of June. The arrangement ensured the parties would maintain a joint Senate ticket, as had been the case for many past elections, and would not contest each other's sitting members. Further, if Joh candidates ran against sitting Liberals, the state National Party would support the Liberal campaigns, with party members helping with door-knocking and manning polling booths.[15] Moppett described the arrangement as a 'de facto coalition', adding 'we thoroughly support it'. It was a highly significant agreement: Joh could never be a serious contender for national leadership if he could not unite the New South Wales Nationals behind him. The New South Wales party's federal representation was similar to that of Queensland – a total of 11 senators and members after the 1984 election, to Queensland's twelve. As Sinclair recently put it: 'The New South Wales organisation ensured that unless you have New South Wales on side you're not going to get a national organisation.'[16]

§

There was still the need to deal with Joh's assertion that he, rather than the elected federal leader, would develop and present National Party policies, including the election policy. The only hope of quashing this was by a decision of the party room. Interestingly, it was not Sinclair but two of his New South Wales colleagues, John Sharp and Charles Blunt, who initiated the necessary action.

By any stretch of the imagination, the notion of anyone other than the leader presenting the policy speech for an election was unacceptable, no matter what political party. The parliamentary National Party had always developed the final policies for an election. Joh was neither a member of the parliamentary party, nor its leader. While he could argue that he and the Queensland party should have some input into policy development, as could any other state, he was in no position to dictate that he would usurp the role of the party room and its leader. The Sharp–Blunt tactic was to move a motion reinforcing the right of the party room to finalise policy. A party meeting was convened on 1 May, when Sharp moved:

> This National Party Room confirms: That after consultation with State National Party organisations, interested groups and consideration of the resolutions of the National Party

Federal Council, the final policy of [the] Parliamentary National Party will be determined by a majority vote of the members of the Parliamentary National Party; that no matter can be regarded as policy of the Parliamentary National Party unless it has been adopted by the Parliamentary National Party.

Some in the meeting said the motion was unnecessary and divisive. However, it was seconded by Blunt and put to a vote – unusual in a party room that normally reached decisions by consensus. It was carried by 21 votes to three. Those who voted against it were all Queenslanders – senators Flo Bjelke-Petersen and Glen Sheil, and Clarrie Millar. Another Queensland senator, Ron Boswell, was absent in Cairns and the New South Wales member, Ian Robinson, abstained.

It was an important vote for Sinclair, even though it did not go to the point of specifying the right of the leader to present the election policy. It was a rebuff to Joh. The premier did not see it that way, although there did seem to be a hint of moderation in his remarks to Brisbane's *The Courier-Mail* the following morning: 'We're all going to work together,' he said. Asked whether he or Sinclair would present the policies, he replied: 'Don't worry about that now. I can't tell you everything.'[17]

The next day, Joh and Sinclair were guest speakers at the Queensland Young Nationals annual conference in Dalby. According to the planning, the two were to miss each other by about half an hour. But Joh was late leaving because of an urgency motion and the presentation of a cake marking his 40 years in state parliament. The urgency motion endorsed his 'leading' role in the continuing National Party campaign, but also called for party unity. It was carried without dissent. By the time it was over, Sinclair had arrived and was standing at the back of the Dalby RSL Hall. As Joh left, he and Sinclair shook hands for the cameras and exchanged pleasantries. Once outside, Joh quipped that the handshaking gesture meant nothing: 'I don't mind shaking hands with Mr Sinclair. I used to shake hands with Mr Whitlam all the time.'[18]

There was a growing view within the party that Sinclair and Joh somehow had to be brought together. A compromise had to be reached. A majority of Queensland federal MPs agreed the party leader should present the election policy speech and were prepared to say so publicly. The Queensland party vice-president, Charles Holm, thought there should be a meeting between Sinclair and Joh to thrash out their differences. Sinclair said he was happy to meet Joh any time, but he was not going to initiate it. He harboured bitter memories of the abortive meeting on 13 February. Sparkes and Holm met Joh on the evening of 5 May. While the premier said he was happy to meet Sinclair, he was in no mind to soften his criticism of him, or agree that Sinclair should deliver the policy speech. He had reiterated his position in that morning's press: 'I will be delivering the speech. … I hope that ultimately he [Sinclair] will accept that what I have [in terms of policy] is what the people want.'[19] Pursuing a meeting was clearly pointless.

§

Sinclair addressed the National Press Club on 8 May, where he forcefully put his case that the majority view of the parliamentary party should be upheld, and criticised what he termed 'conditional endorsements' in Queensland:

> One aspect of the divisions of the past few weeks which concerns me has been the granting of conditional endorsements by the Queensland organisation. The tradition in the National Party is that Senators and Members

are endorsed on the basis of their integrity and their competence. Having been elected, they should be given the respect their Parliamentary office entitles them. They must be allowed, on the merits of an issue before them and having in mind the advice and resolutions of their organisations, to exercise their judgment on the best course to follow.

It is true that in the Labor Party, the discipline of withdrawal of endorsement lies constantly in the minds of every caucus member. Factional disputes are resolved by the continued exercise of the arbitrary threat of withdrawal of endorsement. This has never before been the practice within the National Party.

Ultimately, the policies and programmes pursued by the Parliamentary National Party must be those adopted by the Senators and Members for the time being.[20]

9
THE INDISCRETIONS OF IAN CAMERON

February to May 1987

*We could conceivably dis-endorse him [Ian Cameron],
I suppose.*

Robert Sparkes, *The Sydney Morning Herald*, 10 April 1987

In 1987, Ian Milne Dixon Cameron was 49 years old. A farmer and grazier from south-western Queensland, he was a Country Party boy from way back, having been president of the Queensland Young Country Party in 1962–63. On the retirement of the former party whip and Member for Maranoa, Jim Corbett, Cameron won preselection for the seat and entered federal parliament after the elections on 18 October 1980.

Many in the party regarded him as a bit of a rebel. He certainly had character and a strong mind and was never afraid to say what he thought. This tendency often got him into open argument with Sinclair – for instance, in the weeks leading up to Hervey Bay, Cameron had been a vocal Joh supporter. Yet Sinclair had a grudging respect for him, because whenever he spoke his mind he did so openly and publicly; surreptitious leaks to the press were not the Cameron style. It was because of this openness that Cameron found himself in deep water with the Queensland management committee and the Brisbane organisation at the time of Hervey Bay.

The format for Hervey Bay was that the full central council of 250 delegates was preceded on 27 February by a meeting of the state management committee. Cameron was an observer to that meeting. It put the finishing touches on the complex set of Coalition-busting motions to go before the council. As the meeting concluded, Sparkes told everyone not to talk to the media. Joh emerged reiterating to the press the same message he'd given as when he had gone in – he wasn't interested in the Coalition and it was finished anyway. He didn't give away any details of the management committee's decisions. Instead, he suggested journalists should make up their own minds as to whether or not he looked unhappy, which he clearly did not.

Cameron, however, did talk. He told newsmen that management had passed a motion that effectively called on the federal National Party to split from the Coalition. His comments were covered in *The Courier-Mail* and *The Sydney Morning Herald* the next day, 28 February. Not only had they been made before central council consideration of the recommendations, they had also stolen Sparkes' thunder – he had scheduled a press conference for later that day to announce the details. Cameron had committed a sin for which he would have to pay. That meant facing disciplinary action.

Sparkes proposed to the final session of central council on 1 March that action should be taken against any party member who leaked confidential information to the media. Council carried a motion saying 'the course of action outlined by the State President in regard to the disciplining of a Party Member who provided confidential information to the media be confirmed'. Cameron was not present, having already left to return home.

The first he knew of the matter was when he saw his

25 March edition of *The Courier-Mail* and turned to the lead story on page two, headlined 'Cameron to front National Party for disclosing plans to quit Libs'. According to the story, Sparkes had written to Cameron on the instruction of central council, asking him to show cause why he should not be disciplined for a breach of confidence. The alleged breach was his briefing of journalists on the plans to quit the Coalition. The matter would be considered by the next management committee meeting on 10 April and Cameron risked possible expulsion from the party. Sparkes was quoted as saying he would not divulge the 'details of any confidential Party communication that may or may not have occurred'.

Cameron was incensed. He had not received a letter or any other advice. He telephoned the party's Brisbane headquarters demanding to know what was going on. All he learned was that a letter was in the mail. It was received at his Dalby electorate office on 27 March. Dated 19 March, it read:

Dear Mr. Cameron,

RE: YOUR BREACH OF CONFIDENTIALITY

At the meeting of the Central Council of the Party held on the 27/28 February and 1st March, 1987 it was resolved that consideration should be given to disciplining that member of the Party responsible for the release to the press of confidential information emanating from the State Management Committee held last Friday [meaning Friday 27 February, not Friday 13 March].

I have been instructed by the State President that you have admitted being the person responsible for the release of the information and the purpose of this letter is to advise you that the State Management Committee will consider the matter at its meeting to be held on Friday 10 April, 1987 and you may appear before the Committee to advance reasons why you should not be disciplined.

The State Management Committee has power under Rule 94 of the [party] Constitution to expel or suspend from membership any member. Further powers are contained in Rule 89 of the Party Constitution which powers may be exercised by the State Management Committee in between meetings of the Central Council.

The time appointed for you to appear before the Committee is 2pm.

No doubt you will appreciate that the decision of the Committee may be influenced by your conduct concerning this matter between now and the time of your appearance before this Committee.

Yours sincerely,

H.L. MAYBURY (Mrs.)

Administration Director

Clause 94 of the Queensland party constitution provided that: 'The Management Committee may expel or suspend from membership any member by resolution carried by a majority of those present voting in its favour, and, thereupon, such person shall cease to be a member.' Clause 89 provided that central council could similarly act with regard to individuals, as well as having the power to abolish party branches, state electorate councils or federal divisional councils.

Cameron sent back a short reply on 30 March confirming that he would attend the 10 April management committee meeting and emphatically denying any breach of confidentiality.

He was outraged at the tone of the letter from Brisbane. In his view, he had already been found guilty by the letter's heading of 'Your Breach of Confidentiality'. He also thought the whole thing was a storm in a teacup and wondered why the Brisbane hierarchy was pursuing it so seriously. An obvious theory was that it wanted him dis-endorsed to pave the way for a federal seat for Joh. It made sense. Maranoa, taking up over one third of the state and including part of Joh's state electorate of Barambah, was solid National Party country. Cameron had been re-elected in December 1984 with a margin of 15.6 per cent. Joh would be guaranteed election to Canberra if he was endorsed for Maranoa.

What gave the concept more credence, Cameron knew, was that he had enemies within his divisional council who would have been happy to see him lose endorsement. He canvassed his position with some of his parliamentary colleagues and also took independent advice. Everyone agreed Brisbane was taking a heavy-handed approach. It was carpeting one of its federal politicians, a man with some seniority in the parliamentary party and with long experience and dedication to the Queensland party.

But Cameron was, strictly speaking, in the wrong. He had spoken to the media before the central council decision, despite explicit instructions not to do so. It was decided his best course would be to go to the management committee on 10 April, politely express his objection to the terms of his summons, deny any intention to leak to the media, and apologise if management still considered he had been in the wrong.

The indiscretions of Ian Cameron

As it turned out, he did not have to explain anything; the 10 April meeting was preoccupied with putting into force the full intent of Hervey Bay (instructing Queensland federal politicians out of Coalition), and referred the Cameron case to a disciplinary, or disputes committee, for report to the next management committee meeting on 29 May. Even so, on the morning of 10 April Sparkes was reported in *The Sydney Morning Herald* listing the options that were open to management in the Cameron case – do nothing; reprimand him; take away his endorsement for the next election; or expel him: 'We could conceivably dis-endorse him, I suppose,' Sparkes said, adding that he did not want to say anything else because 'I would be seen to be prejudging the man and I would not want to do that'.

Cameron, no longer as enthusiastic about the Joh campaign given the way events were turning, was on the backburner for the time being, but the issue was still bubbling away. By 22 April, *The Age* in Melbourne was running a story headlined 'Nats push for Bjelke to try for Cameron's seat'. The report said key figures in the Queensland National Party were pushing for Joh to replace Cameron, because Cameron had infuriated the Queensland president and other officials. The same article quoted Cameron in a very unrepentant mood: 'If he [Sir Joh] is desperate to go to Canberra, he should take on the ALP.' Cameron had indeed upset Queensland officials, because only a few days earlier he had been reported saying he might defy the Queensland organisation and return to the Coalition if the new agreement between Sinclair and Howard, announced on 15 April, was likely to lead to a split in the parliamentary National Party. Cameron had to all intents and purposes done a U-turn on his position of two months previously, when he had described Joh as 'the most brilliant leader of people we have here in Australia' and said he supported Joh 'a hundred per cent' in his endeavours to get to Canberra.[1]

While the disciplinary committee was thinking about its report, Cameron's next hurdle was his Maranoa divisional council meeting at St George on 16 May. He had a fair idea he would be faced with some unhelpful motions, but he did not know exactly what they were until almost the last minute. He also discovered two days before the meeting that Sparkes, Holm and the party treasurer, Bill Allen, would be attending – something that was unusual for an ordinary divisional council. The three flew from Brisbane to St George, which was especially unusual for Sparkes, who hated flying. Cameron knew something serious was in the wind.

He discovered there were two motions ready to be put to the meeting.[2] One, from the Dulacca branch, proposed: 'That this Divisional Council strongly supports the Sir Joh for Canberra campaign and issues an invitation to Sir Joh to stand for Maranoa, believing that the endorsed candidate should stand aside in the greater national interest.' The other, from the Roma branch, read:

> That the Roma Branch requests the Maranoa Divisional Council to strongly censure Mr. Cameron, because of certain unsatisfactory aspects of his conduct, especially his indiscreet and reprehensible communication with the media, and his recent derogatory public references for the prospect of the Sir Joh for Canberra Campaign, and therefore this Branch requests the Maranoa Divisional Council to request Mr. Ian Cameron to desist from this type of conduct, which is both contrary to National Party tradition and detrimental to Party interests, and further requests Council to request State Management Committee to take the appropriate action against Mr. Cameron if he fails to comply.

Cameron knew these proposals had to be knocked on the head

before they had a chance to be put. If either was carried, he would unquestionably lose his endorsement. He was furious with them, especially the one from Roma, which assumed his guilt of breaching confidentiality before the disputes committee had completed its inquiries and reported to management. He got on to his supporters. The result was an urgency motion from the St George branch:

> That this Divisional Council strongly supports the Sir Joh for Canberra campaign and moves a vote of confidence in our endorsed candidate for Maranoa, Mr. Ian Cameron. However, we express disappointment in certain of Mr. Cameron's comments, but, having regard to his years of able representation, the prospect of an early election, and in the interests of Party unity, request Management Committee not take any disciplinary action against him on this occasion.

Sparkes was not prepared to let Cameron off the hook completely. He moved an amendment to have the words 'but requests Management Committee to take appropriate action if he repeats these malpractices' added to the end of the last sentence.

The motion, with the Sparkes amendment, was carried comfortably, and the Dulacca and Roma motions withdrawn. Cameron had turned a motion of censure against him into one of confidence – no mean feat. The vote made it more difficult – providing Cameron didn't say or do anything stupid in the meantime – for the management committee to do much more than give him a dressing down at its meeting on 29 May. And it thwarted plans that might have been afoot to get Joh endorsed as the candidate for Maranoa. Sparkes had not entirely lost, either. He had protected his management committee's right to monitor Cameron's conduct and clobber him at any time.

Cameron was effectively muzzled from saying anything that might upset the Joh campaign.

Cameron received a warning when his case again came before the management committee on 29 May, and successfully defended Maranoa at the election in July 1987. However, he lost his endorsement prior to the 24 March 1990 federal election. The new candidate, Bruce Scott, retained the seat for the National Party. Cameron returned to his farming and grazing interests.

10
AN EARLY ELECTION LOOMS

6 May to 13 June 1987

> I believe he [Ian Sinclair] has a grazing property. And he can ride a horse. I don't know what else he would want to do.
>
> Tom McVeigh, *The Sydney Morning Herald*, 1 June 1987

The bickering and infighting in the National Party over who would deliver the policy speech, where, when, and what its status or otherwise would be, continued during the first two weeks of May. So did the jousting as to whether or not Joh would ultimately stand for a federal seat.

Sinclair expressed doubt about this, prompting Joh to retort that he definitely would come to Canberra; it would be to the House of Representatives, not the Senate; and he would decide at an appropriate time when he would stand down as premier and what seat he would contest.

Joh continued to insist he would deliver the policy speech, declaring it was 'quite evident I will have to give the policy speech – that's the only one that's going to win the election for us'. The national co-ordinator of the Joh for Canberra campaign, Fred Maybury backed the premier: 'Given the Premier's political popularity, his campaign would be robbed of that appeal if he does not deliver the main election speech.'[1] The affair reached the ultimate stage of farce when Charles Holm suggested that Joh and Sinclair should each deliver parts of the speech – Joh the economic policies and Sinclair such areas as defence and primary industry.[2]

A government mini-budget came and went amid these wrangles, on 13 May. So, too, did the 25 May Premiers' Conference, at which Joh offered to accept a 3.3 per cent reduction in Commonwealth funding for Queensland in return for a guaranteed similar cut by the Commonwealth to its own spending. He got a 3.5 per cent cut in allocations to Queensland – and no guarantee from the federal government about its spending.

Bob Hawke warmly farewelled Bjelke-Petersen at the end of the conference, wishing him success in promoting World Expo, to be held in Brisbane in 1988, on his trip to the United States. Joh flew out of Australia that evening.

The mini-budget and early Premiers' Conference heightened the probability of an early election. At the beginning of the month, Maybury had said the Queensland organisation was preparing for a federal poll as early as July.[3] As far back as the March federal council, Sparkes had suggested Hawke's best climate for an election would be June–July after a mini-budget. So the Joh campaign's election preparations should have been reasonably well advanced.

The development that finally triggered everybody into the certainty of a snap poll was the announcement on 26 May by the Industrial Relations Minister, Ralph Willis, that the government would not proceed with its Industrial Relations Bill until the next session of parliament. The bill was highly controversial. Employers said it threatened to place unions above the law and make employer actions under Sections 45D and 45E of the *Trade Practices Act*, relating to secondary boycotts, virtually unobtainable. Employer organisations around the country were on the verge of mounting a nationwide campaign, including advertising, against the legislation. Hawke, with his eye on an imminent poll, could not run the risk of such a concerted attack, which would have been strongly supported by the National and Liberal parties.

Shortly after 5pm the following day, 27 May, with Joh barely on the ground in Los Angeles, Hawke announced a double dissolution of parliament, with an election to be held on 11 July – only the second time since Federation that an election would be held in winter.[4] Once again, Hawke was opting for a long campaign – nearly seven weeks – similar to that in December 1984. The trigger for the double dissolution was the Australia Card Bill, which had twice been rejected by the Senate.[5] Its intention was to give all Australians an identity card. The National and Liberal parties opposed the bill, saying it smacked of 'big brother' government and was an infringement on civil liberties.

The immediate priority for the federal National Party was to get its campaign underway, including finalisation and release of policies, given there were no joint Coalition ones. One policy that was ready was Ralph Hunt's on primary industry. It was decided that this should be printed in bulk and launched on 4 June. There were others also nearly complete, including transport and shipping, veterans' affairs, tariffs, social welfare, foreign affairs, defence and fuel. These would be released progressively as early as possible. There would, however, be insufficient time to produce and circulate detailed National Party policies across all portfolios over the coming weeks. The party room agreed that policy summaries should be prepared and published in booklet form for release with Sinclair's policy launch, which had tentatively been scheduled for 18 June. The date was changed to 21 June to coincide with the New South Wales party's annual general conference in the Hunter Valley town of Cessnock, and to boost its campaign in the marginal Labor seat of Hunter.

Joh reacted to the election news from Los Angeles, saying Hawke and Labor had 'dingoed out' because they were frightened; they were running away. He also said Hawke had called the early poll 'specifically to counter me because I have still got a lot of organising to do across New South Wales because of the problems we have had there'.[6] The New South Wales party's refusal to capitulate to the Joh campaign was a continuing and serious problem for its strategists. Privately, the premier was horrified at the early election announcement. New South Wales aside, he knew it would be virtually impossible to get Joh National candidates endorsed elsewhere across Australia in time. Hawke wanted to quash the potential of a nationwide Joh campaign and at the same time capitalise on the divisions within the former Coalition parties. He was being highly successful thus far. Even though the prime minister had promised as recently as 1 April that there would be no early election, he well knew that public outcries about such fibs only lasted for the first day or so of a campaign.

Hawke's hunch about the non-readiness of the Joh campaign proved correct. It immediately became clear that the Joh forces were hopelessly wrong-footed — despite the predictions by Sparkes and Maybury that a July election was possible.

The direction of the Joh campaign was thrashed out during a seven-hour meeting of its campaign committee in Brisbane on 29 May. The meeting decided Joh Senate teams should be fielded in Victoria and South Australia, and House of Representatives seats should be contested in and around metropolitan Melbourne and all of South Australia.[7] Western Australia was already enrolled in the Joh campaign and was endorsing a full Senate team and candidates in all House of Representatives seats. The Northern Territory was similarly up and running with the

NT Nationals. New South Wales remained implacably opposed to the Joh campaign. The threat to run a Senate ticket in Victoria was designed to put pressure on the Victorian party to at least commit to Joh's flat tax policy.

The Brisbane meeting also decided that a new Senate team for Queensland would be selected at a special meeting of the state's central council on 13 June. At the Hervey Bay central council a Senate team of four had been endorsed, on the expectation of a half Senate election. That ticket was made up of Flo Bjelke-Petersen, Stan Collard, Ann Garms and Bruce Laming. With a double dissolution, the ticket had to be expanded to at least include the two other sitting Queensland senators, Ron Boswell and Glen Sheil. The simplest way to do this would have been to endorse Boswell and Sheil in the number three and four positions on the ticket, and place Garms and Laming, new candidates, five and six. However, it was decided that all previously endorsed candidates should recontest pre-selection. This was ominous for Collard – and he knew it.

Joh, cutting short his Los Angeles visit, returned to Brisbane on 30 May and went straight into a series of strategy meetings with Sparkes and other key advisers. In early April, the Joh campaign had engaged the former Secretary of the federal Treasury, John Stone, to develop the detail of Joh's flat tax and economic policy. He was now asked to complete the task much sooner. The campaign committee had been expanded with the appointment of Peter MacDonald, a former Australian Associated Press (AAP) journalist and former press secretary to the premier, as its media co-ordinator. After Joh met with this committee, there was the hint of a change of emphasis on the course of the Queensland campaign. The meeting agreed there was need for a more cohesive approach between the conservative forces during the election campaign. MacDonald said high-level discussions were taking place between the Queensland National and federal

Liberal parties.[8] Joh acknowledged that the conservative parties 'will have to work more on overall strategy. We are all working towards the same objective – that is the defeat of the Hawke socialist Government'.[9] Having destroyed the federal Coalition barely a month earlier, having publicly damned Sinclair for being too close to the Liberals, it seemed the Queensland Nationals were now negotiating with them.

Another feature of the Joh campaign was that it was consumed from the start with finding candidates to run in states other than Queensland for the House of Representatives, and in getting Senate teams together. As a result, the Queensland party failed to properly tend its own interests. For instance, there were three Labor-held target seats for the National Party in Queensland – Leichhardt and Herbert in the far north and Capricornia, centred on Rockhampton, all of which were potentially winnable. Up until the beginning of April, however, not one of the seats had an endorsed National Party candidate. The candidate for Leichhardt was endorsed on 4 April; for Capricornia on 7 June; and for Herbert – the seat that possibly offered the greatest prospect for the Nationals – on 14 June. Not only was the Joh campaign creating havoc around Australia, it was also paving the way for electoral failure within its own borders.

§

From the start of the 1987 election campaign, there were problems between the federal National Party's campaign and that of Joh for Canberra. Under the party's established campaign procedures in the 1980s, the federal campaign headquarters – in other words, the federal secretariat – would prepare and provide all endorsed National Party candidates around Australia with background speakers' notes on key election issues, to help in the drafting of media releases and speeches, and other general campaign material, as well as develop a federal leader's print, radio and television advertising package for nationwide use. The state organisations would look after the advertising and promotional needs of their candidates and undertake any key issues' advertising that they wanted to run. In this way, advertising on a national issue could be tailored to best suit the particular market; for example, a TV advertisement that might appeal to the Victorian electorate might not work for, say, that in Queensland or Western Australia, and vice versa. The system offered more flexibility than a centralised national advertising campaign.

I telephoned Fred Maybury on 29 May to let him know what the federal secretariat would be preparing and sending to candidates. He told me that Queensland would want none of the federal material. He also said that no federal advertising should be booked in the state. I knew Sinclair would never capitulate to such demands, and neither would the federal president, Stuart McDonald. Essentially, the Queenslanders were trying to deny the federal leader the right to mount a comprehensive national campaign, while at the same time they intended to run Joh Nationals advertising all over Australia. Indeed, Sinclair was adamant that he would run a fully-fledged campaign, including across Queensland. He infuriated the Queensland party hierarchy by authorising me to book federal advertisements directly with major regional newspapers, and he went to Queensland on four separate occasions during the campaign to support local candidates.

I spoke to a number of Queensland federal members and senators about the Maybury 'instruction' regarding support material from Canberra. They told me to ignore it, saying they wanted the federal information and especially the overnight courier bags of briefing notes, draft press statements and issues' pamphlets that we would send out every second day or so. There was no email in those days, and sending many pages of information by facsimile to a large number of people was inefficient and time consuming. The party organisations in South Australia and Western Australia were happy to accept whatever we could give them, even though their campaigns were basically under the wing of the Joh campaign structure. From time to time throughout the campaign, the federal secretariat checked with candidates and their offices in all states, and the Country Liberal Party in the Northern Territory, to see if they were receiving our material and if it was of help and use to them. Nobody said they didn't want it or weren't using it. There was also strong nationwide demand by candidates for copies of the federal party's *Election '87 Policy Summary* booklet after its release as part of Sinclair's policy launch on 21 June. The federal secretariat sent material to all endorsed National Party candidates and the two CLP candidates in the Northern Territory throughout the campaign – a total of 105 candidates for the House of Representatives and the Senate.

§

According to *The Age* of 30 May, Joh said from Los Angeles that he would stand down as premier on 16 June, but still refused to say which seat he would contest. Time was running out: nominations closed on 18 June. There was no end to media speculation about which seat he might contest. One suggestion was that McVeigh might be prepared to give up his seat of Groom in exchange for a knighthood and/or a state government job, such as Queensland agent-general in London. McVeigh denied it, saying he was looking forward to 'being a minister in the next Bjelke-Petersen Federal Government'. He took another swipe at Sinclair when asked what he thought the future might hold for him: 'I believe he has a grazing property. And he can ride a horse. I don't know what else he would want to do.'[10] Cameron's seat of Maranoa was again suggested as a possibility, but Cameron wasn't going anywhere. He said bluntly that if Joh 'can't run and win a Labor seat, then there's not much hope for us'.[11]

Joh and Sparkes flew to Melbourne on 1 June for a secret meeting with the president of the National Farmers' Federation (NFF), Ian McLachlan, at the Windsor Hotel. Joh was running out of time to find candidates of national stature to support his campaign and run for parliament under his banner. He desperately needed a national figure to boost his credibility. McLachlan was his last hope. Anyone else of consequence had already declined.

There had been much written about prospective Joh supporters or candidates. Prominent names included yacht designer Ben Lexcen, Mudginberri abattoir owner Jay Pendarvis, businessman John Leard, political commentator Katherine West, Budget Rent-a-Car boss Bob Ansett, former Test cricketer Greg Chappell, businessman Charles Copeman, television announcer Ray Martin and electronics whiz Dick Smith. If any or all of these people were approached, they all declined, as did McLachlan at the Windsor Hotel. On 2 June, he was interviewed on the ABC Radio *AM* program. He confirmed he would not be a candidate. Asked why he had made the decision, McLachlan replied:

> Well, for the same reason as I've made it every other time – not that I'm saying there's a thousand times – but I've been approached a couple of times and I've considered the situation and I've rejected it. I don't find it [being a politician] very attractive and, I mean, that's how it is.[12]

It is easy to see why McLachlan was being courted to enter politics, including by the Liberal Party in his home state of South Australia. A respected wool grower, former South Australian first-class cricketer, keen golfer, successful farmer and president of the NFF, he had the qualities and a well-established national profile that was amply demonstrated in a *Financial Review* survey of 7 May, showing 37 per cent of people polled wanted him to lead the National Party, compared to 30 per cent favouring Joh and 21 per cent Sinclair. McLachlan's refusal of Joh's offer sounded the death knell for Joh's personal Canberra ambitions, as McVeigh later confirmed: 'If Ian McLachlan had come on side, Joh would have taken my seat. But when McLachlan said "no go", it all fell apart.' McVeigh did resign, in February 1988, and he was given the London post. But he insisted it was never related to the campaign: 'Joh had plagued me for 12 months before that [the start of the Joh campaign] to resign and become Agent-General.'[13]

There were further problems for the Joh campaign. The Queensland party's latest nationwide polling, taken between 10 and 22 April and covering 70 per cent of mainland electorates, showed that while the total conservative vote would increase with Joh as National Party leader, the Hawke government would still be re-elected. Joh would increase the National Party's vote from 6.3 per cent under Sinclair to nearly 17 per cent. But most of that support would be siphoned from the Liberal Party. The Liberal share of the vote with Sinclair leading the Nationals would be 28.5 per cent, whereas with Joh as leader, it would fall to 22.7 per cent. The Labor vote would fall only 0.4 per cent with Joh as leader, from 48 per cent to 47.6 per cent.[14] If Joh pursued a seat in federal parliament, the best he could hope for would be election as an Opposition backbencher – not an exciting prospect for the dynamic Queensland Premier.

There were no other prominent candidates and nowhere near enough funds to mount a nationwide media advertising blitz. The question was to what extent, if any, could the Joh campaign be salvaged? Gone were ambitions of Joh becoming prime minister, or of him leading a Nationals-dominated Coalition. Joh agreed after the 1 June McLachlan meeting that Sparkes should open negotiations with Howard, and a meeting was arranged at Howard's Sydney home that evening. Joh did not attend. During discussions lasting about two hours, agreement was reached that the Joh campaign would refrain from criticising or attacking Howard or the Liberals. At the end of the meeting, Sparkes flagged the possibility of Howard travelling to Brisbane to talk directly with the premier, perhaps in the context of Joh pulling out of the race.[15]

Numerous telephone calls were exchanged over the next 24 hours. Howard insisted he would not go to Brisbane unless there was a watertight guarantee from Joh that he would announce that he would not contest the election. Joh prevaricated, but ultimately gave his word. Howard flew to Brisbane early in the morning of 3 June.

Two press statements emerged from the Howard–Joh meeting: a joint statement announcing the determination of both men to work towards the defeat of the Hawke government and a separate statement by Joh announcing that he would not nominate as a candidate for the federal election. Joh's press secretary, Ken Crooke, recalled that the Opposition leader was 'ecstatic' at the development and 'wouldn't leave the office until he knew the [Bjelke-Petersen] press release had been issued – he wanted to be convinced it had really happened'.[16] Joh's retreat and commitment to work co-operatively significantly improved Howard's electoral chances.

The joint release read as though it was a statement by the leaders of the federal Coalition parties, except that in place of Sinclair's name there was Bjelke-Petersen's. Howard and Joh pledged their 'joint determination to defeat the Hawke Labor Government', and declared that 'any important variations between their basic policies for Australia's economic recovery could be resolved co-operatively, and translated into urgent legislation, immediately after a new conservative Government was sworn in'.

Joh's statement confirming he would not seek a federal seat blamed 'some entrenched elements' in the federal National Party for blocking the development of a united front on policy. Sparkes complemented the statements by issuing written explanatory notes which confirmed that the Joh for Canberra campaign had been 'terminated' and which highlighted the co-operative spirit apparently achieved between Howard and Joh:

> I am pleased to be able to report that a meeting took place between the Premier and John Howard today and that the whole philosophical orientation of the Liberal Party had moved to the right (largely you would agree due to the pressure from Sir Joh) and that the Liberal Policies, especially in relation to tax and industrial relations were fairly similar to those of the Premier.

Sparkes said the Joh campaign had 'starched up' the Liberal leadership and concluded that 'In all these circumstances we can justifiably say the Joh for Canberra move has been an extremely well worthwhile political exercise that has made a major contribution towards advancing the cause of conservative politics in Australia'.

There was no mention of Sinclair's name in any of the statements. Joh and Sparkes might be prepared to come to terms with the Liberals, but they were not going to come to terms with Sinclair. Indeed, *The Australian* newspaper's national political writer at the time, Paul Kelly, in an interview with Joh after the Windsor Hotel meeting with McLachlan, gained a fascinating insight into how desperate the Queenslanders were to get rid of Sinclair:

We said to him, 'OK Ian [McLachlan], first of all, we've tried to get rid of Sinclair, but we can't.' I said, 'Ian, what about if you decide to come with us, then we'll have some added strength knowing that you will take his place.'

He said, 'No, Joh, you mucked it up. You fix it. Don't ask me to help you. I won't help you fix it up. You've got to get rid of him [Sinclair].'

That was argued on for a long time. I said, 'Well Ian, we can't get acceptance of the fact that he's a liability and that he should take our policies.' And he said, 'Well that's too bad. I'm not going to be involved in anything with you until you clean up your party.'

Eventually, we said to him. 'Righteo, Ian, say we can achieve that by some means and get rid of Sinclair, would you come with us then?' He said 'I'll make the judgment after I see how you perform and whether you've given Howard the sort of support I want you to give him.'

I mean, he called us all for real suckers. ... But I guess we were. I said, 'Ian, that's not on, tell us now.' We kept pressing him, 'Tell us now, if we do exactly what you want will you then come?' He said, 'No, I won't. I'm not coming. I don't want to be a Member of Parliament.'

It was quite straight, hard. Like that. That was it. In other words, he'd been pulling our leg all this time.

Despite their open lines of communication, Howard did not give Sinclair any 'heads up' about his negotiations with Sparkes or his Brisbane meeting with Joh. All Sinclair knew about the events was what he read and heard in the media. He was not concerned. He knew Joh would not negotiate with him and he recognised that if Howard was able to reach an accommodation with the premier that increased unity among the conservative parties – or minimised Joh's impact on the campaign – that would be advantageous to the federal National Party as well as the Liberal Party. In a recent interview, Sinclair recalled that as he had travelled around the country during the 1987 campaign, he had encountered people who recognised what the Queenslanders wanted to do but did not necessarily agree with their tactics: 'On the other hand, there were all sorts of people who supported what I was seeking to do.'[17]

The Queenslanders were not letting up on Sinclair. Sparkes told the ABC TV *7.30 Report* on 5 June:

> All I want to say is that the National Party in Australia has missed an enormously great opportunity to become the major anti-socialist party in this nation. If it hadn't been for people like Doug Anthony, Ian Sinclair and the New South Wales organisation, if those people had come along with us and used the Joh factor, the National Party would have been the biggest anti-socialist party in this country after the election.

Sparkes made it clear he did not want Sinclair campaigning at all in Queensland: 'Oh, Ian Sinclair would be much better employed devoting his time to shoring up the party's interests in New South Wales and elsewhere. ... He'd be superfluous; he'd be quite unneeded here. We're capable of running our own campaign very effectively.' He also challenged Sinclair on the status of the Queensland tax policy: 'The 25 cents tax policy, although it was pioneered by Bjelke-Petersen and the National Party in Queensland, was subsequently adopted by the federal National Party federal council and therefore is federal National Party policy.'

§

Howard launched the Liberals' tax policy on 10 June. A key feature was to simplify income tax scales. There would be two tax rates – 25 per cent for incomes between $5901 and $31 350 and 38 per cent for incomes above that level. These would replace the four existing rates, which ranged from 24 per cent to 49 per cent. Sinclair described the policy as an 'excellent package', which had a 'large element of National Party support'. Joh acknowledged that it was 'going in the right direction', adding that his policy would be better.[18]

Sparkes launched the Queensland National Party's election slogan, *Joh's Nationals for our Future*, in Brisbane on 12 June and the following day John Stone unveiled the long-awaited flat tax policy, also in Brisbane.

11
TWO MEMORABLE EVENTS

13 June 1987

The only emotion I am allowing myself is disappointment.

Stan Collard after losing his Senate endorsement,
Brisbane, 13 June 1987

Saturday 13 June was memorable for two reasons – the Joh/Stone flat tax policy was finally unveiled, and former locomotive engine driver, Stan Collard, 51, senator for Queensland since 1 July 1975, member of the former shadow ministry, National Party Senate whip and deputy Senate leader from 1981 to 1985 and its Senate leader since then, was dumped from the state's Senate ticket for the forthcoming election.

The tax policy was the main feature of what remained of the Joh campaign. It had been awaited for months – especially by the federal party, which had been kept in the dark about its contents. Neither of the federal leaders, Ian Sinclair or his deputy, Ralph Hunt, was invited to the launch, which took place in the morning at a special meeting of the Queensland central council at the Milton, Brisbane, headquarters of the Queensland Lawn Tennis Association.[1]

Two memorable events

I had telephoned the Joh campaign's national co-ordinator, Fred Maybury, the previous day asking about obtaining a copy of the policy. He said no advance copies were available but undertook to send it by facsimile to the federal secretariat when it was released, which he did. The document spanned 48 close-typed pages. I passed on a copy to Sinclair's office together with a hurriedly prepared briefing note on the highlights that were immediately identifiable.

The policy proposed a 25 per cent single rate tax system to be phased in over a period of 19 months; a reduction in the company tax rate from 49 to 25 per cent by July 1990; a special 'bonus for working' tax rate of 23 per cent for any increases in taxable income from one year to the next; and a balanced budget by 1989/90. It pledged the abolition of Labor's capital gains tax; imposition of fringe benefits tax on the recipient instead of the employer; repeal of Labor's ban on negative gearing; restoration of deductibility for reasonable and bona fide business entertainment expenses; a reduction from 30 to 25 per cent in the top taxation rates for lump-sum superannuation payments; the full rebate of excise for petrol used on farms, together with extension of the diesel excise rebate to the fishing industry; and retention of the 1.25 per cent Medicare levy for 1987/88, but its eventual abolition.

The package was estimated to cost $4.64 billion in 1987/88, which the Stone document detailed precisely. It would cost a further $6.78 billion in 1988/89 and $6.70 billion in 1989/90, which Stone did not detail, because, he explained, he had not had the time to complete calculations in light of the premature election. The cost of the program would be met by cutting deeply into government spending and returning responsibility to the states for a wide range of functions, including health, education, Aboriginal affairs, housing, industry and technology, tourism, sport and recreation, arts, heritage and environment, local government, welfare, community services and transport.

A central problem was that the document did not include some basic and already established policy positions of the federal party. The most glaring omission was no commitment to abolish Labor's pensioner assets test, which had been announced in the 23 August 1983 budget and which the federal party – supported by federal council – had been committed to repealing ever since.

Federal council in August 1984 considered a motion condemning the assets test. None other than Sparkes himself moved an addendum requiring that 'the abolition of the assets test and the increase in taxation on superannuation be a prominent part of the National Party Platform for the next Federal Election'. The motion was carried with the Sparkes addition. A commitment to abolishing the test was also carried by federal council in October 1985, when it endorsed 'the decision by the Parliamentary Party to repeal Labor's discriminatory Pensioner Assets Test'. Even the March 1987 council carried a resolution relating to the test: 'That the National Party calls on the Federal Government to rescind the legislation applicable to the pensioner assets test, and reaffirms its policy commitment to repeal the test immediately on return to Government.'[2]

There were further instances where the Stone package was at odds with pre-existing federal party policy. On fuel, it provided for the full rebate of excise for petrol used on-farm and extension of the diesel excise rebate to the fishing industry. Federal policy, which was developed as a result of an October 1985 federal council resolution on fuel taxes, went further. It provided that the National Party would:

- move progressively to deregulate the petroleum industry
- diminish Government reliance on fuel as a source of revenue

- continue the diesel excise rebate for farming, fishing and forestry
- extend rebate of excise to all fuel used on-farm and in forests and fishing
- remove sales tax on lubricants and oil used on-farm
- review the petroleum products freight subsidy scheme [which had been virtually abolished by Labor]
- abolish automatic fuel excise indexation
- gradually reduce the crude oil excise to ease prices and ensure full development of known resources, and
- reject any resources rent tax.

This policy had been accepted by the parliamentary party at a special policy think tank in June 1986. It had been public since then and was still current. It was inconceivable that the party could now, in the midst of an election campaign, walk away from large slabs of it.

The Stone policy regarding tax on lump-sum superannuation was even contrary to a motion put by Queensland and carried at the March 1987 federal council. The policy proposed reducing the 30 per cent rate of tax applied to lump-sum superannuation payments in excess of $55 000 for people over 55 years at age of retirement to 25 per cent. In contrast, the federal council motion, moved by the Queensland MP, Clarrie Millar, and carried, called on the federal parliamentary party 'upon regaining office to immediately abolish ... the 30% tax on superannuation and revert to the previous level, namely full tax on 5% [of superannuation payment]'.

There were further areas of difficulty. The Stone policy called for a cut of $120 million in 1987/88 in road funding, whereas parliamentary party policy provided for the maintenance of a reasonable amount of road funding and extension of the Australian Bicentennial Road Development Program, an initiative of Ralph Hunt dating back to 1982, beyond its scheduled 1988 termination date.

None of this necessarily meant the federal policies were better than the Stone policy, or vice versa. But it highlighted the hypocrisy of the argument, put time and again by the Queenslanders, that their tax policy was binding on the federal party because it had been adopted by federal council. To apply that argument with any credibility should have made it incumbent on the Queenslanders to ensure their policy was also consistent with other relevant resolutions of council. By not doing so, they effectively proved what they were now arguing against – that resolutions of federal council could be no more than a guide in the development of final policy.

Because of the differences between the Stone policy and that of the federal party, Sinclair was in no mood to give it carte blanche support: 'It has no status within the federal parliamentary National Party except that it is a series of recommendations that a number of members from Queensland presumably would support and will be advocating. It is not the policy of the federal parliamentary National Party.'[3]

Fred Maybury contacted me in the week after the tax policy launch saying the federal secretariat could no longer distribute material supporting the abolition of Labor's pensioner asset test because it was 'not party policy'. While it may no longer have been Queensland party policy, it remained firmly a central commitment of the federal National Party. Maybury and I found it best to agree to disagree.

§

On the last sitting day of the Senate for the 34th Parliament, 5 June 1987, Collard gave a speech praising retiring senators, across political lines, for their contribution to the democratic process over the years and concluding that while he wished Opposition senators all the best for the election, he wished 'Government senators a little less of the best in the next few weeks'.[4] Little did he know it would be his last speech and his last appearance as an elected representative of the Commonwealth Parliament.

Eight days later, on 13 June, Collard and 13 other candidates put their cases before the Queensland central council for preselection to the party's Senate ticket. Eight were selected, but not Collard.

He had previously been through the same process when central council met at Hervey Bay in February. On that occasion he was placed number two on the ticket for a half Senate election. Why wasn't he re-endorsed on this occasion? Simply because in the intervening period he had spoken against splitting the Coalition and in support of Sinclair's right to deliver the policy speech. He had been 'cold' about the overall Joh campaign from the start.

Collard received prominent coverage in *The Australian* and its Brisbane stable mate, the *Daily Sun*, on 16 March. He said if the 12 Queensland federal members withdrew from the Coalition, while the remaining 14 southern National parliamentarians remained, the Queenslanders would become what the media had described as an 'irrelevant rump'. 'We would not even have Party status,' Collard said. 'That would be the worst possible thing that could happen. No-one wants to see that, particularly we who are at the coal face and know what this is all about.' Asked if he thought the Joh for Canberra campaign was losing support, he replied: 'Did it ever have much? I don't think there's much support for it down south. I've been talking to people down there, a lot of people, including media people, and I don't think it's going anywhere.'

Collard said his views were supported by a number of

Queensland parliamentary colleagues. He certainly did not have the support of the Member for Fisher, Peter Slipper, who said Collard would be 'out of step with his colleagues and the Party's rank and file', or of Bjelke-Petersen, who declared no interest in what Collard said or thought: 'If he said that, then he is a hypocrite because it's not what he told us in Hervey Bay.'[5]

Immediately after the Coalition split, Collard made some remarks that were prominently reported in his home town newspaper, *The Morning Bulletin*, in Rockhampton, on 30 April. He described the end of the Coalition as a 'tragedy', and said there was no doubt the Queensland National Party was responsible and precedents showed it would suffer as a result: 'I think the public always exacts retribution from divided parties.' The newspaper carried an editorial strongly supporting its local senator:

> Rockhampton's Senator Stan Collard deserves credit for his forthright statements yesterday about the pressure placed on the Queensland Nationals by their State party machine in the days leading up to the big [Coalition] split.
>
> Senator Collard realises more than anyone that what he has said won't help his career at all.
>
> He has described the split between the National and Liberal Parties as a tragedy, at the same time warning that the consequences could be costly ... .
>
> The weeks and months ahead will tell the story, but at this stage it would appear that the Queensland machine has done a lot of damage to a cohesive opposition unit at a time when it had the Labor Government on the ropes.[6]

It was not only what Collard said publicly that got him into hot water. He had received a copy of a letter that a former senior Queensland National Party minister, Vic Sullivan, had written to the then federal president, Shirley McKerrow, on 23 March.

Sullivan lamented the turmoil in the conservative parties and urged that the Coalition be maintained:

> With the defeat of the Fraser Government, a motion at Central Council of the Queensland Branch of the National Party 'not to serve in coalition with the Liberals in opposition' was defeated. Generally speaking it is unwise to 'change horses in midstream'. United we stand, divided we fall. Let's continue with the Liberals to work towards ridding Australia and its people of that cancerous scourge, the socialists.[7]

In sending a copy to Collard, Sullivan had suggested it might be appropriate to circulate it among his colleagues. Collard did this in May, under a covering note saying 'please find enclosed a copy of a letter that Vic Sullivan, an old Queensland National Party stalwart and former State Minister for Primary Industries, has asked me to circulate among you'.

The combination of these statements and actions was enough to convince the Queensland central council that Collard had been disloyal. Prior to the 13 June meeting, he had privately expected to be dropped down the ticket, possibly to three or four; being thrown off altogether shocked him deeply. His initial reaction was subdued: 'The only emotion I am allowing myself is disappointment.'[8]

Flo Bjelke-Petersen retained the number one spot. Number two went to Stone, who had only just joined the party, after previously saying that the prospect of entering politics was 'quite unattractive' to him.[9] Being number two on the ticket assured him of election. The remainder of the ticket was made up of senators Boswell, from Brisbane, and Sheil, from the Gold Coast; George Cowan, from Jambin in central Queensland; Vicki Kippin, from Cranbrook, near Townsville; Ann Garms, from Brisbane; and Bruce Laming, from the Sunshine Coast.

Privately outraged at the treatment meted out to Collard, Sinclair was cautious to confine his public comments to an expression of sorrow and disappointment, as the endorsement of candidates was properly a matter for state parties.[10] Collard's friend and the Member for Kennedy, Bob Katter senior, was not so reticent. In a 16 June interview on ABC Radio's *World Today* program, he said:

> Look, you know, Stan Collard is someone very special to me, okay? I speak of him in two categories – as a senator, and his performance was absolutely excellent, that's indicated by the fact that he was the leader of the National Party in the Senate ...
>
> Q: Why was he dumped then?
>
> A: I don't know. I wasn't at the meeting. I don't know what the background to it was. All I can say is that I am one who is bitterly disappointed that Stan Collard has been lost to the Senate and been lost to Australia. ... I haven't recovered yet from the shock of losing Stan Collard from the Senate.[11]

§

The Joh camp, in the meantime, was increasing pressure on Sinclair to adopt its tax policy. Sinclair was due to launch his federal campaign in one week's time – 21 June, in Cessnock. There was little time left to force him to accept the Queensland line. On 15 June, Sparkes was asked on ABC Radio *AM* whether the Queenslanders were out to get Sinclair:

> Oh, I wouldn't use that sort of emotive phraseology. We're not out to get anyone. What we're out to do is to ensure that we have competent, strong leadership and above all else, the right policies. And after the election, no doubt the question of leadership will arise automatically; the leadership and the deputy leadership positions become vacant and there'll be an effort made to have people put into those positions that espouse our policies.

It was hardly an endorsement of Sinclair or Hunt. On the ABC Radio *World Today* program on 17 June, Sparkes went further: 'If Ian Sinclair is going to resist the wisdom of our policies obviously we would prefer that he be replaced with someone who was sympathetic, but that's a matter for the parliamentary wing to determine, not the organisation.'

He was also asked why Collard had been dumped – and he didn't mince his words:

> Oh I think what has to be appreciated here is that the central council, comprising of approximately 200 delegates from all over Queensland, took the view that on the basis of the usual criteria of commitment to party solidarity, ability to contribute in the parliament, Stan didn't measure up as well as those that were put on the ticket ahead of him.

Collard responded in a reserved manner: 'When you are in public life, nothing you say or do meets with 100 per cent approval, but I thought I had been an effective and capable senator.'[12] Sinclair also bought into the argument: 'I think that if I were Stan Collard I could have only concluded that he [Sparkes] must have been talking about somebody else.' Sinclair dismissed Sparkes' veiled threats to his leadership, declaring he felt totally secure in his position, and adding: 'I don't intend to be diverted by anyone. I'm not worried about what he [Sparkes] says. My worry is to beat Hawke. I only hope we are in that same battle together.'[13]

Sparkes' allegation that Collard 'didn't measure up as well as those that were put on the ticket ahead of him' hurt Collard. There are many ways by which judgment can be made about how well or badly individuals 'measure up'. When it comes to politicians, one barometer is their attendance and performance in the parliament. Collard asked the parliamentary library to compile the relevant statistics for all National Party senators in the 34th parliament – himself, Lady Flo, Ron Boswell and Glen Sheil from Queensland, and David Brownhill from New South Wales:

Attendance of National Party Senators, 34th Parliament

Senator	Days Present	Days Absent	Days AWOL	Divisions in Senate	Divisions in Committee	Total Divisions
BJELKE-PETERSEN	162	5	35	182	117	299
BOSWELL	189	–	13	210	140	350
BROWNHILL	197	–	5	211	152	363
COLLARD	201	–	1	216	154	370
SHEIL	195	4	3	212	152	364
TOTAL NUMBER OF SITTING DAYS						202
TOTAL DIVISIONS IN SENATE						237
TOTAL DIVISIONS IN COMMITTEE OF THE WHOLE						163
TOTAL DIVISIONS						400

The statistics cannot be regarded as a definitive assessment of any individual senator's performance. Collard, as the party's leader in the Senate, could be expected to have had greater involvement in speeches and questions. Nonetheless, the statistics call into question assertions that he was not 'measuring up'.

Speeches and Questions, National Party Senators, 34th Parliament

	QON	QWN	AD	BI	CO	MISC	MPI	MU	NM
BJELKE-PETERSEN	–	44	3	24	3	4	1	3	2
BOSWELL	5	40	16	55	6	21	4	1	24
BROWNHILL	13	51	5	60	9	22	4	4	5
COLLARD	9	53	4	96	4	59	5	7	4
SHEIL	13	47	1	38	6	19	2	1	–

QON = Questions on Notice; QWN = Questions Without Notice; AD = Adjournment Debate; BI = Bill; CO = In Committee; MISC = Miscellaneous; MPI = Matter of Public Importance; MU = Matter of Urgency; NM – Notice of Motion

SOURCE Federal Parliamentary Library

Collard had his final say as a private citizen. While a senator, he mailed a quarterly newsletter to party branches throughout Queensland. He used this list to send his last message on 21 July – 10 days after the election that saw Hawke returned – beginning with the observation that 'Unfortunately, because of circumstances mainly outside my control, this will be the last newsletter for some time – perhaps forever?' He strongly defended himself against the claimed charges that led to his dis-endorsement:

> The reasons for my dumping have been officially and unofficially put down to lack of effort, treachery and failure to honour undertakings given at Hervey Bay.
>
> No-one who has known me over my twelve years of Parliamentary service could say I did not put in the required effort – and more!
>
> The charge that I failed to honour agreements given at Hervey Bay is false. I undertook to resign my Shadow

Ministry and not to attend joint party meetings with the Liberals if the Party required I should do so. I at no stage said I agreed with these decisions or that they were in any way wise. The events of 11 July proved that my premonitions about the outcome were correct. The fact remains, I did resign my Shadow Ministry and did not attend joint meetings.

The charge of treachery is equally untrue. If I had acted out of pure self interest the charge might have had some justification. Anyone who cares to think about it will soon realise that what I did could not have been in self interest. In fact, the opposite is true.

§

Collard was made an honorary life member of the Queensland National Party in July 1993. He was awarded a Medal of the Order of Australia (OAM) in the Queen's Birthday Honours announced on 9 June 2014 for 'service to politics and to the community'.

A common objective: Queensland Premier, Joh Bjelke-Petersen, and federal Country Party leader, Doug Anthony, worked closely together to help bring about the defeat of the Whitlam Labor government. Brisbane, March 1974.
Photo by News Ltd/Newspix

In more cordial times: Joh Bjelke-Petersen flanked by New South Wales National Party leader, Leon Punch (left), and the then Member for Murray in the state parliament, Tim Fischer, at a fundraising function in Sydney, November 1983. *The Nationals – NSW*

Here we go: Cartoonist Geoff Pryor's interpretation of the start of the Joh for PM campaign. *Geoff Pryor, National Library of Australia, nla.pic-an23385879*

Turmoil: Joh Bjelke-Petersen's threat to run candidates against sitting National and Liberal MPs if they didn't back his policies caused consternation in Canberra. *Geoff Pryor, National Library of Australia, nla.pic-an23475134*

Change at the top: Shirley McKerrow hands over the National Party federal presidency to Stuart McDonald after the March 1987 federal council meeting.
The Page Research Centre Library, PG2717

Above left Man of power: The president of the Queensland National Party, Robert Sparkes, masterminded the Hervey Bay resolutions establishing the Joh for PM campaign and paving the way to smash the federal Coalition in Opposition.

Above right A short life: The Joh for PM campaign was launched by resolution of the Queensland National Party central council in the early hours of 28 February 1987. By 16 March, it was being watered down to the Joh for Canberra campaign. *Photo by David Caird/Newspix*

Good question: Supposed pledges of millions of dollars for a Joh for PM war chest never materialised. *Geoff Pryor, National Library of Australia, nla.pic-an23492445*

The Coalition is finished: Joh Bjelke-Petersen makes his declaration
to the National Party federal council in Canberra, 28 March 1987.
ABC TV News

Ouch: Cartoonist Geoff Pryor senses the frustration and anger in the federal
Opposition leadership at the forced termination of the Coalition.
Geoff Pryor, National Library of Australia, nla.pic-an23515041

Keeping up appearances: A week after the Queensland National Party management committee instructed its federal parliamentarians to withdraw from all Coalition activities, Ian Sinclair and John Howard maintain an outward air of confidence that a Coalition in Opposition can be maintained.

Photo by Ross Duncan/Newspix

My goodness me: Joh Bjelke-Petersen waves a red rag at the federal National Party by declaring he has formed a new organisation, the New Nationals.
Geoff Pryor, National Library of Australia, nla.pic-an23504941

A touch of Alfred Hitchcock: Joh Bjelke-Petersen during the 1987 election campaign. *Fairfax Syndication*

Retreat from Canberra: Geoff Pryor's depiction of Joh Bjelke-Petersen's announcement on 3 June 1987 that he would not seek a seat in federal parliament. *National Library of Australia nla.pic-an23514777*

Away from the hurly-burly: While political pressures were never far from the Bjelke-Petersens, they could find some respite on the family property, Bethany, near Kingaroy. *Newspix 492130*

JOH'S NATIONALS
FOR OUR FUTURE

Authorised by F. Maybury, 6 St. Pauls Terrace, Spring Hill. Printed by Printcraft.

Above No question about it: Geoff Pryor accurately perceived Ian Sinclair's strong belief that being in Coalition in Opposition was the best way for the conservatives to regain government in Canberra. *Geoff Pryor, National Library of Australia, nla.pic-an22668350*

Above left Terminated: With the Joh for Canberra campaign officially terminated on 3 June 1987, a rebadged Queensland campaign slogan was launched by the state party president, Robert Sparkes, in Brisbane on 12 June. *Author files*

Middle left Into the scrum: Ian Sinclair is surrounded by the media as he emerges from the Cessnock Town Hall after delivering his election policy speech, 21 June 1987. *The Nationals – NSW*

Below left Walking the tightrope: To stave off the threat of a Joh Senate ticket in Victoria, the state National Party supported the Queensland flat tax policy, explaining why its number one Senate candidate, Julian McGauran (far left of Joh Bjelke-Petersen) participated in a news conference in Melbourne with the Queensland Premier and his tax and economic policy expert, John Stone (foreground). *Andrew Chapman, National Library of Australia, nla.pic-vn4223207*

Above No change in numbers: The loss of two Queensland House of Representatives seats at the 1987 election was offset by the addition of two senators, meaning the parliamentary National Party's strength of 26 was the same as before the poll: (back row, left to right) Julian McGauran, Michael Cobb, Tim Fischer, (third row) Grant Tambling, Ron Boswell, Evan Adermann, Glen Sheil, John Sharp, (second row) Ian Robinson, David Brownhill, Garry Nehl, Flo Bjelke-Petersen, Bruce Cowan, Charles Blunt, Noel Hicks, Ian Cameron, (front row) Bob Katter senior, Peter Fisher, Clarrie Millar, John Stone, Ian Sinclair, Bruce Lloyd, Peter McGauran, Ralph Hunt, Ray Braithwaite. Absent: Tom McVeigh.

Above left On the stump: National Party deputy leader, Ralph Hunt, uses traditional methods, speaking from the back of a ute, as he campaigns in Gunnedah in his northern New South Wales seat of Gwydir, which he held with a primary vote of more than 57 per cent. *The Nationals – NSW*

Left A safe transition: Ralph Hunt (left) relinquishes the National Party deputy leadership to his Victorian colleague, Bruce Lloyd – a strong supporter of Coalition in Opposition, 23 July 1987. *The Page Research Centre Library – PG2717*

End of the road: Joh Bjelke-Petersen leaves his packed news conference after announcing his immediate retirement as premier and as a member of the Queensland Parliament, Brisbane, 1 December 1987.

Photo by News Ltd/Newspix

12
SINCLAIR DELIVERS THE POLICY

17 June to 6 July 1987

> ... the majority of those Senators and Members elected on July 11 alone will determine our Parliamentary attitude in government. To do otherwise opens the path to corruption, abuse and ultimately, tyranny.
>
> Ian Sinclair, election policy speech,
> Cessnock Town Hall, 21 June 1987

In his *World Today* interview on 17 June, Sparkes commented on the prospect of a new conservative political force in Australia. He was asked whether, if Labor won the election, the Queensland Nationals would pull back and concentrate on Queensland, rather than continue, as some had suggested, to try to hijack the federal party. In reply, he said:

> I think the direction of the Queensland Nationals is inevitably towards building up throughout Australia a conservative party that has the right policies for the nation and, regardless of whether Hawke wins or he doesn't – and

> I am convinced that people have got enough brains to ensure that he doesn't win the election – we'll still be pushing in that direction.

This was not the first time he had floated the idea of a new, or restructured, single conservative party. He had spoken publicly about such a prospect in 1983. His vision was for the National Party to spearhead a combination with right-wing Liberals and other conservatives to develop a new and dominant party.

The significance of his comments on this occasion was their timing. Here was the president of the Queensland National Party, long regarded as one of the shrewdest organisational political leaders in Australia, canvassing the idea of a new conservative force in the middle of a federal election campaign. The implication of his view was that even if the Liberal and National parties won, they would not be good enough; an alternative would still have to be found; disunity would continue. It was, yet again, a comment that undermined the electoral efforts of Sinclair and Howard.

Another concern for the federal leaders was that, despite Sparkes' announcement on 3 June that the Joh for Canberra campaign had been terminated, this was far from the case. The campaign remained alive, although its emphasis had now shifted to the Senate in a bid to win the balance of power. Sparkes thought Joh Nationals could win two Senate seats in Western Australia, one in South Australia and one in Victoria, combining with four National Party senators in Queensland – a total of eight and potentially enough for the balance of power. Sparkes added that financial assistance would be available to Joh candidates and Senate teams 'to a limited extent, depending on what funds we receive'.[1] Joh was more gung-ho, predicting that his candidates would hold the balance of power in the Senate with between 10 and 14 senators and would force a returned Hawke government to another poll within 12 months: 'They [Hawke and Keating] are going to hang themselves as sure as the sun is going to come up tomorrow. ... We're not going to let them mess on like this.'[2]

While predictions of holding the balance of power in the Senate were generally seen as unrealistic, there was nonetheless the possibility that if Joh candidates managed to win representation, through a combination of lower and/or upper house seats in Western Australia, South Australia, Victoria and the Northern Territory, adding to the Queensland party's strength, there may well be the numbers in the federal parliamentary National Party to vote Sinclair out of the leadership – a remaining prime ambition of both Sparkes and Joh.

The Queenslanders were also tightening the screws on the Victorian National Party, with Joh bluntly declaring that unless it completely and publicly supported his tax policy, he would stand a Senate ticket against the endorsed National Party ticket. The Victorian National and Liberal parties were not running a joint Senate ticket, as in New South Wales, and Joh had some starters for his own Victorian Senate team, one of whom was John Clifford, who had unsuccessfully stood for the National Party in the 1984 election for the outer Melbourne seat of Streeton.

Joh wanted to know whether the Victorian state party leader, Peter Ross-Edwards, completely supported his tax policy or not: 'I want a clear-cut statement, yes or no, not a lot of ifs and buts, and then I'll make my judgment [whether or not to stand a separate Senate ticket].'[3]

The Victorians believed they had a strong chance of having a senator elected from their ticket – Julian McGauran, brother of the National Party Member for Gippsland, Peter McGauran, and a former Melbourne city councillor. They could not afford the risk of having a separate Joh Nationals ticket against them, for fear it would siphon away vital votes. On the other hand, they believed a show of solidarity with the Joh campaign was necessary to maximise votes. They buckled to Joh's demands. On 17 June, the state parliamentary leader, Peter Ross-Edwards, after meeting with the premier, issued a short statement saying that 'the Victorian National Party supports the policy of a maximum rate of 25 percent for personal income tax as proposed by Sir Joh Bjelke-Petersen'. This left the New South Wales party as the only state organisation not to support the Joh policy. The Victorian party was spared direct competition from a Joh Senate ticket. It did, however, agree to a number of Joh National candidates contesting metropolitan Labor electorates.

The former federal president, Shirley McKerrow, a good friend of Ross-Edwards, recalled years later how he had been 'visibly shaken' by his meeting with Bjelke-Petersen: 'Peter was not a man given to exaggeration. He came back from the Joh meeting and said to me "the man thinks he has been told by God what to do".'[4]

The Victorian statement was greeted with jubilation in Brisbane. Joh campaign media manager, Peter MacDonald, said the announcement would allow the National Party to present a clear and viable tax policy: 'There is no room for confusion now. This is what we have been working towards.'[5]

There were further strong words from both Joh and Sparkes about which tax policy Sinclair had to adopt and about his leadership. Sparkes said Sinclair could not 'legally' adopt the Liberals' tax policy, or anything other than the Queensland one: 'If he adopts some tax policy that does not provide ultimately for the single 25 cents rate, he is operating unconstitutionally, positively in conflict with our constitution.'[6] Meanwhile, Joh said he was certain there would be a parliamentary leadership spill after the election: 'If Sinclair's still back there, there's no doubt the leadership will come up for sure.'[7] This was mischievous, as he knew that leadership positions were automatically declared open after an election. But he used the opportunity to talk up the possibility of Stone becoming the federal leader, despite the fact that Stone, if elected, would be in the Senate, not the House of Representatives – the chamber from which leaders were traditionally chosen.

All this was going on just days before Sinclair was to deliver the party's election policy. It was also happening on the eve of a by-election for the Queensland Gold Coast seat of Southport, which had become vacant following the sudden death earlier in the year of the sitting state National Party member, Doug Jennings. The by-election took place, virtually unnoticed by the rest of Australia, on 20 June. The Nationals held the seat, but suffered a swing of 4.7 per cent against them. It was potentially an ominous indication of what might happen federally, but the state organisation argued that the party vote had remained solid although, obviously, the personal vote for Jennings had dissipated. Fred Maybury said the premier had been involved 'in the highest possible profile' throughout the by-election campaign, and added:

> So if there were any rejection of Sir Joh and his stance in the Federal political scene, the National Party vote in Southport would have nose-dived. ... The clear implication is that if the Joh/Nationals vote across Queensland remains as constant as it did in Southport on Saturday, then Hawke's Federal ALP is in serious trouble on July 11.[8]

The Southport by-election followed one for the New South Wales state seat of Northern Tablelands a month earlier, on 23 May. In that contest, also not widely observed by most people, the National Party candidate, Ray Chappell, increased the party vote by 4 per cent to win from the Labor candidate,

Thelma McCarthy, who was the wife of the former incumbent, Bill McCarthy, who had died in April. The Northern Tablelands electorate was encompassed by Sinclair's New England federal seat, and he involved himself in Chappell's campaign. The New South Wales party general secretary, Jenny Gardiner, said the result was 'a great fillip to Mr Sinclair, a rebuff for Joh. It is a vote of confidence in orthodox National Party'.[9]

§

Sinclair was acutely aware that his Cessnock launch on Sunday 21 June was a do or die affair. If it was not well received, if the media reported it negatively, his days were numbered.

He arrived in Cessnock on the evening of Wednesday 17 June, and based himself at Peppers Guest House, in the Hunter Valley vineyards. From there he made campaigning forays into other parts of the Hunter electorate, and the adjoining electorate of Calare, also held by Labor. The bulk of his work and concentration went on at Peppers, where he worked over draft and re-draft of his speech, writing most of the final copy himself and not finalising it until late on Saturday night, 20 June. Then came the logistical problem of getting several hundred copies printed in time for release to the media and conference delegates by 11am the next day.

I had already organised a local printer to open on the weekend and do the job. Fortunately, he agreed to begin at 6am on the Sunday morning. The problem was that he did not have a collating machine, so we had to gather a band of staffers and volunteers to help with the necessary sorting and stapling. Given the authorisation and 'printed by' requirements of the *Commonwealth Electoral Act*, the printer's commercial name began moving way beyond the quiet surrounds of Cessnock – into every mainland state and territory of the Commonwealth. The back page of the speech bore in bold type: 'Printed by Goanna Press Pty Ltd., 4 Third Street, Cessnock NSW.'

Shortly before 11am on the Sunday morning, Ian Sinclair walked into the Cessnock Town Hall accompanied by his wife, Rosemary, and delivered what many regarded as one of the best speeches of his life. It had to be.

He released his 36-page *Election '87 Policy Summary* booklet, containing bullet point highlights of party commitments across all portfolios, in conjunction with the speech, in which he trod a fine line on the economy, basically adopting Howard's economic and tax policies but signalling additional areas the National Party would press as priorities in a Coalition government – areas such as an ultimate 25 per cent personal and corporate tax rate. He picked up and supported Stone's 23 per cent working tax bonus and injected some new ideas, such as allowing tax deductibility for the first $5000 worth of interest earned on personal savings each year. To show he was not completely buckling to the Queensland policy, he maintained support for the abolition of Labor's pensioner assets test and for the federal party's fuel policies. He put forward the tax element of his policy in the following terms:

- Experience shows that tax reform without simultaneous legislation to implement related expenditure cuts could lead to rejection of the latter and a deficit blow-out.
- This, of course, would be totally unacceptable.
- Accordingly, as a first step to major tax reform and in light of the consideration given to National Party concerns in the tax policy of the Leader of the Liberal Party, Mr. John Howard, the National Party will support his programme, both for expenditure savings and immediate tax reform.
- Above all the capital gains tax and the fringe benefits tax introduced by Mr. Keating will go in legislation

introduced in the first session of the new Parliament.
- Labor's negative gearing measures will be repealed.
- Bona fide entertainment expenses met in the course of doing business again will be tax deductible.
- However, the Party does not see this as the end of tax reform nor of expenditure cuts.
- Labor's lump sum superannuation tax scales will be modified to be taxed at 25%.
- We will seek further changes in due course.
- The corporate rate must be reduced to the maximum personal rate.
- Further personal and corporate tax reductions should then be pursued so that the maximum rate of tax would be no more than 25 cents in the dollar.
- The 'bonus for working' concept involving the introduction of a flat 23% tax rate for increases in taxable income from one year to the next should be carefully assessed and if achievable PAYE scales amended accordingly.
- Fuel is a major cost item for all Australians. Automatic fuel indexation should be terminated as soon as possible.
- For farmers, fishermen and the forestry industries there will be a full rebate of excise on petrol and diesel used off-road.
- An exemption of sales tax on lubricants used in these industries will be provided.
- For most taxpayers in primary industry the cyclic effect of variable incomes has meant large tax payments and penal provisional tax rates in a year of drought or other financial exigency.
- The National Party, therefore, will seek once more the reintroduction of full tax deductibility for Income Equalisation Deposit Bonds in the year of deposit with tax

payable in the year of withdrawal. Interest rates on IEDs will be at lower than market rates.
- Australians for too long have been encouraged to be a nation of spenders, not savers.
- The National Party recognises the worth of achieving greater personal savings. If a scheme could be developed to allow for all taxpayers a deduction for up to the first $5000 of interest earned it would increase enormously the domestic funds available for investment in this country.
- Were this possible without facilitating tax evasion and within deficit priorities it would have the strong support of the National Party.

In his conclusion, Sinclair sounded a note of warning, aimed directly at the Joh campaign:

> Over the last few months, divisions among those who share our beliefs in the urgent need for a new national direction for Australia have gained a lot of media attention.
>
> That these differences have been public rather than private does not affect the essential strength of the National Party around Australia. The Party has always been a loose federation of strong State organisations.
>
> However, the majority of those Senators and Members elected on July 11 alone will determine our Parliamentary attitude in government. To do otherwise opens the path to corruption, abuse and ultimately, tyranny.

Sinclair received a spontaneous standing ovation from the 700 delegates that went on for several minutes. He was mobbed by well-wishers as he walked back through the Town Hall and into the winter sun. One year later, in her report to the 1988 annual meeting of the party's central council in Dubbo, Jenny Gardiner reflected on the atmosphere in Cessnock:

> When it was time for the Federal Leader to launch the Party's Australia-wide campaign, those [party] members' expressions of loyalty and goodwill towards the Party and their desire for a return to commonsense politics could be felt through the floorboards of the Cessnock Town Hall. The irony in such heartfelt emotions being demonstrated towards this party inside a building most often occupied by dyed-in-coal Laborites was profound. It was as if the Party had rediscovered faith in itself and that rare public exhibition of emotion carried many a Party worker through the succeeding difficult months.[10]

The question in the wake of Sinclair's speech was how would the Queenslanders react? He had decided that if they were critical, he was going into full attack. He wasn't going to tolerate any more sniping from the north.

Sparkes' initial reaction was critical. Contacted in the afternoon of 21 June by *The Australian* newspaper, he foreshadowed that Sinclair's 'two bob each way' tax policy would be thrown out by majority vote of the party room immediately after the election. He accused Sinclair of maintaining deep divisions within the party by embracing the Liberals' tax policy in defiance of the National Party's federal council and all states except New South Wales: 'All the other States have adopted the Joh–Stone tax policy, which I hope ultimately will be adopted by the party federally after the election. The party will make its own judgment on Sinclair's action after the election.'[11] While *The Australian* ran these comments, they were not prominent elsewhere in the media, largely because Sparkes issued a written statement later in the afternoon of 21 June, in which he expressed a very different view:

> The National Party in Queensland says today's Sinclair tax statement clears the way for clear-cut choice for voters on July 11 – between more ALP deficit budgeting or a tax relief-driven national recovery under the Coalition. ...
>
> Sir Robert [Sparkes] said Mr. Sinclair had clearly confirmed his support for the taxation strategy adopted by the National Party's Federal Council last March.
>
> 'Nationals around Australia will be spurred on by Mr. Sinclair's statement, just as all Australians are being excited by the economic recovery programme spelt out in the 25 cents in the dollar National Party tax policy,' he said.[12]

Even Joh appeared to have modified his views: 'I am pleased Mr. Sinclair has picked up the threads of our 25% tax policy and our industrial relations policy. He seems to be picking up our threads a bit and, at last, starting to follow our lead. I guess you could say he's finally seen the light to some degree.'[13]

With this newfound acceptability of Sinclair and his policy directions, the Queenslanders even decided to invite him to their election campaign launch by Joh in Brisbane the following Friday, 26 June. Sinclair was not scheduled to go to Queensland that day. He had a long-standing commitment to attend a small business lunch in Tamworth, in his own electorate. Nonetheless, the Queensland vice-president, Charles Holm (now Sir Charles after being knighted in the 4 June Queen's Birthday Honours), confirmed on 22 June that he had been trying to contact Sinclair to ask him to the launch, and he would continue trying.[14] Sinclair believed his Tamworth commitment had to be kept. He suggested a joint news conference in Brisbane with Queensland party leaders on the morning of 26 June, prior to the Queensland launch, so that he could then return to Tamworth in time for the business lunch. This was agreed. Joh had developed a bout of laryngitis and would not be present. Neither would he be the key speaker at the party launch. Instead, Sparkes would do the introductions, and Stone would deliver the main speech, which, not surprisingly, would largely be a further exposition of the Queensland tax statement.

Sinclair went to Brisbane for the joint news conference. It was a gamble, as there were some reports that the Queenslanders were undecided about attending it.[15] He arrived to find no senior officials from the Queensland party at the Brisbane headquarters. He held the press conference on his own, the bulk of which was centred on how embarrassing it must be for him not to be supported by anyone from the state hierarchy. He put on a bold face, saying he did not need anyone to prop him up; he was quite capable of conducting his own news conferences. With that, he flew back to New South Wales, convinced he'd been set up – which was how the next day's headlines portrayed it: 'Qld. Nats fail to appear with Sinclair' was *The Age* headline; 'Queensland Nationals snub Sinclair' in Melbourne's *The Sun News-Pictorial*; 'Qld Nat no-show sinks unity bid with Sinclair', *The Weekend Australian*; 'Joh's Nationals stand up Sinclair at press conference', the Sydney *Daily Telegraph*. While Sinclair was angered, he was persuaded not to react. By saying nothing, it was the Queenslanders who looked petty, negative and obstructive, not Sinclair. He had gone out of his way to go to Brisbane. He had done the right thing; they had not.

§

On 6 July, Bjelke-Petersen went to Canberra to support the two Joh Independents standing in the ACT seats of Canberra and Fraser. Both men were members of the New South Wales National Party's ACT branch. The premier held a news conference at the National Press Club, where he refused to endorse or support Sinclair's leadership. The conference was almost exclusively concerned with the Joh–Sinclair split, to the point where the candidate for Canberra, John Farrell, interrupted and tried to get the subject on to local issues. The media was not interested, and neither was Joh. He said he would leave his Joh Nationals structure in place across Australia after the election: 'We are pursuing it. We will put an organisation across Australia in every state, including New South Wales, that will support this [flat tax] policy.'

Joh did, however, indicate support for a Coalition with the Liberal Party after the election, if necessary to enable the formation of a conservative government, and warned that if Labor was to win: '… then I'll tell everyone in Australia to go straight home, batten down your house and tie it down, go into your room and put a safety belt on, put your head between your knees because you are going to run into some pretty rough weather'.[16]

A few weeks earlier, the premier had delivered a classic 'Johspeak' of the campaign. Appearing on Channel 9's *Today* show on 17 June, he warned people against voting for Labor: 'Who wants to stick together with them and get your stick feet? You know, if you get, stick foot on sticky paper, you get both of them on, you fall over and Mr Hawke asks us to stick with him. You put your foot on sticky paper with him, his and Keating, his Government's got their feet on sticky paper, my word they have.'

13
THE IRRITATION OF JOH INDEPENDENTS

June to July 1987

He [Bjelke-Petersen] told us to call ourselves Joh Independents.

Joh candidate for New England, Bevan O'Regan, *The Australian*, 5 June 1987

Sparkes gave an assurance to the federal management committee prior to federal council on 27 March that the Queensland organisation would not run Joh candidates against sitting National Party MPs: 'There is no intention on our part to run candidates against sitting National Party Members anywhere.' On 15 April, he gave a similar assurance to *The Age*, which reported that he had ruled out standing Joh's 'New National' candidates against sitting National MPs 'anywhere in Australia. We won't be running against them'.

These sentiments recognised the motion of federal council, which called on Joh to work within the constitutions of the state and federal parties. They were also in line with those of the federal management committee at its meeting in Sydney on 5 February, when it agreed that the state constitutions of the party were supreme. The sentiments were even consistent with the set of objectives drawn up in the meeting with Peter Nixon during federal council, which required the acceptance or recognition of each state organisation's rights and powers. Clearly, no Joh Independent candidates should have been run in any of the affiliated states without the agreement of the relevant state organisation. Joh was required to work within the constitutions of the parties, and Sparkes had confirmed this would happen.

Joh was not interested in any of this. His Independent candidates stood in Treasurer Paul Keating's seat of Blaxland, in Sydney, and in the two ACT seats of Canberra and Fraser – without the support or agreement of the New South Wales National Party. For party constitutional purposes, the endorsement of candidates in the ACT was the responsibility of the New South Wales National Party. These candidates were not a major problem, as they were standing in seats held by the Labor Party that were not being contested by the NSW Nationals. But it was still unconstitutional for a National Party other than that in New South Wales to support candidates within the state's responsibility without the organisation's knowledge and agreement.

More significant were Joh Independents standing elsewhere – against Sinclair, Hunt and the National Party Member for Parkes, Michael Cobb, as well as against the Liberal Member for Hume, Wal Fife, in New South Wales; and against sitting National members Peter Fisher and Bruce Lloyd and the endorsed National candidate for Indi, Phillip Pullar, in Victoria. These mattered very much indeed. So, too, did the threat of rebel Senate tickets in Victoria and New South Wales. The threat was averted in Victoria by that party endorsing the Joh flat tax policy, although Sparkes would later try to credit the Joh campaign for the election of Julian McGauran as a Victorian senator. McGauran had participated in a news conference in Melbourne during the election campaign with Bjelke-Petersen and John Stone. In New South Wales, it seems that two Joh Senate tickets were being planned, one by a group that was in touch with the premier and another that was in contact with the Queensland party vice-president, Charles Holm. Ben Lexcen's name was cast around as the potential 'big name' to head a ticket. Whatever plans were afoot fell through when none of the supposed candidates lodged nominations prior to the midday deadline on 18 June.

Technically, Sparkes lived up to his assurances that the Queensland party would not endorse candidates against sitting National Party members beyond Queensland. The party did not formally nominate the Joh Independents. The candidates nominated and contested the election as Independents. The Queensland party organisation felt it necessary to make some clarification about this, specifically so far as the Senate was concerned. On 16 June, Australian Associated Press carried a statement by Peter MacDonald, in his capacity as state campaign director, saying that while Bjelke-Petersen's feelings were understandable, the premier 'was not speaking for the State National Party when he promised to run independent Senate candidates in New South Wales and Victoria':

> 'It has no relationship to the National Party Queensland Branch which can only support endorsed National Party candidates,' he [MacDonald] said.
>
> 'However, we can well understand the Premier's feelings when all other State Branches have supported his tax plan and New South Wales remains outside that Australia-wide National Party stance.'
>
> The Queensland National Party is expected to announce tomorrow it has endorsed two candidates to stand for the Senate in the Northern Territory.
>
> The Party's central council on the weekend passed a special resolution allowing it to endorse and fund candidates outside Queensland.

The irritation of Joh Independents

While Joh Independents standing against sitting nationals in New South Wales and Victoria might not have been endorsed by the Queensland party, its campaign staff undoubtedly gave them moral support and actively cast around for potential seats to contest. The New South Wales general secretary, Jenny Gardiner, remembered being asked for information about the Hunter electorate: 'The Queenslanders were planning to run a Joh candidate in Hunter, but didn't even have a map of the electorate – and they actually expected to be helped by the New South Wales head office!'[1]

Some Joh candidates were supported financially, either directly or indirectly, by funds from Queensland. Neither South Australia nor Western Australia would have been able to field candidates in all of their lower house seats, as well as run Senate campaigns, without outside financial support.[2] To what extent, if any, the premier procured funds for Joh candidates is questionable. Bevan O'Regan, a former spokesman for the North West New South Wales Joh for Canberra Committee and Joh Independent candidate for New England, said he had personally been contacted by Joh within hours of the premier's announcement that he would not run for Canberra (3 June) and encouraged to stand against Sinclair. O'Regan said Joh had given riding instructions on how to run campaigns: 'He told us to call ourselves Joh Independents.'[3]

The Joh Independent for the ACT seat of Canberra, John Farrell, said his campaign was receiving some financial support from Queensland, but not from official channels: 'We have no funding from the Queensland National Party.'[4] The other Joh Independent in the ACT, Larry O'Sullivan, contesting the seat of Fraser, said some of his campaign money had been arranged through 'Joh's good offices', although he did not know the specifics of its origins: 'Joh said we had the money,' so he had not questioned it.[5] Joh actively campaigned for the ACT

Independents, as well as for his Independent, Philip Black, in Blaxland, and for the NT Nationals.

Ultimately, the Joh Independents running for the House of Representatives were more of an irritant than a serious threat, although the Queensland-backed Senate teams in South Australia and Western Australia each came close to winning a seat. One Joh Independent, Neil Lehmann, standing against the Victorian National Party Member for Mallee, Peter Fisher, directed his preferences away from the Nationals. His how-to-vote card asked people to vote one for him, two Liberal, three National and four ALP. The ACT Independents used the slogan 'Joh's Nationals for the National Capital'. Even though the New South Wales party was not contesting either ACT electorate, legal opinion obtained by the party supported the federal party's contention that use of the term 'Nationals' could have been confusing to electors, as this was widely used in National Party advertising and election material, and could have been in breach of the *Commonwealth Electoral Act*. The electoral commissioner, Colin Hughes, disagreed. In another instance, O'Regan produced a pamphlet containing a how-to-vote, in which he changed the order of how the New England candidates would appear on the ballot paper, so that his name headed the list. Again, this potentially contravened electoral rules – specifically section 329(1) of the *Electoral Act*, which made it an offence for any person to distribute material that was likely to mislead or deceive an elector 'in relation to casting his vote'. It seemed clear that O'Regan's how-to-vote was confusing and misleading to the electors of New England. I wrote accordingly to Colin Hughes on 29 June, and he replied the same day, saying he would not 'seek to prohibit the distribution of this pamphlet'.

None of the Joh Independents running against Sinclair, Hunt, Cobb, Fife, Fisher and Lloyd won 10 per cent of the primary vote, and of those sitting members, all of whom were returned, only Fisher in Mallee, with 48 per cent of the primary vote, was taken to preferences.[6]

14
THE RECRIMINATIONS FLY

11 to 20 July 1987

It is because of Joh this election was called and he and nobody
else has to accept responsibility for that defeat.

Ian Sinclair, news conference, Bendemeer, NSW, 12 July 1987

On the Thursday before the election, 9 July, I received a surprise telephone call from the Queensland National Party vice-president, Charles Holm. We had known each other for several years and generally got on well, despite the recent difficulties. He said he was confident of a good result on the Saturday, after which we would 'all be back in the same camp'. He predicted the Queensland party would win five additional seats, plus a fifth Senate position. I wished him well, saying I hoped his prediction would prove correct – which I seriously doubted.

In fact, from the conservative point of view, the 11 July election was a disaster. Labor increased its representation to a record 86 seats and won a record third term in office. Never before had a Labor prime minister achieved three consecutive terms.[1] On

The recriminations fly

this occasion, Hawke won the right to be prime minister during the prestigious 1988 Bicentennial celebrations, which would include the opening of the new Parliament House by Queen Elizabeth II – a milestone in Australian political history.

Joh and the Queensland Nationals bore the brunt of the blame for the conservative loss. The Joh campaign was largely responsible for the division and disunity that had dogged non-Labor politics all year, and particularly during the election campaign. To that extent it was culpable. The Liberals also had not been entirely united during the year. It was not long before the election that Peacock had been sacked from the front bench and Senator Peter Baume had resigned. There had been frequent speculation, although not during the election period, about a Peacock challenge to Howard, despite Peacock's denials.

There were mistakes in the Liberal campaign – serious miscalculation on the cost of its tax policy and confusion over health policy. The Liberals' refusal, or inability, to release their tax policy until 10 June gave insufficient time for the electorate to come to grips with it. Compounded with mathematical errors, it became unbelievable to many voters, and thus unacceptable. A future Liberal Opposition leader, John Hewson, failed to learn from this lesson in the March 1993 election, when he launched his complex *Fightback!* economic package, which proposed a goods and services tax and was a contributory factor in the Coalition losing what became known as the unlosable election.

The 1987 campaign got off to a rocky start for both the Liberals and the Nationals. Labor forged ahead. By the end of June, the conservative campaign had picked up and Labor became bogged down – all its policies were launched; there were no more goodies in the bag to offer the electorate, yet there were still two weeks to go. The conservatives ploughed on during the first week of July, picking up ground. Then, they too ran out of steam in the final week. In the end, Labor was home and hosed.

While its overall percentage of the House of Representatives vote dropped from 51.8 per cent after preferences in December 1984 to 50.31 per cent, it increased its number of House seats by four.

While a combination of factors led to the failure of the conservatives generally, one overriding factor dogged the National Party – the Joh campaign. It deeply divided the party and it confused the electorate. Even in Queensland, many supporters were worried about where their National Party candidate stood – was he a Joh man, or a Sinclair man? Did he support the Joh tax policy or some other policy? Did he support the Coalition, or not? These concerns were compounded by the continual undermining of the federal leadership and the highly public war of words between Sinclair, Sparkes and Joh. The National Party had several campaigns running – the Joh campaign, the Sinclair campaign, Joh Independent campaigns, use of different logos and slogans and even different policies in significant areas.

Before the Joh campaign, Labor was unpopular in many parts of regional and rural Australia. The National Party should have had a serious chance of retaining all its existing seats, and winning, at the very least, the additional seats of Leichhardt, Herbert and Rankin in Queensland, Hunter and Calare in New South Wales and Bendigo in Victoria. It could also have stood a chance of picking up Capricornia in Queensland, Eden-Monaro in New South Wales and McMillan and Indi in Victoria. Instead, it lost its two most marginal seats, Hinkler and Fisher, both in Queensland. It won no new seats in the House of Representatives and only picked up one new Senate position, Julian McGauran, in Victoria, although South Australia and Western Australia came close to clinching a Senate seat each with their Queensland-backed Senate teams. The Country Liberal Party lost the seat of Northern Territory, primarily because a large percentage of the preferences of the NT Nationals went to Labor. The CLP did, however, win a Senate seat and its candidate, Grant Tambling, would sit with the National Party. This meant the Nationals' numbers in parliament would remain at 26–19 in the House of Representatives and seven in the Senate. Interestingly, the Liberal Party's two lower house losses were also in Queensland – Forde and Petrie.

The Joh campaign failed completely, even if it had, as Sparkes had said, 'starched up' conservative policy. Beyond Queensland, it won no seats in the House of Representatives or the Senate. As the results went up in the tally room on election night, Sparkes might have recalled his comment on the *Willesee* program on 16 March – 'If the price [of the election] is further success for Labor, then we've made a very serious mistake. We've gambled and the gamble has not come off.'

On an Australia-wide basis, the National Party's share of the primary vote increased from 10.6 per cent in the December 1984 election, to 11.5 per cent in July 1987. This reflected the fact that, for the first time, National Party candidates, supported by the Queensland party with the agreement of the state organisations, had stood in all House of Representatives seats in both South Australia and Western Australia. The party's share of the primary vote in those states increased by 2.26 per cent and 5.58 per cent respectively, helping to boost the nationwide proportion. It did nothing to achieve the only thing that matters in politics – winning seats. No fewer than 10 of the 13 National candidates for the House of Representatives in Western Australia failed to poll as many votes as the informal vote in their electorates, and two of those lost their deposits. In South Australia, 12 of the 13 House of Representatives candidates failed to pass the informal vote, and 10 lost their deposits.

In Victoria, the party's share of the vote went down by 1.0 per cent to 6.35 per cent, while in New South Wales it increased by 1.25 per cent to 11.78 per cent. In Queensland, the party's share of the vote dropped by almost three per cent to 28.77 per cent. The biggest swing against the Nationals in any state was in Queensland. Moreover, the Queensland party was now surpassed by New South Wales in its federal parliamentary representation – ten senators and members compared to 11 from the southern state.[2]

Tom McVeigh, who was returned in his Queensland seat of Groom, said the Joh campaign was not all negative. He pointed to the fact that the two hopeful Senate candidates, from South Australia and Western Australia, were so close to being elected that they were invited to the first post-election meeting of the parliamentary party:

> They attended because it was likely that they were going to be elected senators. In the final analysis, they weren't. But they attended the party meeting. Sinclair, quite rightly, and agreed by us, didn't allow them to vote. But we thought they were going to get elected – hadn't happened for years [in those states]. So it wasn't all negative.[3]

Joh immediately distanced himself from the outcome, declaring on election night: 'I do not accept any blame. … The only thing I blame myself for is that I didn't continue to go [to Canberra] myself'.[4] Sparkes' initial reaction was that the election had turned out exactly as the party's private polling had predicted if Joh was not a candidate.[5]

By Monday 13 July the recriminations were flowing thick and fast. Joh focused on Sinclair and Howard: 'No wonder they got nowhere. We want leaders, people who are prepared to fight and accept the verdict, not start thrashing around looking for someone else to blame.'[6]

Sinclair had no doubt where the blame lay: 'It is because of

Joh this election was called and he and nobody else has to accept responsibility for that defeat. Anybody who is out there fighting people who are of his own party ... I don't know how he [Sir Joh] lies safely in his bed at night.'[7] Howard was scathing:

> I have spent 75 per cent of my time putting out bushfires on my own side and 25 per cent fighting the Labor Party. I have no doubt in the world that if the push from the Queensland National Party had not occurred, we would not have had an election in July. The Hawke Government would have run its full term. The coalition, which led in the opinion polls last year, would have gone to the election with the perception of unity.[8]

Sparkes told *The Age* of 13 July that he would ask John Stone, who won election to the Senate, replacing Collard, to consider contesting the leadership because he was probably the most talented member and because Sinclair's record was 'tarnished'. In *The Australian* the same day, he claimed 'our problem was that we didn't have time to get the whole [Joh] show rolling. Apart from that, we were virtually sabotaged by Sinclair in New South Wales'.

Sinclair countered that Sparkes was looking for scapegoats: 'If he wants to blame someone for the failure of the National Party in the election, he should look at his own camp. The campaign run by the Queensland National Party was totally obstructive – they even ran candidates against me. Sir Robert should do some thorough self-examination before he meddles in federal politics again.'[9]

The general secretary of the New South Wales party, Jenny Gardiner, was publicly critical of the Queensland party. In a press statement on 15 July, she noted:

> Our no nonsense support for the duly elected Parliamentary Leadership and the concept of Coalition with the Liberals was appreciated by the Liberals. If it had not been for the diabolical self-defeating activities of the Queensland organisation, then presumably the National Party result here in New South Wales would have rocketed to its highest ever.

Perhaps in an effort to deflect the post-election debate in another direction, Sparkes revived the possibility of a new conservative party being formed:

> I think you'll find you'll either have the two parties operating as independent entities with a co-ordinating committee to co-ordinate their activities on major issues, or ultimately, you'll have some sort of a major structural realignment of conservatives with the establishment of one party federally. ... I think there's much to be said for it philosophically, but whether it's achievable practically is another matter.[10]

Meanwhile, both Sparkes and Joh were beginning to come in for criticism from within the Queensland party itself. The state's Local Government and Main Roads minister, Russ Hinze, appeared on the ABC Radio *PM* program on 13 July and did little to hide his belief that the Queensland party had been seriously wrong in its campaign and tactics:

> Q: Why do you believe it was that traditional National Party supporters didn't vote for the National Party in this election in Queensland?
>
> A: Because they didn't want to see us scrapping with our partners or our colleagues in the south and that's the

reason and there's no other answer.

Q: But shouldn't shrewd political analysts have realised that that would have been a result?

A: Oh yes, it surprises me that Sir Robert Sparkes became embroiled in the squabbling with Sinclair. All my political life as a minister, he's [Sparkes] always told me to cut it out, to stop it, but he publicly came out and had public arguments and it just wasn't accepted.

The veteran Member for Kennedy, Bob Katter senior, wrote a long letter to Sparkes on 14 July evaluating 'the circumstances of our deplorable performance in Queensland'. He said that at no stage prior to basic decisions being taken were the Queensland members and senators consulted, that their letters were not answered and their telephone calls to party headquarters were 'disregarded'. He went on to be highly critical of the decision to break the Coalition and of the 'crucifixation' of Collard from the Senate ticket:

Two major developments led to our present situation …

A. The ill advised decision to break the Coalition. I will concede, I even supported, the concept that there may be no need for a Coalition in Opposition, but to split the Conservative forces in an election year while any sort of risk existed of Hawke and his vicious policies being our scourge for another three years was unthinkable.

I agreed to it because I had no option, and what concerned me, and almost every other Member and Senator were two glaring, undeniable facts …

    i. The Coalition arrangement since 1949 had kept the Socialists out of government, with very few exceptions.

    ii. The Coalition, in spite of heavy criticism of the two Leaders, for the past eight months, had gradually climbed on the Morgan Gallup Poll edging up to 50%, while ALP support was approaching 40%, which reinforces my comment that the real world of politics was not considered.

B. Now we come to Senator Collard … What I cannot understand is how a lifetime of loyalty and service to an organisation can be wiped out by one misdemeanour – or two, or three … I sat at Management and listened to the bitterness of the attack on Stan Collard. No-one mentioned that his father was one of the first Life Members of this organisation. No-one mentioned the fact that his entry to politics began a new era for Conservative Politics … an ordinary railway man becoming a Senator, and finally Leader of the National Party in the Senate.

Katter put forward ideas on what the Queensland party should do for the future, including reverting its policy emphasis back to its traditional support base, inviting greater policy input from branches and electorate councils, and reorganising state conference so that rank and file members had greater opportunity to express themselves.

In conclusion, he acknowledged that his views would 'not be regarded very favourably', but insisted he had 'the right to be honest' and to bring the facts to the attention of the party.[11]

§

Joh told journalists in Brisbane on 15 July that he would not be talking to the media any more after what he described the 'greatest concoction of lies ever written' in recent weeks.[12] He said that apart from one or two, the newspapers had become the arm of the left wing of the ALP, and nominated *The Australian* and *The Courier-Mail* as the only two he would talk to in the future. The ban did not last long. Joh – long renowned for his willingness to 'feed the chooks' – soon found he had views he wanted widely published and broadcast. After the parliamentary Liberal Party met in Canberra on 17 July and re-elected John Howard as leader, with Andrew Peacock replacing Neil Brown as his deputy, Joh could not contain himself. He called a news conference to deplore the 'more of the same' leadership, and followed the Sparkes' line that something new would have to emerge on the conservative front: 'The only hope is that an organisation will emerge, like we are trying to build. That is the only way to gain the initiative. Howard and Sinclair are not winners. We need winners.'

Meanwhile, there was more flak on the way for Sparkes. This time, the Queensland Member for Dawson, Ray Braithwaite, took him to task in a long letter, dated 17 July. He expressed his 'disgust' at what had happened within the party over the past six months and chronicled his grievances about how the Joh campaign had been conceived and executed. He concluded by saying he would 'no longer receive instruction from the Executive, Management, or Central Council which I believe is in conflict with, or not in the best interest of, National Party members or my constituents of Dawson, nor which, in my opinion, are not in the best interests of our State or Federal organisations'.

The federal president of the Young Nationals, Julian Anderson, himself a Queenslander, issued a critical press statement on 19 July: 'The single greatest contributing factor to the swing against the Party here in Queensland is the disruption caused by constant criticism of the Federal Party and its former Coalition partner. There is absolutely no way that the Australian people will support a Party that is disruptive and destructive.'

§

In the federal National Party, speculation was growing that Ralph Hunt would not stand for re-election as deputy parliamentary leader, opening the way for a Melbourne Cup field of contenders.

Sinclair wanted Hunt to continue. But Hunt had canvassed his future – even to the point of admitting he would not contest the next election – too openly with some of his parliamentary colleagues. The 'young turks' smelled the prospect of promotion. It reached the point where if Hunt did stand – which he had already decided he would not do – he might not have the numbers. He stuck to his view that it was time to give leadership experience to someone else. On 20 July, he announced he would step aside, saying that it was 'wise to make way for younger members to be given experience in positions of responsibility' and adding that the party was 'fortunate that it has a number of keen and talented members from which to choose'.[13] Sinclair said Hunt left the position with 'my greatest respect and affection. ... In the problems and difficulties which we have faced in the last eight months, no party could have had a stronger or more loyal Deputy Leader than Ralph Hunt'.[14]

15
BACK TOWARDS COALITION

20 to 27 July 1987

> Our branch [Western Australia] is adamantly opposed to Coalition in Opposition – the sooner the Federal Parliamentary Party accepts this stand, the sooner we will be able to get on with the business of formulating our policy and identity to permit us to fight the next election as an effective political force.
>
> John Paterson, general president, National Party of Australia (WA), media release, 24 July 1987

A week after the election, Sinclair had still not scheduled a parliamentary party meeting, largely because considerable uncertainty remained about the Senate election outcome. The party in Queensland was confident, but still uncertain, that its fourth senator, Glen Sheil, had won his seat. The Victorian party had claimed victory for Julian McGauran, but the result was not finalised. South Australia and Western Australia were each in with a chance of returning a senator, thanks to the Senate tickets sponsored by Queensland.

Sinclair received a number of calls from members asking when he would call a party meeting. This, coupled with increasing speculation about the deputy leadership, made him call a meeting in Canberra on 23 July. He included the undecided, yet prospective senators in the meeting notice, which was sent out by the whip, Noel Hicks, on Monday 20 July. He advised the prospective senators the party room would decide what participation or voting rights they might have. They all accepted the invitation to attend and the consensus view of the party room that they not be allowed to vote.

By the time of the meeting, the race for the deputy leadership favoured Bruce Lloyd from Victoria. Other contenders who had nominated were Ian Cameron and John Stone, from Queensland; Charles Blunt, Tim Fischer, Noel Hicks and Ian Robinson, from New South Wales; and Peter McGauran, from Victoria. Queenslander Bob Katter senior, who had earlier suggested he might contest the position, did not do so. John Sharp, from New South Wales, who the press had been tipping as a strong contender and who was favoured initially by Hunt, also decided not to stand. He felt the time was not right, having recently been married and having only been a parliamentary member since 1984.

Before the deputy leadership ballot came that for the leader, where the surprise development was the decision by Ray Braithwaite to oppose Sinclair. He gave no advance warning and Sinclair, while half expecting some late development, was being tipped for re-election unopposed. Braithwaite decided to stand so that there would actually be a ballot. His reasoning was that had there been none, anyone opposed to Sinclair could claim his tenure was under a continuing cloud because it had not been put to the test. He also felt that Sinclair had not given an adequate indication of the direction he intended to take the party in the wake of the Joh experience. He had no illusion of beating Sinclair, but he wanted to impress upon him the party room's general desire for new ideas and greater cohesion.[1] Sinclair won a resounding vote. *The Sun News-Pictorial* in Melbourne suggested a fairly narrow win of 16 votes to ten. It was actually 20 for Sinclair and six for Braithwaite.[2]

In the bid for deputy leader, the numbers were clearly coming down in favour of Lloyd. He was more experienced than his fellow Victorian, McGauran. He had the backing of Sinclair and Hunt, both of whom were concerned to ensure a deputy who would be loyal to Sinclair and who was a firm coalitionist. Lloyd had these qualities. He had considerable experience, both in the parliamentary party, where he had been since 1971, and in the Victorian party organisation where he had served as state president from 1969 to 1971. He was solid and safe.

As the ballot progressed, it came down to a tussle between Lloyd and Stone. The fact that Stone did so well enhanced his prospects of being elected party leader in the Senate and having an important Opposition portfolio, such as finance, especially if a new Coalition agreement was established. Ultimately, Lloyd was elected.

The ballot for the Senate leadership positions was deferred. Sinclair had wanted to change the system for these elections. Up to now, the elected senators alone chose their leader, deputy and whip. Sinclair wanted the whole party room to do it. His reasoning was that so long as the Queenslanders held the majority party representation in the Senate, there would be little if any opportunity for someone from another state to hold leadership positions. He also believed, given the antics of the Queensland party over recent months, and especially their dumping of Collard, that they simply did not deserve to hold any positions. He was unsuccessful in this bid. The status quo remained and the senators agreed to postpone their ballot until after the Senate election results were finalised.

The party room also discussed Coalition, where Sinclair won a partial but useful victory. He received unanimous support to begin preliminary discussions with Howard. He was directed not to reach any final decisions before reporting back to the party room, and was also requested to consult the party organisation, in view of the resolutions of federal council. Of further encouragement was an interview on ABC Radio *AM* on 24 July, in which Ian Cameron – originally a pro-Joh man – came out strongly in favour of re-forming the Coalition and acknowledged the failure of the Queensland campaign:

> I believe the results of the election, not just in Queensland, but in other areas of Australia, have proved to us conclusively that it's wise for us to work together in Coalition, and I, personally, have never been able to understand why it is that we're prepared to go into Coalition after being elected to government and not in Opposition, and certainly the result in Queensland highlighted the fact that the Queensland voters weren't very happy about the way we broke the Coalition, the timing of the breaking and also the fact that we were out of Coalition.

On the same program, Joh remained implacably opposed to re-forming the Coalition: 'They make their bed, they have to sleep on it ... . I have said that I have never been in agreement with it [Coalition] when they're in Opposition ...'

Joh was supported by the general president of the party in Western Australia, John Paterson. When he heard that Sinclair was apparently seeking to restore Coalition, he issued a press statement, on 24 July, reiterating the Western Australian–moved motion at federal council requiring the party not to enter into Coalition in Opposition. Paterson emphasised that there was no doubt where the Western Australian party stood: 'Our branch is adamantly opposed to Coalition in Opposition – the sooner the Federal Parliamentary Party accepts this stand, the sooner we will be able to get on with the business of formulating our policy and identity to permit us to fight the next election as an effective political force.'

Sinclair wasted no time beginning talks with Howard. He met him for a short time in Sydney on Friday 24 July. As a result, he decided that a federal management meeting should be convened as soon as possible – sometime the following week. He contacted the federal president, Stuart McDonald, to discuss logistics.

Apart from discussing Coalition, the management committee would have to consider a further re-application for affiliation from the NT Nationals. It would be important to try to have all management delegates present. At such short notice, this was going to be difficult. The party treasurer was not available at any time during the week, except possibly Monday, and on top of this, he was suffering a severe bout of influenza. The secretary could only make it on the Thursday. McDonald telephoned the Queensland vice-president, Charles Holm, on Saturday morning, 25 July, and was advised that Tuesday looked like being best for him and he would see about Sparkes' availability. Tuesday 28 July was ultimately fixed as the day, mainly because it appeared the most convenient for the Queensland delegates.

At about 11pm on the Sunday evening, Holm rang McDonald and told him the Queenslanders would not be able to attend a federal management meeting until after their own state management had convened the following Friday. But notices for the federal meeting, to be held in Sydney, had already gone out, and both the Western Australian and South Australian presidents had confirmed they would attend. Paterson pleaded with the Queenslanders to have some representation, but to no avail.

16
A QUEENSLAND NO SHOW

28 July 1987

1. That Federal Management confirms the traditional autonomy of the Federal Parliamentary Party (carried unanimously).

Federal management committee resolution, Sydney, 28 July 1987

The federal management committee normally had a strength of 14, but with the party's Senate leadership election still pending at the end of July, this was reduced to thirteen. Seven delegates – one more than required for a quorum – attended the Sydney meeting. Present were Sinclair and Lloyd, the federal president, the presidents of Victoria, Western Australia and South Australia, and the state chairman of New South Wales. Apologies were received from the treasurer, secretary, president of the Young Nationals and president of the Women's Federal Council.[1]

Sparkes and Holm, while not sending apologies, sent letters protesting that the meeting was being held. As well as complaining that the meeting was being called 'at such short notice', when the election result for the Senate in Queensland had not been finalised, Sparkes argued that the management committee had no right to consider the potential re-forming of the Coalition because of the resolution of federal council in March that the party should not enter into a Coalition in Opposition. He said that instead, the management committee should convene a special meeting of federal council 'as soon as practicable to deal with these matters in depth'. Holm's letter was in similar vein and attacked Sinclair for wanting to 'go on his merry way' on Coalition 'and to hell with the Organisation', when the Liberals were 'a nest of hornets at present'. McDonald circulated the letters at the meeting for the information of delegates. There was no debate on them. Later in the morning, word was received that Sparkes had released his letter to the media. All delegates were unimpressed. It was simply not the 'done thing' to make such internal correspondence public.

The first business of the meeting concerned the Northern Territory. McDonald tabled the correspondence he had received in May from the Northern Territory CLP confirming that, contrary to the advice received at the last federal management meeting, the CLP had disaffiliated from the National Country Party on 3 February 1979. This was duly noted.

There was considerable discussion about the NT Nationals' renewed application for affiliation, which had been lodged despite the federal management committee's request in March that the party defer its application for 12 months. Sinclair said the application should be rejected. He pointed out that up to 35 per cent of NT Nationals' preferences in the federal election had gone to the ALP. Also, while the CLP senator-elect, Grant Tambling, would prefer to sit with the National Party in Canberra, he would not do so if the party agreed to affiliate the NT Nationals – the very party that Tambling had been fighting in the election. Further, not affiliating the NT Nationals would increase the chance of them reuniting with the CLP. Sinclair remained convinced the CLP offered the best future for conservative politics at the federal level in the Northern Territory. The South Australian and Western Australian presidents, Neville Agars and John Paterson, did not agree. Agars said Tambling was effectively holding a gun at the federal party's head by threatening to sit with the Liberals if the NT Nationals were affiliated.

Eventually Sinclair moved that the application be rejected. It was carried by five votes to two. Even if all management committee delegates had been present, the motion would have been carried by a similar margin. McDonald had been given assurances by the treasurer and secretary that they were opposed to affiliating the NT Nationals. Julian Anderson, the Young Nationals' president, and a Queenslander, sent a facsimile letter that morning expressing total opposition to the affiliation: 'It is my opinion that the Northern Territory Country Liberal Party is better suited to our sort of politics and is more likely to be stable than their pretender faction that is known as the Northern Territory National Party.'

Sparkes, Holm and the women's president, Jean McIntyre, also from Queensland, would almost certainly have favoured affiliation. That would have resulted in a vote of eight against and five for. Even if there had been a Senate leader in favour of affiliation, the vote would have been eight to six and not require any casting vote from the president, who, had it been necessary, would have voted against. The numbers were never there for the NT Nationals.

On Coalition, Sinclair briefed the meeting on the 23 July party room decisions and the preliminary discussions he had held with Howard. He explained that he was not seeking management's endorsement of a return to Coalition, but rather its agreement to the continued autonomy of the federal parliamentary party. He had spent a lot of time on the telephone over recent days talking to parliamentary colleagues. He had also asked Peter Nixon to talk directly to Sparkes. Nixon's brief was to find out exactly what Sparkes would say or do if a majority of the parliamentary party wanted to rejoin a Coalition with the Liberals. Nixon was able to give to Sinclair word for word what Sparkes had told him, and Sinclair used this to the letter in wording a motion to put to management.[2] He presented his case convincingly and won overwhelming support for the motion, which was in four parts, each one voted on separately:

1. That Federal Management confirms the traditional autonomy of the Federal Parliamentary Party. (Carried unanimously).
2. That should the majority of the Parliamentary Party opt to go back into Coalition with the Liberal Party, so be it. (Carried, with Paterson opposing).
3. That Federal Management has no reason to believe that State Management of any affiliated branch of the National Party will cause Senators or Members any problems if the Parliamentarians decide to go back into Coalition. (Carried unanimously).
4. That Federal Management recommend to Federal Council that it endorses the above resolutions as the view of the Federal Council. (Carried unanimously).

It was the wording of the second and third motions that were based on Sparkes' conversation with Nixon.

The meeting also rejected the suggestion by Sparkes that it should call a special meeting of federal council as soon as practicable. Immediately after the March council meeting, it had been agreed a further one would have to be held later in the year, to get the meeting schedule back into its normal cycle of being held towards the end of each year. The reason for this timing was to enable the council to consider resolutions that came from the various state party conferences, which were held earlier in the year, usually between May and August. Preliminary venue bookings had already been made for a federal council in Canberra between 15 and 18 October. The management committee agreed that, as this was only ten weeks away, there was no point in altering arrangements. Paterson moved that the dates be confirmed. The motion was carried unanimously.

The day had been quite a victory for Sinclair. A short press statement on the federal council date and the major resolutions carried was issued under McDonald's name. The only remaining task was to respond to the letters from Sparkes and Holm. McDonald was both infuriated and amused by them. He was angered that Holm, as senior federal vice-president and a contender for the federal presidency in March, had adopted an entirely Queensland-oriented position, rather than think about the broader party interests. He was stung by Holm's allegation that Sinclair 'wants to go on his merry way and to hell with the Organisation'. He was unimpressed with the other arguments in the letters. He was especially amused that Holm's letter bore the rider: 'Dictated by Sir Robert Sparkes and signed in his absence as instructed'. It was a secretarial error; the line should have been on the Sparkes letter, but the impression that Sparkes was writing Holm's letters for him seemed amusingly appropriate.

McDonald realised that as a new federal president he was being put to the test by these letters. He wanted to make it clear to Sparkes and Holm that he was not going to be intimidated by them. Before leaving Sydney to return to Melbourne, he drafted a lengthy letter in reply to those of both Sparkes and Holm and instructed that it be faxed immediately to Brisbane. In it, he regretted that neither Sparkes nor Holm had come to the meeting, saying that their stated reasons were no excuse; he told Sparkes that his argument that the management meeting should not have been convened because the party had yet to elect a

Senate leader was 'frankly, fatuous'; he said Sparkes' assumption that management would take a vote on the issue of Coalition was wrong; he said delegates had been 'singularly unimpressed' to learn that Sparkes had released his letter to the Brisbane media; and he rounded on Holm's claim that Sinclair wanted to 'go on his merry way', saying the very purpose of convening the management meeting was to enable Sinclair to 'INVOLVE the Organisation'. He concluded by assuring Sparkes that 'I will not be releasing this letter in any form whatsoever to the media'.

17
THE COALITION RE-FORMS

29 July to 14 August 1987

We have to be absolutely certain that the Queensland problem in the National Party is behind us. I am not interested in resuming a Coalition only to see that problem re-emerge in some form or another.

John Howard, Channel 9 *Sunday* program,
2 August 1987

With his resolutions on the autonomy of the parliamentary party carried by the federal management committee, Sinclair was in a stronger position to continue negotiations with Howard. He arranged for further talks in Sydney the following day, 29 July, and called a party meeting for the day after, also in Sydney.

For Sinclair, time was now getting extremely tight. Howard had already announced that his deputy, Peacock, would be the shadow Treasurer and that he intended to announce the full shadow ministry by the end of the week. If Sinclair could not shore up his party by then, it would be too late; there would be an all-Liberal front bench. Howard was playing tough. He had to. There were many in his parliamentary team who remained

The Coalition re-forms

bitter about the Nationals, blaming them entirely for the election loss. They would be happy to see the 'Nats' left out in the cold.

Howard laid down strict conditions for resuming Coalition. He wanted virtually ironclad guarantees that it would last the distance to the next election. It had to be 'honourable', and part of this would require that only Coalition policies be put to the electorate – no independent National Party ones. Sinclair knew this could be problematic. Coalition or not, there was a strong feeling throughout the National Party that it had to highlight its own identity and policy priorities. If the party could not differentiate itself, then it truly was little more than a rump of the Liberal Party.

Sinclair remained convinced that a united Coalition was the only answer to beating Labor. The non-Coalition days in 1972–74 had failed. So, too, had the brief split between April and now. Sinclair did not believe in Coalition for the sake of Coalition. He saw it as the best way for the National Party to have an influence on the development of policies that could ultimately be implemented by a non-Labor government. Moreover, working co-operatively with the Liberals in Opposition enhanced the National Party's justification to be a partner in government, particularly if and when the Liberal Party won enough lower house seats to govern in its own right, as had been the case after the 1975 and 1977 elections (and would again be the case after the 1996 election). At the same time, however, on this occasion, Sinclair was aware that many in the party were eyeing him critically. The Queenslanders, Western Australians and South Australians supported the federal council resolution that the party should not again enter into a Coalition in Opposition. Sinclair needed clear majority support from his party room to re-form the Coalition. It was the only way to negate the federal council position.

He had further talks with Howard in Sydney on the morning of 30 July. The two worked out the basis of what they regarded as an honourable proposal. Sinclair drafted a set of motions that he took to his party meeting, which got underway in the conference room of the Commonwealth Parliamentary Offices, in Chifley Square, shortly after 1pm. It was the same room in which the federal management committee had met two days earlier.

Twenty-six people were asked to attend. These were the elected members and senators as well as Julian McGauran from Victoria, who was almost certain to be elected to the Senate but whose position had yet to be confirmed. The prospective senators from South Australia and Western Australia were not invited on this occasion. While their positions were still unclear, their prospects of being elected were now viewed as unlikely. Two returned members, Bob Katter senior in Kennedy and Bruce Cowan in Lyne, did not attend; Katter had electorate commitments and Cowan was overseas. Twenty-four attended the meeting.

Sinclair proposed seven motions detailing how the party would work in a future Coalition and reaffirming the autonomy of the parliamentary party and its right to make its own decisions. Each was voted on separately. While the voting numbers changed marginally, all were overwhelmingly carried with only a handful – all from Queensland – voting against:

1. That the Parliamentary National Party believes the most effective way to defeat the Labor Government is to work co-operatively with the Liberal Party in Coalition.
2. That the Parliamentary National Party enter into a Coalition in Opposition in the Federal Parliament with the Parliamentary Liberal Party, with a view to forming a Coalition Government after the next federal election.

3. While noting the resolutions of the National Party Federal Council and Federal Management, this Party Room reaffirms the autonomy and independence of the Parliamentary Party and agrees that the establishment, maintenance or termination of the Coalition will be determined by the majority vote of the National Party Senators and Members and not be subject to direction by any affiliated State organisation of the Party.
4. That the Coalition arrangements acknowledge and preserve the National and Liberal Parties' independent identities, meeting procedures, platforms and organisational policy processes to ensure public recognition of each Party and their respective Parliamentary candidates but present joint policies at the next election.
5. That the Coalition arrangements ensure fair and equitable representation of the National Party in all Parliamentary processes such as Matters of Public Importance and Question Time and in Shadow Cabinet, Shadow Ministry, Joint Committees and in Coalition policy development.
6. Where there are differences in approach by the National Party to that of the Liberal Party whether in policy or in response to legislation or otherwise and they have not been resolved in Joint Party meetings, they be referred to the leadership group of the two Parties for decision.
7. The foregoing resolutions are the basis for the leadership to conclude the negotiations with the Liberal leadership to form a Coalition.

Sinclair had won a commanding victory. He had met the obligations placed on him by the party room at its meeting a week earlier, on 23 July, by consulting the organisation through the federal management committee, and he had reported back to the party room before reaching any final decisions. Moreover, the party room, through the third resolution, had sent a clear message to all states and the federal council that its members and no-one else would determine matters of Coalition. And, equally important, he had negotiated with Howard the right for the National Party to maintain its independent identity and develop its own platforms and organisational policy processes, even though joint policies would be presented at the next election. The road to re-forming the Coalition was open, but there were still potential problems ahead, not the least being how the Queensland party would react and whether the parliamentary Liberal Party would want to reunite with the Nationals.

Sinclair did not release the party room resolutions to the media. He held an informal news conference after the meeting, which he opened by telling reporters: 'The Party overwhelmingly permitted me the responsibility for concluding the arrangements for a Coalition. There were only four members of the party room who voted against a Coalition and an overwhelming majority asserted the autonomy of the federal parliamentary party in line with the resolution of [federal] management the other day.' His reference to 'only four members' voting against Coalition upset Tom McVeigh, who the next day said he had checked with his colleagues and found that five had in fact voted against Coalition and it had been incorrect of Sinclair to say what he did. McVeigh's point was pedantic, but it was clearly intended to embarrass Sinclair.

Howard was encouraged by the outcome of the Nationals' meeting, but remained coy: 'In the nature of things, I am not going to start committing the Liberal Party to anything at the present time.'[1] He began canvassing the views of senior colleagues and set Wednesday 5 August at 10.30am in Canberra as the date and venue for a parliamentary Liberal party meeting to consider the issue.

§

The Queensland party's management committee met for a marathon ten hours in Brisbane on Friday 31 July. Much of the time was taken up by Sparkes giving his assessment of the election result. He argued that the party had done well in the state, containing Labor's primary vote for the House of Representatives to almost the same as in 1984 and to the lowest level in all mainland states. But this ignored the fact that the ALP had taken two seats from the Nationals and two from the Liberals, increasing its number of seats in Queensland by four.

On Coalition, the state management committee decided to support the federal council position that the party should not be in Coalition in Opposition. However, Sparkes, in a significant capitulation from the Hervey Bay position, said there would be no directive to Queensland federal MPs on the matter:

> No, we won't be directing our members on this occasion. What we've done is express our view on the matter which, of course, is simply that the decision taken by the federal council last March should be adhered to, should be observed. But, in the final analysis, we're prepared to allow our parliamentary members to make the decision.[2]

Despite the 'on this occasion' qualification, there were two significant points about this statement. First, that Sparkes had held true to the assurances he had given to Peter Nixon prior to the 28 July meeting of the federal management committee; and second, an implicit acknowledgment that a majority position of the federal parliamentary party would prevail.

Howard remained cautious, confirming to the Channel 9 *Sunday* program on 2 August that there were 'quite strong' reservations among Liberals, including those who were normally pro-Coalition, about resuming the arrangement. He even conceded that he personally had 'some reservations':

> I think it would be fair to say that from a long range point of view we'd be better off having a Coalition, but it's got to be a Coalition for keeps. ... We have to be absolutely certain that the Queensland problem in the National Party is behind us. I am not interested in resuming a Coalition only to see that problem re-emerge in some form or another.

The same day, Sinclair issued a statement urging the Liberals to endorse a return to Coalition. He included the first four Coalition resolutions of his party room, to indicate to potentially wavering Liberals that the parliamentary Nationals were serious about re-forming a lasting partnership: 'The National Party has put forward significant proposals and it is hoped that the Liberal Party Members and Senators endorse a return to coalition when they meet on Wednesday.'[3]

Any wavering Liberals might have wavered more in the two days leading up to their Wednesday party meeting. Bob Katter senior appeared on the ABC Radio *AM* program on Monday morning, 3 August. In trying to be supportive of Sinclair as his leader, he claimed there was a 'deep and continuing detestation of Ian Sinclair' within the Queensland party organisation: 'They will not have him under any circumstances at all.' Charles Holm responded on the ABC's *World Today* program in the early afternoon and gave, to say the least, highly qualified support for Sinclair: 'Perhaps there are segments within the [Queensland] party who are really gunning for Ian, but the position is, as far as I'm concerned, he's elected as the leader and I suppose until such time as the members of parliament toss him out, well that's that.'

The New South Wales party chairman, Doug Moppett,

decided to weigh in. In a statement from his Quambone home in the state's north-west, he praised Katter for his 'courage and insight in his forthright remarks' and then said that media reports of Sparkes' marathon exposé to his management committee of the federal election result in Queensland suggested that Sparkes had learnt nothing: 'If this is so, then the Queensland organisation will not return from space until he [Sparkes] is replaced by someone who can come to terms with the fact that Ian Sinclair is the undisputed Leader of the Party, both personally and in strategy direction.' The statement also criticised McVeigh for his 'unbridled and gratuitous comments' regarding the voting numbers on the motion to re-form Coalition at the previous week's party meeting, saying that they qualified McVeigh for 'suspension, at least from the Parliamentary Party'.[4] That brought a quick response from McVeigh:

> Mr Moppett makes statements which are absolutely incorrect. He said Mr Sinclair was unchallenged. History will recall that Mr Ray Braithwaite did challenge him for the position of leadership. A statement was issued last week indicating that four people had voted against a Coalition in Opposition. The fact of the matter is that there were five. I publicly corrected that error.[5]

This was all disconcerting for Sinclair and Howard, both of whom wanted a new Coalition agreement. The view among a growing number of Liberals, however, was that the Nationals were still bitterly divided and should be left on the crossbenches.

When he went into his party meeting on 5 August, Howard was armed with all the resolutions from the National Party federal management committee and parliamentary party meetings, as well as the public commitment from Sparkes that the Queensland organisation would not direct its MPs on Coalition. After several hours, Howard won majority support to negotiate a new Coalition agreement. The following day, 6 August, he delivered a letter to Sinclair's Canberra office outlining the terms under which the Liberals would conclude such an agreement:

1. That each of our Parties preserves its independent identity, meeting procedures, platforms and organisational policy process. Our Parliamentary Parties would continue to meet separately as and when desired by each Party.
2. There will be joint Coalition policies both in relation to Government legislation and issues generally. It will be the obligation of each member of our Parties to support and advocate Coalition policy both inside the Parliament and elsewhere. No member of either Party shall advocate in the name of his or her Party policies in any area which differ in substance from Coalition policy.
3. All members of the two Parliamentary Parties shall fully accept and participate in the Coalition arrangements.
4. That the Coalition arrangements ensure fair and equitable representation of both Parties in all Parliamentary processes such as matters of public importance and question time and in shadow cabinet, shadow ministry, joint committees and in Coalition policy development.
5. Where differences in approach between the two Parties emerge either in policy development or in response to legislation, the Joint Party Meeting may refer such differences to the leadership group of the two Parties for decision or resolution.

This was acceptable to Sinclair. To a large extent the proposal mirrored the terminology of the National Party room resolutions. He knew there could be some apprehension about clause 2 of the Howard proposal, yet it did not specifically forbid the development of National Party policy objectives. Moreover, Howard had raised no objection to the wording of the fourth resolution of the National Party meeting. There was room for flexibility. Sinclair and his deputy, Lloyd, began ringing MPs to brief them and recommend acceptance. They received clear majority support.

Sinclair then held a further meeting with Howard. The two agreed that a new Coalition could be formed. Sinclair gave Howard a formal letter of reply. Howard released both letters with a brief press statement announcing that the Coalition had been re-established and calling on Liberals and Nationals throughout Australia to put aside past divisions and commit to a united Opposition to the Hawke government.[6] It had been exactly 100 days since the previous patched-up Coalition had fallen apart on 28 April.

The exchange of correspondence and the Sinclair–Howard meeting occurred against the background of continuing debate on the merits of Coalition. Joh declared no interest at all on the ABC's *AM* program on the morning of 6 August: 'I couldn't be less interested in them [the federal parliamentary National Party]. They don't seem to have learned a lesson. They just still want to be in the shadow and shrivel up even further, to be a prop to the Liberal Party, to be at their behest and control and direction. ... They might as well join the Liberal Party.'

McVeigh, speaking on the ABC Canberra radio program, *The Morning Show*, just after *AM*, flagged the possibility of sitting as an Independent Queensland National in the parliament: 'If after an analysis of all the facts, if after discussion with the people on whom I rely to put me in parliament, it appears to me that the best position for me to adopt and one consistent with my own conscience and strong feelings on certain matters, is to become an Independent or a member of parliament representing the Queensland National Party, I would not lack the courage to do so.' Ultimately, after consulting party branches in his electorate, he accepted the new Coalition.[7]

Later in the day, the Queensland Member for Wide Bay, Clarrie Millar, told the ABC's *World Today* that the party should not be in Coalition in Opposition. However, he would accept the majority decision of the party room: 'When I expressed that view [that the party should not be in Coalition in Opposition] on a number of occasions for the party room, I qualified it unequivocally with the undertaking that if it was the will of the party room to go into Coalition, I would accept that without demur and address myself as a responsible member of Coalition from that point on.'

On the same program, Katter said that any of his colleagues who refused to accept a majority party room decision should 'get to hell out of it. ... I think if we don't go into Coalition we're going to have the fragmentation the people in Australia will not accept'.

Sinclair and Howard began working on a new Coalition shadow ministry. Howard would not now announce the front bench by the weekend of 8–9 August, when he was due to undergo minor knee surgery. It would be delayed until the following week. He would have to juggle prospective positions to allow for seven or eight Nationals being included.

Meanwhile, the South Australian National Party was in no mind to heed Howard's call for unity. Its annual conference in Bordertown over the 8–9 August weekend carried two anti-Coalition motions, despite Sinclair's attendance and his explanation of the majority party room position:

(1) That the South Australian National Party:
    1. Not be bound by any Coalition arrangements that would impede the development and promotion of its own identity, principles and policies at future

State and Federal elections, and,
2. Advise Federal Council of our disapproval in principle to Coalition in Opposition.

(2) This Conference recommends to Federal Council that the Federal National Party embark immediately on new policy formation so that the National Party can be seen as having its own identity.

The motions, carried unanimously or without dissent, would be submitted for consideration at the October 1987 federal council. The Western Australian party's annual conference was to be held the following weekend and could be expected to similarly oppose the re-establishment of a Coalition in Opposition.

§

Ralph Hunt, having stood down as Sinclair's deputy after the election, was turning his mind to the future. He wanted to retire. Had it not been for the Joh campaign, he would have done so at the last election. He perceived that it was possible that two or three of his New South Wales colleagues might retire at the next election. By about 10 August, he came to the view that he would retire mid-term, thereby creating a by-election and taking some of the pressure off the New South Wales party organisation seeking to retain seats at the election with new candidates. He then reasoned that if he was not going to complete the parliamentary term, he should retire to the backbench, enabling Sinclair to promote new blood on to the front bench. He told Sinclair of his plans on 12 August. Sinclair accepted his rationale with reservations. He had wanted Hunt to continue as his deputy and he wanted him to continue on the front bench, preferably still as shadow Minister for Primary Industry. But it was hard to argue against the logic of what Hunt put to him. Later in the day, Sinclair finalised negotiations with Howard on which National parliamentarians would be promoted to the shadow ministry.

The media by now was becoming critical of the delay in finalising the Opposition's line-up. It was more than a month since the election. The government had taken a number of initiatives, like restructuring the public service and amalgamating departments, establishing a royal commission into Aboriginal deaths in custody, overhauling its parliamentary committee system, considering an Australian Council of Trade Unions (ACTU) report on industrial relations, titled *Australia Reconstructed*, and receiving recommendations from the Constitutional Commission on several proposals for constitutional reform. All of these had gone virtually without comment from the Opposition.

By the afternoon of 14 August, Howard was finally able to announce a shadow ministry of 30, eight of whom were from the National Party – Ian Sinclair, trade and resources; Bruce Lloyd, primary industry; John Stone, finance; Charles Blunt, community services and assisting the leader of the National Party; Ray Braithwaite, territories; Tim Fischer, veterans' affairs; John Sharp, tourism and sport; and Ian Cameron, local government.[8]

Given his background as a former head of Treasury, promoting Stone to the finance portfolio – the tenth most senior position in the shadow ministry – was logical. It also raised interesting questions. How would Stone reconcile his shadow ministerial position with the tax policy he had devised for the Queensland National Party? Would he feel in any way obliged to pursue it? From a professional point of view there was no reason why he should, because he had merely accepted a contract from the Queensland party as an economic adviser to develop a policy that met the Queensland party's objective of implementing a single rate income tax system. But how would

The Coalition re-forms

he stand if the Queensland hierarchy demanded that Queensland federal parliamentarians support its tax policy over that of the Coalition? Fortunately, the issue did not arise. The Queensland party did not try to force its federal MPs on tax policy. Stone did, however, express his belief that there was room for discussion within the Coalition about the single rate concept, describing it as 'an exceptionally good policy'.[9]

The Queensland party was also in no position to be too disruptive because, despite everything, Sinclair had been generous; three Queenslanders were on the Coalition's front bench – Stone in the shadow cabinet; Braithwaite, back in the shadow ministry, albeit in a more junior role; and Cameron into the shadow ministry for the first time. Some in the parliamentary party believed, given the chaos the Queenslanders had caused, that they should have been given virtually nothing.

18
ONCE MORE UNTO THE BREACH ...

14–21 August 1987

A Coalition in Opposition is the political equivalent of a cartel. It is a conspiracy to limit choice and is a political manoeuvre more appropriate for the Labor Party.

Hendy Cowan, speech to the Western Australian National Party annual conference, Perth, 14 August 1987

While Howard was putting the finishing touches to the shadow ministry on 14 August, Sinclair was winging his way to Perth for the annual conference of the Western Australian National Party. He knew it would not be an easy visit. But if he had been disappointed with the outcome of the previous weekend's conference in South Australia, he would be hurt by what awaited him in the west. The 150 delegates did not want to know him.[1]

The state parliamentary leader, Hendy Cowan, who had successfully moved the motion at the March federal council that the party not enter into a Coalition in Opposition again, gave the opening speech. No shrinking violet, Cowan did not mince his words:

Once more unto the breach …

> While I welcome the participation at this Conference of our Federal colleagues, it must be apparent to all of you I feel no obligation to patronise them by shielding them from what WA Nationals feel about their actions. The steadfast refusal of the Parliamentary National Party to stand proudly as an independent Party is a fundamental error of judgement. The new Coalition agreement … is a form of political censorship which we in Western Australia could never endorse. …
>
> A Coalition in Opposition is the political equivalent of a cartel. It is a conspiracy to limit choice and is a political manoeuvre more appropriate for the Labor Party. There is no benefit in the National Party attaching itself to the coat tails of the Liberal Party.

Cowan said the resumption of Coalition in Opposition would 'never be condoned in Western Australia'. His address was followed by that of the party's general president, John Paterson, who was equally scathing:

> Having had a position of no Coalition in Opposition carried at Federal Council and now opposed by the Federal Parliamentary Party, we can either –
> 1. Withdraw from the Federal Council on the grounds of a waste of time and finance and go it alone in Western Australia,
> 2. Accept that the Federal Parliamentary Party doesn't have regard for Federal Council motions carried and stay a reluctant partner,
> 3. Stay in and change the [National Party federal] Constitution so that it does have some meaning when motions are carried at Federal Council.
>
> This Conference should decide exactly what the Western

Australian attitude is to Federal Council and the Federal Parliamentary Party.

Both addresses were enthusiastically received by the delegates. Sinclair's speech was another matter altogether. Delivering a strong argument in favour of the parliamentary party's decision, he was confronted by some delegates waving placards with slogans such as *Sinclair's tough – so tough he's rusted* and *Federal faint-heartedness*. The conference wanted to get on with a block of urgency motions dealing with Sinclair, the federal parliamentary party, the Coalition and federal council. They were brought on as the first items on the agenda.

The first motion was moved by James MacDonald, the man who had headed the party's Joh campaign–supported Senate ticket and who had lost by only 507 votes. He was seconded by Cowan:

> That this Conference resolve to serve notice upon the Federal Council of the National Party that:
> (a) The action of the Federal Parliamentary Leader, the Rt. Hon. Ian Sinclair, MP in effecting a Coalition-in-Opposition with the Federal Parliamentary Liberal Party and thereby negating the integrity and independence of the Federal Party is in total violation of the resolution of Federal Council, and contrary to the best interests of the Party and conservative politics as a whole;
> (b) Subject to ratification by the State Council at a Special Meeting of State Council to be convened in the month of November 1987, the National Party of Australia (WA) Inc. withdraw from Federal Council on the first day of December, 1987; and that

(c) In the period August to November a special Constitutional Committee be formed comprised of:
   (a) The State Leader Mr Hendy Cowan MLA
   (b) The State President
   (c) The Proposer of this Resolution; and
   (d) Four Party Members elected by this Conference

to examine and report to State Council upon the viability of the National Party of Australia (WA) Inc., together with such other State organisations of the National Party as shall similarly agree and resolve to establish a new Federal Party structure to be called the 'Australian Conservative Party'.

This had all the hallmarks of having been influenced by Queensland. It was an extraordinary motion to come from the candidate who had headed the state party's Senate ticket, on the endorsement of the state National Party, even if that ticket had been facilitated by the Queensland party. It was also extraordinary that the state leader of the party should second a motion suggesting the potential establishment of a new federal political party, which, if formed, could be in direct competition with the National Party.

The conference agreed to consider the motions separately. Part (a) was overwhelmingly carried. It was then agreed that parts (b) and (c) be considered as one. They were lost.

Three other critical motions were, however, carried:

That this conference expresses its utter disappointment with the insistency by Mr Ian Sinclair and some of his colleagues for continually craving for Coalition in Opposition and urges the Federal Council to severely reprimand the Federal Parliamentary Party for acting contrary to the direction of Federal Council.

That the National Party (WA) calls for changes in the National Party of Australia's Federal Constitution which will give the Federal Council all the necessary power to direct the Federal Parliamentary Party on matters of involvement in Coalition in both Government and Opposition.

That in view of the disappointing Federal election result and the lack of positive independent action by the Federal National Party, the National Party (WA) establishes a Committee of Review to reassess its Federal affiliation and future direction, and the National Party (WA) unequivocally sets as its first priority expanding and becoming the major conservative force in WA.

There was no comfort for Sinclair in these. He was dejected by the reception he received, by the mood of the conference and by the tenor of the motions carried. He returned dispirited to the east. Well he might. The scene was now set for another bitter federal council gathering, unless some circuit-breaker could be devised. Even though the strong anti-Coalition sentiments had come from the party's smallest states – neither of which had any federal parliamentary representation – their motions would be submitted for the federal council agenda, and Queensland would almost certainly support them. The federal parliamentary party was facing a censure at federal council from at least three state delegations.

§

The leadership elections for the parliamentary party's seven-member Senate team took place at a meeting in Sydney on 21 August. Queenslander, Ron Boswell, had been lobbying hard and was tipped by the media as a strong contender for the leadership.

He backed out at the last minute, apparently at the suggestion of Sparkes, clearing the way for Stone's election and his continued rapid rise in the parliamentary party. In the space of a week, Stone had gone from being a newly elected backbench senator to shadow Finance Minister and now party leader in the Senate.

Flo Bjelke-Petersen was elected deputy leader, while the Northern Territory's Grant Tambling won the position of whip. This was highly significant. The Queenslanders, with four of the seven senators, held a controlling vote for all positions. Queenslander, Glen Shiel, had been the whip in the last parliament. The Queensland organisation, and Joh himself, were still strongly supporting the NT Nationals. By electing Tambling as whip, however, the National Party senators – and especially the four from Queensland – had effectively acknowledged the association of the NT CLP with the federal party. They had given a CLP man a formal job within the federal parliamentary National Party. It would make it all the harder for the NT Nationals to press their claim for affiliation. It would make it even more difficult for the Queensland party, or anyone else, to justify a claim in the federal management committee or federal council that the NT Nationals should be affiliated. It was the best news Sinclair had received in weeks.

19
FLAMES FLARE IN QUEENSLAND

September–October 1987

*If Flo and I went out of politics there would be such a
big black hole and most of you [media] would fall into it as well.
I will go when I want to go.*

Joh Bjelke-Petersen, *The Age*, Melbourne, 1 October 1987

The federal Coalition soon swung back into its normal activities as though it had never been broken. Joint parliamentary committees were formed, planning for future policies resumed, proportional sharing of parliamentary questions and speakers in debates restored, and meetings of the leadership group back on track. Normal contact between the National and Liberal federal secretariats was re-established. The Liberal Party's federal director, Tony Eggleton, convened regular strategy meetings – known as 'prayers' – with his staff. I also attended these, although not after the break in the Coalition. During the election campaign, Eggleton and I co-operated with each other as far as possible. Now we returned to the status quo. The 35th parliament opened on 14 September and was immediately consumed with the election-delayed

1987/88 federal budget, brought down the following day.

On the surface, politics in Canberra settled down; the Joh show was history, water under the bridge. Under the surface, however, the intrigue was raging unabated in the National Party. The only difference from the pre-election period was that now its emphasis was shifting wildly. Sinclair's leadership remained susceptible to potential challenge, with Sparkes increasingly intent on replacing him with Stone. But the Queensland party had another problem, much closer to home – a deepening rift between Sparkes and Bjelke-Petersen and their respective supporters.

The premier was becoming erratic and obstinate. He was seen to be the root cause of a raft of difficulties that beset the state government. He created unnecessary tension by doggedly rejecting recommendations to liberalise Queensland laws in areas such as allowing condom vending machines on university campuses, legalising prostitution and providing AIDS education in schools, squashing in cabinet the recommendations of his Health Minister and heir apparent, Mike Ahern. There was also concern over what was being unearthed by the Fitzgerald inquiry into alleged police corruption in Queensland.

The inquiry was initially established by the deputy premier and Police Minister, Bill Gunn, when he was acting premier, on 18 May 1987, while Joh was out of the state. Gunn and the cabinet, meeting in Roma, were persuaded into a rapid decision after the ABC Television *Four Corners* program, which had been investigating corruption in Queensland for some time, broadcast an explosive episode on 11 May, titled 'The Moonlight State'.[1] Gunn agreed to what was intended to be a highly limited four-week investigation by Tony Fitzgerald QC into allegations of prostitution, illegal betting and police corruption in Brisbane's Fortitude Valley over the past five years. On his return, Joh reluctantly agreed to go along with it.[2] The initial terms of reference were approved by the government on 26 May, but the inquiry's severe limitations made its task almost impossible. Fitzgerald requested and was granted more time to complete his task and allowed to delve into the past for a period of ten years. The terms of reference were accordingly expanded on 24 June, and again on 25 August. By September–October 1987, Fitzgerald was unearthing some very nasty allegations about crime and corruption implicating top-ranking police officers and even some state government ministers. The state's police commissioner, Terry Lewis, was stood down on 21 September.[3]

Against this background and in the wake of the Joh for Canberra disaster, there was a distinct sense of unease in the Queensland National Party. The government's stocks were falling in the opinion polls, as was Joh's personal rating. Every time Joh opened his mouth in public he seemed to upset someone. Far from being infallible, the man who just four months earlier was seriously aiming to be the next prime minister of Australia was struggling to hold his job as Premier of Queensland. His use by date appeared to be nearing after almost 20 years in the job. His most recent questionable comments came when he supported the second military coup by Colonel Rabuka in Fiji at the end of September, adding that he did not care what the Queen, whose British government opposed the coup, thought.[4] Criticism of royalty was virtual treason to many in the Queensland Nationals. It added to the growing view that Joh was losing his political touch. Labor's Foreign Minister, Bill Hayden, said Joh reminded him of a 'worn out brahman bull that's lost its lift power'.[5]

§

Sparkes extensively toured Queensland in September to get firsthand feedback from party branches on the federal election and the general standing of the party. He reportedly picked up 'the strong feeling from all sections that Joh should gracefully retire as Premier within a year'.[6] He also must have picked up serious concerns about the conduct of the Joh campaign, the disappointing election result and the dumping of Collard from the Queensland Senate ticket, all of which prompted him to write a six-page explanatory letter to all party members.

Dated 28 September, it was heavily critical of Sinclair and the New South Wales National Party for not backing the Joh campaign: 'The great stumbling block was the failure of the Federal Parliamentary Leader, Ian Sinclair, and the New South Wales National Party organisation to join this historic move. ... Undoubtedly, the verdict of history will be that the National Party lost its greatest opportunity to become the major conservative Party in this Nation because of the lack of vision of these people and their unwillingness to subordinate their personal ambitions to the good of the Party and the country.' He acknowledged that the 'massive funding' that was essential to the Joh campaign 'was not materialising rapidly enough'. He said the ultimate decision by Ian McLachlan not to join Joh's Nationals and stand for parliament denied the campaign 'a very significant element of support which would have acted as a catalyst to bring other prominent Australians and resources behind us'. His letter was totally supportive of Joh's decision to abandon his quest for a seat in federal parliament:

> Beset with these insurmountable difficulties [lack of funds and prominent candidates], there was no alternative but to abridge the Joh for Canberra campaign. Obviously with this severe abridgement it would have been almost impossible for the campaign to achieve sufficient National Party members in the next Parliament supportive of the Premier to enable him to assume an effective role. Therefore, naturally not

wishing to be relegated to an ineffectual back bench role, the Premier rightly decided, with the full concurrence of the Joh for Canberra Committee, that he would no longer seek a seat in the Federal Parliament.

His defence of the election result in Queensland was centred on the percentage of the primary vote won by the National Party compared to that won by the party in other states, the fact that Hawke and Keating came across 'as more effective leaders', and Howard's stumbling over his tax policy. He reiterated that those seeking to blame the Joh campaign were mainly 'misguided people seeking a scapegoat and refusing to accept the unpalatable realities'.

On Collard, he wanted to refute claims that Collard was dumped by the party hierarchy manipulating 'a massive number of proxies' at the central council selection meeting. There were, said Sparkes, only 13 proxy votes involved, not the 47 or 90 alleged by some. Further, the decision to reject Collard 'was a popular one in the sense that it was overwhelmingly supported by over 200 delegates present'.

On 29 September, the day after Sparkes had written his letter, he dropped the bombshell that he believed Joh, now 76 years old, should retire from the premiership by the middle of 1988 in the interests of the party and to give his successor at least 18 months before the next state election.[7] Joh had previously indicated, vaguely, that he would stay on as premier at least until the end of Expo 88 in October that year, or shortly before the next state poll, due in late 1989. Sparkes' statement, significantly coming just four days before the party's central council was due to meet in Rockhampton, prompted an angry response from the premier, who said Sparkes should concentrate on getting his own house in order – meaning the party organisation – and declaring: 'If Flo and I went out of politics there would be such a big black hole and most of you [media] would fall into it as well. I will go when I want to go.'[8] He questioned Sparkes' consistency, saying the party president was renowned for being 'absolutely ruthless' with any member who criticised the party publicly, which was precisely what he was now doing by calling for the premier's resignation.[9] The relationship between Sparkes and Joh over the years had frequently been difficult; now it was toxic. Sparkes had joined the growing number of senior party members and parliamentarians who believed Joh was now such a liability he had to be replaced. A showdown was looming between the two most powerful men in Queensland politics. But it was not all going Sparkes' way. There was growing speculation that he could face criticism, even censure, at the forthcoming central council for his handling of the Joh campaign and the organisation's direction to its federal parliamentarians to leave the Coalition.[10]

§

The vitriol, all vividly documented in newspaper headlines and radio and television interviews and commentaries, ran thick and fast. Holm backed his president, as did the Local Government and Main Roads Minister, Hinze, who thought the premier should 'at least be allowed to continue [as premier] until the opening, or the start of Expo' – in other words, until April 1988.[11] Joh continued his erratic behaviour to the point where he floated the prospect of setting up his own National Party political liaison office to bypass Sparkes and the state machine.[12]

The state management committee met ahead of the central council on Friday 2 October. Joh was not present and was not due to arrive in Rockhampton until the Saturday evening. Sparkes emerged from the management meeting, if anything, emboldened: 'It is an indisputable fact that he [Joh] should retire sooner than later. I have to act by what I believe is in the best interests of the Government and the Party. I think the view I express is such an indisputable one that the majority of [party] members would concur with it.'[13]

On the Saturday, Sparkes fielded criticism for taking the party into the Joh for PM campaign and other perceived organisational failures.

Joh addressed the council soon after his arrival in Rockhampton on Saturday evening. He concentrated most of his time defending his right to set his own retirement agenda and blaming the state government's recent poor performance in the polls on lack of co-operation by the organisation with the parliamentary wing. By the early hours of Sunday morning, the council had talked itself out, ultimately settling on a resolution that:

> NOTES the very many years of dedicated service of Sir Joh Bjelke-Petersen to the people of Australia and Queensland, culminating in his record-breaking term as Premier during which time he has shown outstanding qualities of leadership, strength, integrity and tenacity.
>
> NOTES Sir Joh Bjelke-Petersen's stated intention to retire prior to the next State general election.
>
> NOTES that the date of his retirement is ultimately a matter for himself and the Parliamentary National Party.
>
> REAFFIRMS the long-standing Party convention that Ministers of the Crown proposing to stand down at or before an ensuing general election should do so appropriately in advance of the anticipated date of the poll, and calls on Sir Joh and the Parliamentary National Party

to time the retirement of Sir Joh and the election of a new leader accordingly.

NOTES suggestions of difficulties having developed in communications between the organisational and Parliamentary wings and calls upon the President and the Premier to implement such steps as may be thought necessary to remedy any such difficulties for the benefit of the Party and the people of Queensland.[14]

Joh told a later news conference that the central council had given him 'unqualified support, completely and utterly, unanimously, no deadline whatsoever was put on when I have to retire. Joh will decide'. He confirmed he would not contest another state election, but then amazed onlookers by speculating that he 'might run in the [next] federal election, because what have Ian Sinclair and John Howard done?'[15]

The premier told the weekly cabinet meeting in Brisbane on 5 October that Sparkes was 'tearing the party apart' and should resign. After the meeting, he accused Sparkes of trying to 'force the Party down the road of condoms, legalised prostitution and sex education for people who are not ready for it'.[16] He was, however, mindful of the possibility, unlikely at this point, but still possible, that the parliamentary party meeting in two days' time, on 7 October, could move a spill motion for the leadership. He decided a truce was needed. He telephoned Sparkes on the morning of 6 October, following which he issued a press release saying the two had sorted out their differences:

There's no problem. Bob and I have had a good talk and we are to work much more closely together. I'm pretty pleased. Sir Robert and I have a good understanding again between us and the roles we are each trying to play for our Party and the

Government. We certainly agreed that we will keep our lines of communication open … and we agree that we don't want to enter into any criticism of each other in the public arena.[17]

This assurance initially seemed to placate a worried government backbench. But it soon backfired when Sparkes, after hearing of the statement that evening, sent an urgent letter to all state National Party MPs flatly denying that any agreements had been reached:

> As you are probably aware, the Premier and I had a telephone conversation today. I am most concerned that the Premier's Department has issued a media release (copy of which is attached) without any consultation with me in regard to that discussion. This release completely misrepresents our conversation.
>
> I believe it is essential that I should acquaint you with the facts. For obvious reasons, I would require that you treat the matter as <u>strictly confidential</u>.
>
> The release suggests quite erroneously that the Premier was able to satisfy me on a number of issues of great concern to the Party and further it alleges that an arrangement had been put in place for regular consultation and communications.
>
> The facts of the matter are simply that in the course of the telephone conversation a number of areas were discussed but neither was there any resolution of our differences nor any consultative mechanism established.
>
> Regretfully I must reiterate that suggestions to the contrary in the release are misleading.

Sparkes had signalled that his relationship with Joh was now finished. His letter seriously embarrassed the premier, effectively calling him a liar, and increased the prospect of a spill against him.

When the party meeting convened at 9am on 7 October, Joh told his MPs that if there was any move against him, he would immediately call an election. The implication was plain for all to see. An election now would see many members lose their jobs. The threat worked, in that there was no motion for a spill. But the fact that Joh was prepared to risk the government and dump his colleagues in his determination to retain power hardened feelings – and numbers – against him.[18] Hinze was the first of several senior MPs to visit Joh on the morning of 8 October. He told the premier bluntly that he faced a 40–8 vote against him in the party room.[19] Joh appeared unconvinced, but privately decided there was only one option left to stave off his immediate demise – announce a firm date for his retirement.

He called a press conference just before six o'clock in the evening of 8 October. As the cameras rolled in the media room of the government's Brisbane Executive Building, he made a brief statement:

> I wish to announce to the people of Queensland that I have decided to retire on 8 August 1988. The date will mark 20 years as Premier. It was always my wish and intention to step down near the end of Expo. I was always against setting a date. However, to end confusion and speculation, I do so now.

Reaction was mixed. The chairman of the Kingaroy Shire Council in Joh's Barambah electorate, Warren Truss, who would go on to become the National Party's federal leader from December 2007 and deputy prime minister from August 2013, said the local community could 'hardly remember having another member and the town [Kingaroy] is saddened'.[20] Many in the party believed Joh had done the right thing and should be allowed to serve his time until August 1988, or 8/8/88 as it was being dubbed. Others feared he had placed himself in a lame duck position for the next ten months, which could further damage the government. And there was still the rift between Joh and Sparkes, which the latter inflamed on 11 October by saying the premier still risked being dumped if he conducted a witch-hunt against any members who had forced him to name his retirement date. Joh hit back: 'There's something wrong with the man. This has been the trouble all along. I've got nothing to say to Sparkes when he says this sort of thing.'[21]

In Canberra, Sinclair watched the unfolding crisis in the Sunshine State with a mixture of satisfaction and despair: satisfaction at seeing Sparkes and Bjelke-Petersen face the sort of pressure to which they had subjected him; despair at the damage that was being done to the party in Queensland and the broader national context.

20
LET'S HAVE A COMMITTEE!

October 1987

The ultimate objective of the review shall be to devise means to enhance and improve the National Party's position in Australian Federal politics.

Opening sentence, terms of reference, Committee of Review into the Future Direction of the National Party of Australia, 17 October 1987

While events moved dramatically in Queensland, the federal party organisation was concentrating on the federal council meeting, scheduled for Canberra between 15 and 18 October. The council normally met once a year at this time. The meeting in March had been the 1986 meeting, which had been deferred because of the state election in Queensland. This second council for 1987 would re-establish the calendar for annual federal council meetings.

A significant challenge for the meeting was to minimise disunity and the potential for further negative publicity. The March federal council had carried the resolution calling on the parliamentary party not to enter into Coalition in Opposition. That had clearly been contravened, even though Sinclair had acted with the agreement of the party room and the acknowledgment of the federal management committee that the parliamentary party was autonomous. Nonetheless, there was a real prospect that an urgency motion could be moved from the floor of the council meeting to censure the parliamentary leader and party – hardly a helpful headline and a scenario that had to be avoided.

Even if there was no such motion, there were seven others on the agenda that could again seriously split the party. Little had changed since March. The motions were:

Review of National Party Federal Constitution (proposed by Queensland)

That in view of the ambiguities and omissions which have been noted in relation to our Federal Constitution, this Council appoints a Committee to review our Constitution with a view to:
    a. defining the power and responsibility of the Council in regard to Federal Policy Formulation;
    b. defining the power and responsibility of the Council in determining whether or not a Coalition shall be withdrawn from or entered into and the associated conditions;
    c. defining the powers and functions of the President and the Management Committee;
    d. generally tidying up the sequence and mode of expression of the various provisions of the Constitution; and,
    e. making any other recommendations for the improvement of the Constitution and enhancement of Party efficiency.

Let's have a committee!

Federal Council (proposed by New South Wales)

That a Committee be formed to review the function and Constitution of the Federal Council for report and recommendation within the Constitutional time frame to allow action to be decided by Council at its next Annual meeting.

Parliamentary Party Autonomy (proposed by the federal management committee)

a. that Federal Management confirms the traditional autonomy of the Federal Parliamentary Party.
b. that should the majority of the Parliamentary Party opt to go back into Coalition with the Liberal Party, so be it.
c. that Federal Management has no reason to believe that State Management of any affiliated branch of the National Party will cause Senators or Members any problems if the Parliamentarians decide to go back into Coalition.
d. that Federal Management recommend to Federal Council that it endorses the above resolutions as the view of the Federal Council.

Federal Constitution (proposed by Western Australia)

That a committee be established to review and report on the changes to the National Party of Australia's Federal Constitution that are necessary to:-
a. empower the Federal Council to give direction to the Federal Parliamentary Party on the entry and

terms and conditions of entry into Coalition both in Government and Opposition;
b. establish a triennial conference of delegates representing the Federal divisions.

Coalition Arrangements (proposed by South Australia)

That the South Australian National Party:-
a. not be bound by any Coalition arrangements that would impede the development and promotion of its own identity, principles and policies at future State and Federal elections;
b. advise Federal Council of our disapproval in principle to Coalition in Opposition.

Policy Formulation (proposed by South Australia)

That this Conference recommends to Federal Council that the Federal National Party embark immediately on new policy formulation so that the National Party can be seen as having its own identity.

Separation of Roles (proposed by Queensland)

That this Council rejects past practice whereby the National Party Federal Parliamentary Leader has frequently intervened in and assumed a large degree of responsibility for the running of the National Party Federal Organisation. Accordingly, this Council, whilst recognising the need for close cooperation and coordination between the Federal Parliamentary Leader and the Federal Organisational Leader, i.e. the Federal President, directs that their roles shall be kept separate for the following reasons:

a. the duties and responsibilities of both positions, but especially that of the Federal Parliamentary Leader, are now so onerous that it is impossible for the Parliamentary Leader to perform both successfully; and,
b. there is no provision in the Party's Federal Constitution which authorises the Parliamentary Leader to intervene in the operation of the National Party Federal Organisation. In fact it would seem to be implied in the Constitution that responsibility for operating the organisation is the sole prerogative of the Federal President and Management Committee acting for Federal Council.

Turning my mind to these motions, a common thread appeared to be a desire, held at least by Queensland, New South Wales and Western Australia, for some kind of review of the party's structures and operation, including the federal constitution. If an all-encompassing review could be devised, one that was established by federal council, these contentious motions could be referred to it and so removed from the federal council agenda without acrimonious debate. Also, the recommendations of a federal parliamentary party review into the federal secretariat, which had been established under the chairmanship of Ralph Hunt on 11 September 1987 and was expected to be finalised within weeks, could similarly be sent to the broader inquiry.[1]

The appeal of this approach was first, that it would avoid the prospect of a further public breach over Coalition. The party, especially with the turmoil in Queensland, was in no position to withstand more internal conflict. Second, the concept of undertaking a comprehensive, nationwide review of party structures, processes and relationships at federal and state levels was a positive initiative. If its terms of reference and membership could be designed to ensure that it was objective and not simply a whitewash, if the committee could complete its task and report within a fairly short time frame, it could provide the basis for a reinvigorated and fresh approach – a rebirth of unity and common objective. The party had never before undertaken such an exercise. The practical logistics might become complicated, but the federal secretariat could provide the necessary research and other support.

Sinclair and Stuart McDonald agreed the strategy was worth pursuing. As we left Sinclair's Parliament House office, McDonald took some delight in saying to me: 'This was your idea. If we get it off the ground, you can be the committee's secretary!' We set about meeting the first challenge – coming up with a committee whose membership would be acceptable to all state parties. If this could not be achieved, the whole plan would be doomed. It also had to be small; we both agreed that large committees were rarely successful. Then there was the need to develop terms of reference that would be supported by the federal management committee, so that they could be proposed to the federal council as a recommendation from management.

The chairman of the committee would have to be someone who was well versed in the workings of the party and federal politics, but preferably who was no longer directly involved. Peter Nixon met such requirements, if he could be persuaded to do the job. This suited McDonald and I personally as we both knew him well. McDonald was a long-standing friend, and I had been Nixon's principal private secretary for more than three years in the Fraser government. More importantly, however, from the point of view of this exercise, he was accepted and respected by the state parties, including Queensland. Further, as a Victorian he could be mindful of that state's interests. Sinclair agreed that Nixon would be a good choice and left McDonald to do the persuading. McDonald discussed the idea of the review with Nixon but did not immediately suggest he should be its chairman. He surmised that if Nixon thought the exercise would be a waste of time, he would have to go back to the drawing board. Nixon, however, thought it was probably a good idea, so McDonald then asked if he would chair the committee. They discussed the concept further – potential committee members and the time frame involved – after which Nixon agreed in principle. However, he would not give a firm 'yes' until he had cleared the proposition with a number of company boards on which he was serving. McDonald gambled that it was possible to proceed further.

There had to be a representative of the federal parliamentary party. Ralph Hunt was the obvious choice. He was well regarded in the party, had been a minister, shadow minister and deputy leader, as well as chairman of the New South Wales party from 1964 to 1969 and federal president from 1968 to 1969. Being from New South Wales, his appointment would also ensure that state's representation on the committee. And he was chairing the parliamentary party's review into the federal secretariat.

The Queensland party clearly had to be represented, otherwise it would almost certainly reject the whole concept. David Russell seemed a good prospect. He was a member of the Queensland party's executive, a close adviser to Sparkes, and, importantly, a Queen's Counsel. His legal expertise would be valuable in any consideration of party constitutional issues.[2]

As a fourth member, McDonald favoured John Paterson, the general president of the Western Australian party. He could represent the interests of the smaller states and had considerable experience within the party organisation, being the second most senior of the federal council vice-presidents.

The committee outline, together with draft terms of reference, was drawn together on the basis of this four-man committee. A 'proposal paper' was prepared for consideration by the federal management committee, which would meet on the morning of 16 October, prior to the opening of federal council. If management agreed, it would go to council as a recommendation from senior representatives of all affiliated states. Such endorsement would make it hard for council to reject.

The management committee agreed, with some minor modifications. Sparkes said he would press to have the senior vice-president, Charles Holm, included on the committee. New South Wales indicated that if Queensland wanted greater representation, then it would too. McDonald's objective all along had been to keep the committee membership small. A compromise was reached to recommend to federal council that Holm and McDonald be appointed as ex-officio members, and the draft terms of reference be amended to enable the committee to co-opt additional people as necessary. The proposal paper, adjusted to take into account these changes, was circulated to members of federal council during the afternoon, with consideration of the matter set for the next morning, giving delegates time to study it closely.

When the council reconvened on the Saturday morning, Sparkes put forward the motion to include Holm and McDonald as ex-officio members. It was lost and he did not pursue the matter. The review proposal, the committee's composition of Nixon, who had confirmed his availability to be chairman, Hunt, Russell and Paterson, and the amended terms of reference were overwhelmingly accepted. The committee would be required to present its final report by 31 March 1988. The report would be circulated to affiliated state parties for their consideration prior to the convening of a special federal council in June 1988, which would make the ultimate decisions on its recommendations. The committee's terms of reference were:

The ultimate objective of the review shall be to devise means

Let's have a committee!

to enhance and improve the National Party's position in Australian Federal politics. The Committee shall therefore examine, report and make observations, recommendations, or present options on:

1. The origins and purpose of the National Party of Australia.

2. The National Party's position in present and future Australian society and politics.

3. A general review of the Federal Constitution of the National Party of Australia.

4. The motions as contained in 1 to 7 inclusive of the October 1987 Federal Council Agenda.

5. The structure, operation and relationship between the Federal and State National Parties of Australia at Parliamentary and Organisational levels.

6. The role and responsibility of the Federal Secretariat of the National Party of Australia, taking into account the report of the Parliamentary Party's Secretariat Review Committee (The Hunt Committee).

7. The Liaison and division of responsibilities between the Federal and State Parties in all matters relating to Federal Elections.

8. The role of the Women's Federal Council and Young National Party of Australia.

9. The financial relationship between the Federal and State Parties.

10. Any other matters that the Committee considers relevant.

The Committee shall complete its written final report no later than March 31 1988. In the course of its work, the Committee may co-opt additional members as deemed necessary. It shall also have at its disposal the resources of the Federal Secretariat.[3]

Nixon's agreement to chair the committee had been based on a fundamental proviso: it would not paper over any nasty home truths. If he was to put his name to the report, it would be comprehensive, objective, possibly embarrassing at times, and be made public. The last term of reference gave him the sweeping power he needed to look into anything he wanted. It would be an interesting exercise: Nixon and Hunt were coalitionists; Russell and Paterson were opposed to Coalition in Opposition.

§

The Northern Territory continued to be a problem for the federal management committee. While the NT Nationals had not resubmitted an application for affiliation, the Country Liberal Party had put forward a request that negotiations be entered into for it to affiliate with the federal party. Its request was considered by the management committee on 16 October. It was not an application for affiliation, so management received the correspondence and agreed that the CLP president, Grant Heaslip, be advised that his party was entitled to apply for affiliation and such application would be 'treated in the normal way'. The meeting further authorised McDonald 'to discuss reconciliation with CLP and NT Nationals' leadership and the general question of afffiliation'.[4] Basically, federal management was hoping the two parties would resolve their differences and reunite.

However, an indicator that this was not, at least in the near future, in prospect was the fact that the NT Nationals had lodged an application with the Australian Electoral Commission for registration as a political party. This was necessary under the *Commonwealth Electoral Act* for political parties to receive financial reimbursements from the Commonwealth for federal elections under public funding provisions. The act required the electoral commission to advertise that it had received an application for registration and notify that objections to the application could be lodged within a period of one month.

The NT Nationals' application was lodged with the commission on 26 May 1987. Because of the July federal election, the commission was not able by law to process it until after the return of the writs on 3 September. It advertised its receipt of the application on 14 October, meaning any objections had to be submitted by 14 November.

The advertisement notified that the Territory party was seeking registration in the name of Northern Territory Nationals, with an abbreviated name of Territory Nationals. Neither of these were the names the party had used in its application for affiliation with the National Party of Australia. It had sought affiliation as the National Party of Australia – Northern Territory.

The federal management committee on 16 October discussed the implications of the application for registration, ultimately agreeing that an objection should be lodged because the name and abbreviation were too similar to those of the National Party and could cause confusion to voters. The letter of objection was delivered to the electoral commissioner, Colin Hughes, on 13 November.

Stuart McDonald and I were required to appear before a public hearing of the commission into the NT Nationals' application in Darwin on 21 April 1988. We were both well across our 'brief of evidence', having discussed the matter extensively in the lead-up weeks. So the flight to Darwin offered me a few hours when I could read over the final proofs of the Nixon committee's report. (As will be seen, the committee had been granted a short extension of time.) Sitting beside me on the plane, McDonald was trying, and totally failing, to get interested in a Wilbur Smith novel. He was itching to know what was in the papers I was going through. He also knew I would not let him see them: this was a document that was still confidential to the committee and, as its secretary, I could not divulge any of its contents, even to my president. Remembering that he had unilaterally appointed me secretary to the committee, I enjoyed making this point to him, to which he laughed, replied 'You bastard!' and ordered a scotch for himself and a beer for me. It was a pleasant flight.

On 8 July 1988, the electoral commission ruled in favour of the National Party's objection, which had been strongly supported by the Northern Territory Country Liberal Party. The NT Nationals began fading from the political scene.

21
THE EYE OF
THE STORM

November 1987

The Labor Party has for years denigrated Sinclair and has for years failed to get his head. You are on the verge of giving it to them on a plate.

Stuart McDonald, letter to Robert Sparkes, 27 November 1987

With the quiet passing of federal council, attention again turned north – to Townsville, where the Queensland National Party was holding its 1987 state conference, attended by more than 650 delegates. It had been postponed from July because of the federal election.

In the lead-up to the conference – at Townsville's Sheraton Breakwater convention centre between 5 and 8 November – there was considerable speculation about the future of both Joh and Sparkes. There were growing views within the party membership that Joh had to go and that Sparkes deserved to be rolled for his part in the Joh for Canberra debacle.

The relationship between the two men was now non-existent. Joh encouraged Hiram Caton, a professor of politics and history at Griffith University in Brisbane, to stand for the presidency. The anti-Sparkes campaign reached a particularly nasty stage when, in the days immediately preceding the conference, a photograph allegedly showing Sparkes, Holm and Vincenzo Bellino was published in the media. Joh may have had nothing to do with this.

Bellino had been named in the Fitzgerald inquiry's extended terms of reference, which asked if he or four other men 'either directly or indirectly, made a payment of $50 000 to any political party'. The Queensland National Party denied having received any money, but the hint of a connection with anything adverse to do with the Fitzgerald inquiry was potentially explosive to the re-election of both Sparkes and Holm. Sparkes was angered and dismayed at the attempt to denigrate him, describing it as 'gutter' tactics: 'I've been in politics 40 years and this would be the dirtiest piece of work I've ever encountered.' Sparkes and Bellino both had vague recollections of meeting at Bellino's House On The Hill nightclub in Cairns, where the photograph was purportedly taken, in late 1981 or early 1982. Sparkes said an application Bellino had lodged with the state government for a casino licence may have been discussed. In any event, the licence was granted to Townsville.[1] Far from undermining Sparkes' standing in the party, the incident worked in his favour. Most people saw it for what it was – a dirty trick.

In short, the conference ended well for Sparkes, but not for Joh. The premier's personal opposition to condom vending machines, AIDS education, legalised prostitution and abortion was swept aside by conference decisions supporting them in the opening session on 5 November. When Joh arrived after this session, he had a swipe at the fact that people had paid a thousand dollars or more each to attend a conference that only concerned itself with such matters. Then he stayed very much to himself. The following day, before he was due to address the conference, he left, suffering a bout of laryngitis. Despite his voice troubles, he gave an interview to ABC Radio on Friday morning, 6 November, in which he reiterated his belief that the conference was 'talking about nothing really. ... The first item on the agenda is about condoms and legalised prostitution; nothing about the problems confronting business people, small people, unemployment, high interest rates'. Asked for his reaction to Sparkes' assessment that the party's stocks were low because the state government was out of touch, Joh replied that it was 'sheer stupidity to say that'.[2]

The conference was due to go into a closed session on the Friday afternoon to discuss the Joh campaign and the alleged dictatorial stance of Sparkes and the party hierarchy in directing the state's federal MPs to quit the Coalition in Canberra. In view of his absence, Joh arranged for a lengthy type-written explanation of his Canberra push to be made available. Copies were left on tables around the conference foyer. Few people picked them up, although the paper gave an interesting insight into how Joh perceived the campaign.

He said in the early months of the year 'more and more eminent people were urging, in even stronger terms, that I should marshal a drive that would defeat Hawke'. It would include the multitude of people who wanted to be part of an anti-Hawke crusade, but who did not want to be tied to political machines they no longer respected. Part of the reason for the campaign's failure, he asserted, was that necessary work to establish organisational structures was not done: '... this proved eventually to be the beginning of our failure.' Ultimately, there was 'no sensible option but to abandon the endeavour. And so began one of the worse [sic] periods of my life'. The premier concluded by reflecting on current Queensland politics and the relationship between the parliamentary and organisational wings of the party. Ironically, given the attempts by Queensland at the federal council in March to make council decisions binding on the federal parliamentary party, he attacked his own organisation for doing the same in Queensland:

> Over the years, our Organisational wing has developed a disturbing tendency to tell our Parliamentary wing what it should do on particular issues that develop from time to time. Advice is one thing, but if framed in forms that can be constructed as instruction, then that is another. ... Unlike the Labor Party, we do not direct our Parliamentary Members. They are properly expected to act within the Platform, but they mustn't be made to publicly appear as puppets whose strings are pulled by Party room masters. The Party is in peril if it appears to the electorate as modelling itself on an authoritarian Socialist party.[3]

Sparkes was able to defend his position more effectively than Joh. For a start, he was present, while the premier was absent. Second, he was running the conference and had total control. Just before the conference went into its closed session, he gave his presidential report, which he skillfully used to lobby for his re-election as state president. He said the federal election result in Queensland had been 'a minor reversal of the sort every political party must be prepared to weather from time to time', and called for an end to 'destructive self-criticism, needless knocking and senseless scapegoat hunting' within party ranks. He attacked the 'gutter politics' of the 'infamous House on the Hill photograph', the 'deplorable tactic' of phone calls by an anonymous caller to branch officials urging them to vote against him 'because he condones and encourages homosexuality', and an allegation 'that I am an immoral person who is preoccupied with ushering in an era of condoms, prostitution and abortion – a person who is leading the Party away from traditional values and principles'. This was 'utter malicious garbage'.

He called for 'an immediate end to all feuds and factionalism' and a rekindling of 'the traditional National Party spirit of loyalty and unity'.[4] While this was aimed at the Queensland party and state politics, it could equally have been applied federally. Many hoped it was – that the party overall was on its way back to a cohesive effort and sense of purpose. Such hopes were short-lived as the conference then moved into its closed session. There were five motions for consideration, none of which were ultimately voted on. But they reflected the depth of concern among the broad party membership at the party's position in both state and federal politics. The motions were:

- That this Conference recognise the deep concern of all National Party members in Queensland and Australia with respect to the Parliamentary and Party Leadership of the State and Federal National Party.
- That this Conference require a full analytical debate on the 'Joh for Canberra' campaign and further require State Management Committee through the State President, to make a clear report available to all Branch Secretaries on all the advice given to Sir Joh Bjelke-Petersen pertaining to that campaign, including the content and sources of that advice and on the tactics that resulted from that advice.
- That the National Party of Australia – Queensland recognise its structural shortcomings as a major contributing factor to the poor result achieved at the July 11th Federal election and adopts the following programme as the minimum necessary to restore the Party's credibility. The appointment of:
  (a) a full time State Director with responsibility for Media Liaison and Party structure within the Greater Brisbane area,
  (b) a full time assistant to the State Director with

> responsibility for all Party structure outside the Greater Brisbane area,
>
> such appointments to be subject to the approval of two-thirds of Central Council.

- That this Conference express its concern at State Cabinet decisions which demonstrate a lack of research into their effects and consultation with those people most likely to be disadvantaged by such decisions.
- That if the Premier intends to retire he be requested to consider doing so at least 12 months before the next State election, in the interests of the Party.[5]

Sparkes laid the motions on the table and allowed a general debate to run for about two and a half hours. Delegates aired their grievances one by one. By and large, they were quite tame and criticism kept to a minimum. Only one Queensland federal MP, Ray Braithwaite, contributed to the discussion. Delegates were generally prepared to accept Joh's stated intention to stand down on 8/8/88, allowing him to retire with dignity and at the time of his choosing. Once the floor had talked itself out, Sparkes replied. He cast some doubt as to whether Joh would remain premier until August 1988 when he conceded that it saddened him to have to say that his relationship with the premier was now 'terminated'. He was effectively saying Joh was finished, irrespective of any timetables. He said he had agonised long and hard at the start of the year about the Joh for Canberra campaign, concluding that if the Queensland organisation had not taken control of it through the Hervey Bay resolutions, it would have split the party in the state. He reiterated his reservations about the federal Coalition's leadership, and especially that of Sinclair, saying: 'We will have difficulty achieving success in the future while we have the leadership we have. However, I have great hopes for John Stone.'[6]

It was a popular concept among delegates. Stone had become the flavour of the month after he, with the aid of a retired public servant, Ewart Smith, on 19 September had uncovered a fatal flaw in Labor's proposed Australia Card identity system. As a result, the Hawke government was embarrassingly forced to announce ten days later that the legislation would be abandoned. The core justification for Hawke calling the early double dissolution election had collapsed around him. Stone was a hero in Queensland. But it was an amazing contradiction for Sparkes, who barely three hours earlier had been imploring the party to rekindle its traditional spirit of 'loyalty and unity', to again be undermining Sinclair.

The federal president, McDonald, had been at the conference for the past two days, but had left to catch an afternoon flight back to Melbourne about an hour before Sparkes made his comments. Had he still been there, he would no doubt have had something to say. Of the Queensland federal members and senators present, not one rose in defence of the federal leader – a leader who had been re-elected by the party room only 15 weeks earlier, on 23 July.

Sparkes invited Stone, who was sitting with him on the top table, to respond. Stone was diplomatic, saying he would allow the nice things said about him to 'go through to the keeper'. While he made no effort to support Sinclair, he did give a resounding endorsement of Sparkes as state president – significant, given the organisational elections would be held the next day.

§

Sinclair did not arrive at the conference until Saturday, 7 November. He was invited to give a short address and was politely received. Then came the office bearer elections. Sparkes was opposed by Hiram Caton, and an insurance broker from Toowoomba, Les Whykes. It was a no contest. Sparkes won 528 votes, Caton 89 and Whykes 47. It was only the second time Sparkes had been contested for the presidency since he was first elected in 1970 – the previous challenge being at the 1986 conference. The anticipated challenge to Holm as senior vice-president failed to emerge; he was re-elected unopposed. The hierarchy of the Queensland party remained firmly intact. Sparkes' power base had been comprehensively reaffirmed, which was bad news for Joh and little better for Sinclair.

The worst setback Sparkes suffered – although it was only a minor one – was over the Northern Territory Nationals. The conference had been expected to carry a motion congratulating the party on its achievements of the past ten months. However, a persuasive delegation from the CLP, which attended as observers, was successful in its lobbying. The conference carried a motion that recognised that the interests of the Northern Territory and the federal National Party would be best served by 'a single united conservative party as a constituent unit of the National Party of Australia'. It further stated that if such unity was not achieved, 'this Conference support Federal affiliation status being granted to the Northern Territory conservative party most genuinely committed to the Federal Platform of the National Party of Australia'. That could, of course, have insinuated the NT Nationals. But the broader resolution brought the Queensland party virtually into line with the position of the federal management committee, urging a reunification of the non-Labor forces in the Territory, and was a long way from the previous hard line view of Sparkes that the NT Nationals should be fully supported.

After his re-election, Sparkes spoke to journalists. He was asked whether he believed he now had greater power to force the decisions of conference, notably on condom vending machines and legalised prostitution, on the state government. He said he would expect the government to adopt the policies of conference, but then added: 'I don't want to create the impression that the Government is some sort of a puppet on a string to the National Party organisation. We've never operated that way.'[7] He was acknowledging the autonomy of the state parliamentary party – something he refused to do for the federal parliamentary party with regard to the resolutions of the March federal council, particularly that on the single rate tax policy.

Sinclair did not tackle Sparkes on the matter, or on his endorsement of Stone for the leadership. McDonald, however, was furious when he learned what had happened while he was in flight to Melbourne. He gave the matter careful consideration, before some days later sending Sparkes a letter saying he was 'appalled' to learn of his comments: 'The point is not the personalities involved, but the principle. This Party has always accepted that the Federal Parliamentary Party has the sole right to elect its Leaders and that, having done so, those Leaders are entitled to the support of the Party throughout Australia – and in particular, the support of senior Party officials.' McDonald said Sparkes had fallen 'hook, line and sinker' for the bait set by the ALP: 'The Labor Party has for years denigrated Sinclair and has for years failed to get his head. You are on the verge of giving it to them on a plate.' Noting that over the years, Sparkes had been rightly critical of anyone in the party who made statements that could be regarded as disloyal, McDonald advised Sparkes to 'take a cold, hard look at some of the public comments you have made about Ian Sinclair during the course of 1987 and apply your own standards to them'.[8] McDonald received no reply.

§

In the meantime, Stone fell foul of Joh. There was much falling out within the senior ranks of the Queensland party during these critical times. Stone's 'crime' was that he told the Townsville conference, in a wrap-up address on Sunday 8 November, that no-one was more important than the Party:

> Above all, Conference has done what it is the duty and responsibility of Conference to do – to give to our Parliamentary team, particularly in the Legislative Assembly of Queensland, the clear guidance from the Party as to where it wishes to see the Government of this State go, and the manner in which it should go about that task.
>
> In so doing, Conference has also expressed its considered view – which is in the end the only view possible in a democratically structured Party such as ours – that no single man is more important than the Party, and that however deeply the Party may feel indebted to individuals, the personal passions even of those individuals cannot be allowed to prevail where the future good of the Party is at stake.

Joh took exception to this. He believed that had it not been for his Canberra campaign, Stone would never have won election to the Senate, let alone appointment to the party's Senate leadership: 'A man that I helped and got into power – and he got in, hanging on to Florence's dress. He hung on there that tightly you couldn't prise him off. And he got there. He's not even worth commenting on.'[9] Stone again decided the best way to handle such remarks was to let them 'go through to the keeper'.

Another who had not endeared himself to the premier was Joh's deputy, Bill Gunn. Relations had been strained between the two anyway – mainly, in recent times, because of the Fitzgerald inquiry. Gunn knocked the stuffing out of Joh's campaign to have Sparkes ousted as party president by nominating Sparkes for re-election. After successfully making the nomination, Gunn suggested that Joh should take a holiday and go fishing, telling newsmen: 'I don't know where he likes fishing – Fraser Island's a wonderful place. We'll look after things, we've done it before.' On ABC Radio *AM* on 9 November, he went further, saying Joh was 'out of tune at the present time and doesn't realise what's happened here [the Townsville conference]'.

Tensions were mounting rapidly. Sparkes, at the close of the conference, was not even trying to hide the communications impasse between himself and Joh. He told reporters at a press briefing:

> If the premier is not willing to engage in that necessary communication [with the party organisation] then I suppose an alternative mechanism for liaison between the two wings of the party will have to be put into operation. I have quite a good rapport with the deputy premier and other ministers and will use that means to convey the thinking of the party on issues to them.
>
> Q: So what are you saying there – bypass the premier?
>
> A: I'm not desirous of bypassing him, but it would appear that adequate communication with the premier is not possible at this point in time and one has to live in accordance with reality and the only alternative is for me to communicate through the deputy premier and the ministers.[10]

§

Despite Sparkes' 'terminated' relationship with the premier, a feeling of affection for Joh was evident at the conference. It basically said to him 'Joh, you can go in your own time, at your own date of 8/8/88. We deeply appreciate what you've done for Queensland, the National Party and Australia, and we want you to be able to retire with the dignity and praise you deserve – providing you don't rock the boat in the meantime'.

For a few days – just a few – it began to look as though this would happen. Joh was conciliatory to both his cabinet and parliamentary party. If this attitude lasted then so would he for the months until August 1988. Certainly, there were those who were sceptical of the proposed retirement, believing it was all a bluff. Even so, the party generally was prepared to forgive to a certain extent, and let him have his way.

Joh was even able to win an important political victory in the state parliament in the week immediately following the Townsville conference. The Labor Opposition tried to capitalise on the chaos within the government on 10 November, with the Opposition leader, Neville Warburton, moving a motion of no confidence in the premier and the government and challenging disgruntled National MPs to vote with Labor.

The vote was taken in the small hours of 11 November. No National members crossed the floor. The parliamentary Liberal Party, under the leadership of William Knox, abstained from voting. Knox said his party would support neither the government nor a motion that was merely a political stunt. The motion was lost along ALP/National Party lines – 28 to 48 votes.[11] Joh had received 100 per cent support from his parliamentary party – significant under the circumstances.

The spell of comparative calm lasted only two weeks. On 24 November, Joh detonated a new bomb when – out of the blue – he tried to sack five ministers, including his deputy, Gunn, and his greatest perceived threat, Mike Ahern. He precipitated a new crisis within the government. It was a staggering gamble on his behalf – staggering in that it would drastically aggravate feelings against him within the parliamentary party; staggering also in that it was literally Joh against the rest. The action had nothing to do with Sparkes, the party machine, or even Sinclair. It was entirely Joh's own doing, and he would sink or swim as a result.

22

JOH'S LAST CAMPAIGN

November to December 1987

The National Party of today is not the party that I took to the election last year. The policies of the National Party are no longer those of which I went to the people. Therefore I do not wish to lead this Government any longer.

Joh Bjelke-Petersen, press conference, Brisbane, 1 December 1987

On the evening of Monday 23 November, Joh's private office contacted Bill Gunn, Mike Ahern, Mines Minister, Brian Austin, Tourism Minister, Geoff Muntz, and Industry Minister, Peter McKechnie. Each was requested to be at the premier's office the following morning.

When they duly arrived, at 15-minute intervals, each was asked to sign a pre-prepared letter of resignation. Each refused. Ahern called a news conference and said he was challenging for the leadership forthwith. Brisbane became the focus of Australian politics. Joh had begun his last campaign.

He went to see the state governor, Walter Campbell, and asked him to withdraw the commissions of the five ministers. Campbell counselled caution, saying he could not do so unless the premier could demonstrate he had the backing of his cabinet. Joh returned to his office, apologised to Gunn and Muntz, saying there had been a mistake and invited them back into cabinet. He then called a cabinet meeting for 5pm. There he again asked for the resignations of Ahern, Austin and McKechnie. They refused. By 6pm, the meeting ended in confusion. Joh went back to the governor, who this time agreed to sack the three ministers. Then Gunn and Russ Hinze joined Ahern in announcing they would contest the leadership.

Anxious National Party MPs were returning to Brisbane in anticipation of a regular parliamentary party meeting on Wednesday morning. But Joh was refusing demands to confirm the meeting, so Sparkes was hurriedly arranging an urgent state management committee meeting so that, under clause 93 of the party constitution, it could force an extraordinary meeting of the parliamentary party. The virtually sweep-all clause gave the committee power to 'exercise full control over all members and units of the Party …'.

It had been a day of turmoil and intrigue – reminiscent of the 11 November 1975 sacking of the Whitlam government; there was the whiff of constitutional crisis in the Queensland air.

Nobody seemed to know why Joh had wanted the heads of the five ministers, although it was apparently because of their alleged disloyalty to him. In Gunn's case, it was put down to his nomination of Sparkes for re-election as state party president. *The Courier-Mail* quoted Joh explaining the sackings in the following terms:

> All I have done as a responsible minister, Premier, which is my right to replace men, I have changed three of our Ministers. Now that is my right. I cannot continue in good Government with the leaks, with the disloyalty that I have had to experience for so long. It is impossible and imperative

and that is my right and my responsibility and exactly why I have done just that. We have done it before. It is nothing new, nothing sensational.[1]

At the news conference announcing his challenge for the leadership, Ahern hinted at more sinister reasons behind the sackings – the prospect that the premier was trying to close down the Fitzgerald inquiry prematurely: 'I am concerned at the action that has been taken this morning and the machinations in respect of the eventual outcome of the Fitzgerald inquiry in Queensland. ... I am fearful in the current climate that it will not have the outcome that the people of Queensland are looking for if this situation is to proceed unchallenged.'[2] Terry Lewis had been stood down as the state's police commissioner on 21 September, and there were now rumours that the inquiry was on the verge of revealing new information, or a new witness, that would be highly embarrassing for the government. This added weight to Ahern's indirect suggestion that Joh was trying to truncate it. To be able to do so, the premier had to have cabinet approval – and all five of the men he had moved against were in favour of letting the inquiry run its full course.

The drama continued on 25 November. It began with a 9am cabinet meeting, called by Joh to discuss the proposed ministry changes. The meeting ended in disarray, with ministers rejecting the proposals and Joh walking out.

Next, the premier prepared for the swearing in at Government House of new ministers to replace Ahern, Austin and McKechnie. This was arranged for 10.30am but was postponed for a number of reasons until shortly before 3pm. The new ministers were the speaker, Kevin Lingard, who had to resign the speakership before being able to accept a ministerial commission, and the Member for Cooroora, Gordon Simpson. Joh had been unable to find anyone to take on the third vacancy.

In the meantime, the state management committee met at party headquarters in Spring Hill – Bjelke-Petersen House. Joh refused to attend because he did not recognise its validity or relevance. He insisted everything was under control – his control – and it was business as usual. The committee decided by 29 votes to one that a meeting of the parliamentary party had to be held as a matter of urgency. It was set down for 10am the following morning, 26 November. The single dissenter was Gordon Simpson, an accredited parliamentary delegate to the management committee. As soon as he had voted, he left for Government House to be sworn in as a minister.

At a press conference to announce the management committee's decision, Sparkes tried not to pre-empt what the parliamentary party might decide: 'It is for the parliamentary wing to determine the question of leadership.' In answer to a further question, he said: 'I have always hoped Sir Joh would make his political exit with dignity and honour.' That still did not satisfy journalists. They wanted to know if Sparkes believed Joh would still be premier the following afternoon. Finally he capitulated: 'You people are certainly persistent, and I guess I have to reward persistence and say, "no".' He was also asked his views on the new ministerial appointments, to which he replied: 'At present they are ministers. They may of course displace Senator Sheil in the *Guinness Book of Records*.' This was a reference to the fact that Sheil had been appointed Minister for Veterans' Affairs after the Fraser government's re-election in 1977 and been dismissed two days later for making comments that were sympathetic to the white minority regimes of South Africa and Rhodesia (Zimbabwe) and against the imposition of sporting and economic sanctions on them.

Just as he had refused to recognise the management committee meeting, so Joh refused to acknowledge the legitimacy of the party meeting it had called. He said the parliamentary party had given him the right to convene party meetings and he was not going to convene one. He didn't believe the organisation had any right to convene a meeting, so he would not attend. A solid majority of the parliamentarians believed the management committee did have the right and were determined to bring the farce to a head as quickly as possible. They would do this in Joh's absence, if necessary.

§

Thursday 26 November began in a messy way, with Joh and Sparkes criticising each other in separate interviews on ABC Radio *AM*:

Q: Sir Joh, what happens if the meeting of your parliamentary colleagues this morning votes Mr Ahern into the premiership?

A: Well, that's not anything for me to decide what they're going to do there at the meeting. That's a meeting that has been called out of context of the usual procedure which is one where, down the years and traditionally, I've always called all these meetings together at the appropriate time. And, indeed, at our last meeting before the House adjourned, they moved that I, the premier, should be the one who determined the time and date of the next meeting. This is a meeting, of course, that has been stirred up by the people on the hill [meaning Spring Hill party headquarters]. Anyway, be that as it may, that's just a sideline and we've got good government. We haven't got a crisis. We've got people sworn in by His Excellency yesterday, fine men. I'm sure there'll be no leaks.

> Q: But Sir Robert Sparkes says the meeting is legal. Are you … do you not accept that?
>
> A: Oh, I'm not arguing with him. He's outside parliament. He's trying to interfere in this, obviously, by what he's saying and doing. And it's quite wrong, completely wrong. And if he's not careful he'll undo all the good work that I've done down the years and destroy this party the way things are going, tearing it apart. I'm trying to keep it together, and I'll keep on trying to keep it together today, don't you make any mistake about that.

The interview with Sparkes followed:

> The problem that we've got today of course is that the premier refuses to accept the rules of democracy, namely that the majority should prevail. He refuses to call a meeting of the parliamentary wing so that the whole question of leadership can be tested. Anyone really believing in democracy would be prepared to call such a meeting, would want to call such a meeting, to determine the level of parliamentary support, and if it wasn't majority support, then they should stand down and make way for the person that does obtain majority support. It's as simple as that, nothing sinister, nothing untoward at all.
>
> Q: Sir Robert, the man who's now accusing you of having political blood on your hands was the man who only five months ago you were touting as the potential prime minister for Australia. What's gone wrong?
>
> A: Well, you know, it's very difficult to specify the details of the problem in a short period of time but there have

been a number of events that have intervened since the time that you refer to, events which I think unfortunately indicate that the leadership of the government in the state has gone off the rails, has been out of touch with the thinking of the vast majority of the people in the community and out of touch with the vast majority of party members. And in that situation of course, the party dramatically loses support and that's precisely what's been happening. The public have been drifting away from the party because of these government decisions, state government decisions, and unless there's a change of leadership, a change of direction, I don't mean an abandonment of our fundamental philosophy or policies or our standards at all, but a change of style and direction, unless we have that change of style and direction then of course the party, I believe, is heading for disaster.

At 9.30am – half an hour before the party meeting – Joh called a cabinet meeting. He tried to persuade his ministers to either not attend the party meeting, or vote against any motion on leadership. The ministers refused. The party meeting then got underway – minus the premier. Ahern moved that the leadership be declared vacant. The motion was carried by 39 votes in favour, eight against and one abstention. Ahern, Gunn and Hinze then nominated for the leadership. Ahern won on the first ballot with 30 votes – Gunn received 16 and Hinze two. Gunn was then re-elected deputy leader unopposed.

Ahern rang the governor to advise him of the result. He made an appointment to visit Government House with Gunn at 12.30pm and deliver a letter signed by 47 of the 49-member parliamentary National Party supporting his leadership and requesting the governor to withdraw Joh's commission. The two missing signatures were those of the premier, who did not attend the party meeting, and Ahern. Ahern and Gunn expected to be sworn in as premier and deputy premier, but the governor advised that the matter should be resolved either by Joh resigning or by a vote of parliament.³ Ahern then called a press conference and promised an Ahern-led government would be open, accountable and innovative: 'The wheels are back on the green and gold bus,' he declared, in reference to the green and gold colours of the National Party.

Joh refused to accept the party room decision, saying the meeting had not been called by him and was therefore not proper. He said the appropriate place to test whether his government and leadership had confidence was on the floor of the parliament, adding that he would recall parliament the following Thursday, 3 December.

Queensland drifted into a state of virtual non-government. Joh was the premier in name, with virtually no support from his own party or cabinet. Ahern was the elected parliamentary leader of the government party, but not the premier. Indeed, he was a mere backbencher, having been sacked from the ministry two days previously. The following morning's *The Courier-Mail* editorialised: 'Yesterday Sir Joh Bjelke-Petersen made Queensland a laughing stock. In any conventional political system, Mr. Ahern would today be Premier and Sir Joh in retirement. Instead, Sir Joh is pushing his party to the brink.'⁴

Despite Joh's refusal to resign, negotiations were underway to persuade him to do so, in his own interests as well as those of the state and the party. Retirement packages were mentioned. Joh was still not convinced that he had lost, although during Friday 27 November he began packing his personal effects from his Executive Building office and the penthouse suite at the Parliament House annex. He flew back to Kingaroy in the afternoon in the government aircraft for the weekend – to canvass possibilities and options and discuss the situation with his family.

On Sunday 29 November, the Bjelke-Petersens went to their local Lutheran church, as was their normal practice. Television crews went as well and the evening news bulletins carried footage of the premier and his wife in the congregation. Leaving the church, Joh gave little away: 'I'm completely happy and relaxed because I know I'm going the right way.' Asked if he had made up his mind, he replied: 'Yes, I made up my mind long ago.'[5]

Also on the Sunday, Sinclair, who had remained silent on the Queensland crisis, decided it was time to make a statement. It was aimed at strengthening Ahern's position, should the affair proceed to a vote in state parliament. Sinclair said that following the election of Ahern as party leader, it was appropriate that Joh should resign:

> While I respect the contribution Sir Joh has made to Queensland he has ceased to have the confidence of the Party and he must go before he does any more harm. …
> I have great regard for Mike Ahern and believe that he can heal the wounds in Queensland. He needs the total support of the Parliamentary Party and the organisational wing.
> If there are people in those organisations who cannot give 100% support and loyalty to Mike Ahern, they too should resign.[6]

§

Joh's promise to have parliament recalled had not been put into action. No notices had been sent out to members. The reason was because when parliament had adjourned for the summer recess, it had agreed that it would reconvene on a date to be fixed by the speaker in consultation with the government. With the former speaker, Lingard, now in Joh's ministry, there was no speaker.

Cabinet met at its usual time of 10am on Monday 30 November. Joh was present but did not chair the meeting, which agreed parliament should be recalled on Wednesday 2 December, not the day after as Joh had wanted.[7] If the premier needed any further proof that he no longer had the control or support of his cabinet, that decision was it. It was a far cry from the situation 180 days earlier, when Joh said on 3 June that one of the reasons he would not seek a seat in federal parliament was because of the hundreds of requests he had received, including from 'my entire Cabinet', to stay in Queensland to 'Keep Queensland strong'.[8] Now he had no support in cabinet. But he had worked this out anyway. He had already made an appointment to see the governor at 4pm on Tuesday afternoon, 1 December. There seemed no other reason for such an appointment unless it was to resign.

In the meantime, plans and counter plans were being devised for the parliamentary recall, which had been approved by the governor. Various possibilities arose. There was speculation that Labor and Liberal MPs might support Joh in an attempt to ensure he stayed as premier. If Joh could find just four Nationals to also stay with him, the tactic would work, almost certainly forcing an election. Conversely, if Joh could not find sufficient support, he faced enormous humiliation on the floor of parliament.

By Tuesday 1 December, it was clearly all over. Joh had no support in the parliamentary National Party. If he went into parliament the following day, he would be politically mutilated. He visited the governor at the appointed time of 4pm. The meeting took three minutes. He then called a news conference for 5pm Queensland time, when the major television news bulletins would be going to air in the southern states – 6pm daylight saving time.

The end might have finally come for Joh, but he was not going quietly or meekly. In a statement, which he read with considerable emotion, he said he did not want to remain leader of a party whose policies were no longer those under which the last state election had been won:

> I have an announcement for the people of Queensland. The National Party of today is not the Party that I took to the election last year. The policies of the National Party are no longer those of which I went to the people. Therefore I do not wish to lead this Government any longer. It was my intention to take this matter to the floor of State Parliament. However, I now have no interest in leading the National Party any further. I have decided to resign as Premier and retire from Parliament, effective immediately. As this is the last time I will address you as Premier, I wish to say that in the last 40 years I have had but one objective – to make Queensland a better place in which to live and work. I have always given of my best. Thank you for your support down the years. I do appreciate your prayers and your messages of love to me and to Flo. I wish you well. Thank you all. Goodbye and God bless.

As he rose to leave the room, questions were thundered at him. Most of them were indecipherable, except one that asked 'Who's got your blood on their hands, Sir Joh?'

He turned to face the cameras: 'I want to say to you all, thank you for your attendance this afternoon. I wish you well. Happy Christmas.' As a further barrage of questions was thrown at him, he continued: 'Mr Speaker … ah, [smiling] ladies and gentlemen, I'm a free man.' He spread his arms wide, clutching the notes of his statement in his right hand and standing in front of the Queensland state flag: 'I'm free. I'm going to celebrate tonight up at the Sheraton with my family; tremendous! All the best.' With that, he walked out of the room looking relieved.

If he was relieved so, too, were many others. Ahern and Gunn immediately formed a two-man executive government to administer the state until they were able to form a full ministry.[9] Sparkes said that for the sake of good government the party welcomed the resolution of the difficulties associated with the leadership. John Howard said he felt not the slightest sorrow. Ahern said he was sad at the criticism contained in Joh's parting statement, but added: 'It was a statement made by a retiring man for whom I have the greatest respect. He is full of emotion and disappointment tonight.' Sinclair expressed little regret: 'I think without any doubt there are those who worry about the judgement shown in the Queensland National Party federal campaign which no doubt led to the re-election of the Hawke Government.' He sent a congratulatory message to Ahern, and told *The Sydney Morning Herald*: 'The premiership baton has been well and truly passed to Mike Ahern. I regret the former Premier did not have the grace to pass on the baton with the dignity his long record of achievement might have expected.'[10]

§

Before he went to see the governor on 1 December, Joh gave an exclusive interview to John Moses, a Canberra-based freelance journalist. It was for *The Australian* newspaper and was published the following day. In it Joh said of his former National Party colleagues: 'They've all gone soft. Nothing will get done.' He was unrepentant in his attitude to such things as condom vending machines: 'They're cluttering up the values of our young people. There is light and darkness. There is right and wrong.

Joh for PM

Politics is about what is good and what is right. About Christian belief.' He also bluntly revealed his view on the emergence of the Joh for PM campaign, blaming Sparkes for everything:

> I never wanted to be Prime Minister. I wanted to change things in Canberra and it was not until I had been campaigning for five weeks that Sir Robert Sparkes and the rest of them could see how successful I was being and wanted to come in on my coat tails. Sir Robert Sparkes, not me, made the wrong judgment. They gummed it up for weeks. I knew in my heart he was wrong, and I warned him, but he wouldn't listen. They all sit up there in their bunker [National Party headquarters] and won't listen to advice.

23
NIXON DOES HIS JOB

January to July 1988

There is no electoral statistic in existence today to support an argument that the National Party would be better able to win power in Federal Parliament by standing outside Coalition.

Nixon report, 6 May 1988, p. 35

Labor's fortunes were taking a turn for the worse. It lost the normally safe federal seat of Adelaide to the Liberals at a by-election on 6 February 1988, and just retained Port Adelaide at a further by-election on 26 March, suffering a two-party preferred swing of nearly 11 per cent. In the meantime, the New South Wales Labor government of Barry Unsworth was defeated by the Coalition of Nick Greiner and Wal Murray on 19 March, and there were substantial swings against Labor in state by-elections in Victoria and Western Australia, and in the Brisbane City Council election, which saw the Liberal lord mayor, Sallyanne Atkinson, returned with 63 per cent of the vote.

There were two catastrophic by-election results for the National Party, both in Queensland. Two weeks before resigning as premier and from parliament on 1 December 1987, Bjelke-

Petersen appointed McVeigh as the state's agent-general to London. A by-election for McVeigh's seat of Groom on 9 April saw a swing of 20 per cent against the National Party candidate, Nixon committee member, David Russell, with the seat going to the Liberal Party. One week later, on 16 April, Bjelke-Petersen's seat of Barambah, which he had held for almost 37 years, fell to a new political entity, the Citizens' Electoral Council (CEC), with an almost unheard of swing of 35 per cent against the Nationals. Joh had endorsed the CEC candidate in Barambah and the Liberal in Groom over those of his own party.

Russell's campaign in Groom, together with the New South Wales election, forced Nixon to seek a short extension of his deadline. He was given until mid-May, with the special federal council rescheduled to 28–31 July. The Nixon committee held formal hearings in Brisbane, Sydney, Canberra, Melbourne, Adelaide and Perth, received formal and informal information, verbal and written, from many other areas, and studied political party constitutions, organisational structures and reviews from the United Kingdom, United States, Canada, Australia and New Zealand. Once all the hearings had been completed and submissions studied, the committee agreed that Nixon should work on an initial draft report. He outlined what his approach would be to a meeting on 22 March. After much interchange of draft chapters between committee members involving many hours of telephone discussions and some – although surprisingly little – compromise, a final draft was ready for consideration at a meeting in Melbourne on 14 April. Further minor amendments saw all committee members agree with the contents. Divergent views had come together, a point that Nixon highlighted in his foreword: 'Throughout our internal meetings, all members of the Committee vigorously argued their strong and individual points of view. On every occasion, we were able to reach common ground, which demonstrates what can be achieved through proper and rational debate based on a thorough consideration of the available facts.'[1] If the rest of the party could do likewise, there was hope that a new era of unity could be achieved at all levels across the country.

The method of actually presenting the final document was also considered at the 14 April meeting. The NSW party had asked for a draft to be circulated to state presidents before the report was finalised, on the grounds that it would be useless to present a report which the party at large would not accept. Nixon rejected this. So far as he was concerned, he had been commissioned to present a report. The document would be just that – a final report. There would be no draft in advance. The reaction of the various parties was a matter for them, not Nixon. It was agreed by all committee members that the report should be finalised and printed before being circulated to anyone. A substantial print run of the 86-page document was ordered, with presentation to the federal management committee set for Sydney on 6 May. Nixon demanded absolute confidentiality from his committee members on the content of the report. He wanted it kept 'as tight as a drum', and it was. Even Ian Sinclair did not receive an advance copy. However, with the committee's concurrence, Nixon did give Sinclair a verbal briefing a few days before the federal management committee met.

The report, titled *The Future: A Report by The Committee of Review into the Future Direction of the National Party of Australia*, became known as the Nixon report and is still referred to as that to this day. It examined historical perspectives on Coalition at state and federal levels, noting among other points that the Queensland National and Liberal parties had been unable to break 'Labor supremacy in Queensland' until they formed a Coalition in Opposition in 1956, which resulted in them winning the state election in August 1957. Nixon's key conclusion found that historically in the federal sphere, being in Coalition had provided the party with the best opportunity of achieving government: 'There is no electoral statistic in existence today to support an argument that the National Party would be better able to win power in Federal Parliament by standing outside Coalition.' He continued:

> The Party has a record of legislation on the statute books dating back to 1923, when Earle Page formed a Coalition Government with Stanley Bruce. That record of legislation amounts to the implementation of the Party's policies. Had the Party not entered into respective Coalition arrangements, it would today have nothing to show for all its efforts, or its policies. No National Party Minister's name would be on the statute books. The fundamental objective of politics is to win Government so that policies can be translated into legislation. That objective must never be overlooked.

Nixon canvassed the idea of a new, single conservative party based on the National Party, which he said was in essence what was behind the Joh for PM campaign, and which history had shown 'failed dismally'. He found that a new conservative entity was not an option:

> A new conservative party would be most unlikely to bring about the demise of either the existing National or Liberal Parties. It would therefore further complicate the political scenario and could even lead to wider splits within conservative forces. For example, the Committee was told in evidence that any attempt to form a new conservative party would undoubtedly see the reforming of an Australian Country Party at least in New South Wales.

The report broached amalgamation, saying there was 'an undeniable truth' that maintaining two separate non-Labor parties was bad economics, involving 'a waste of money and valuable human resources' and requiring 'enormous duplication of effort'. It acknowledged that any change in the voting system for federal elections, such as the introduction of optional preferential voting, 'could force a decision on the question'. Overall, however, the committee believed the issue required 'far greater and deeper consideration by all the State Parties before proper conclusions can be drawn'.

The report contained 68 recommendations and conclusions, as well as a totally revised federal party constitution. Key conclusions concerning the parliamentary party and leader, policies, Coalition, relations between the parliamentary and organisational parties, and the activities of state parties beyond their state boundaries – issues arising directly from the Joh campaign – included:

- It is the exclusive right of the Federal Parliamentary Party to elect its Leader.
- The Federal Parliamentary Leader must have the freedom to implement and promote the Federal Party and its policies in any way he and his Parliamentary colleagues judge to be the best under the political circumstances of the day. At the same time, there must be proper coordination and liaison between the Federal Leader and the Organisation.
- If the argument of National Party Parliamentarians is good enough, there is no reason why their policy attitudes should not dominate Coalition policies.
- The Federal Parliamentary Party must be able to take a different stance on [party] policy, but must explain why to the Organisation.

- The Federal Parliamentary Party must fully take into account the views of the Federal Management Committee before determining its position on Coalition, either in Government or Opposition.
- Whatever decision is ultimately adopted by the Federal Parliamentary Party on Coalition, it must be accepted by the Parties right around Australia.
- No Affiliated Party may seek to endorse candidates for Federal elections or Federal by-elections outside its own State or Territory.
- If the Federal Organisation wants to stand a National Party candidate in a State or Territory where there is no Affiliated Party, then the Federal Management Committee should have the power to call for nominations, select and endorse candidates.
- In areas where there are Affiliated Parties, no other State should seek to intervene in that Affiliated Party's affairs in any way whatsoever, unless specifically asked or invited to do so by a vote of the Central Council of that State.
- Any member of an Affiliated Party who stands against a candidate endorsed by an Affiliated Party for a Federal election or a Federal by-election should be automatically expelled from his or her Affiliated Party.

These required a total rewrite of the party's federal constitution, which at the time comprised 44 clauses covering five pages and was little different from that first adopted in 1926. Nixon's constitution ran to 83 clauses, with many more sub-clauses, and covered 16 pages. If adopted, it would necessitate substantial amendments to state party constitutions to make them compatible.

The federal management committee agreed the report should be released to the media immediately and circulated widely throughout the state parties, so that maximum time could be given to considering its recommendations before the special federal council.

When it did meet at the end of July, federal council was quick to settle the amalgamation question, resolving that, against the background of recent anti-amalgamation statements having been made by the leaders of all affiliated National parties, and by the federal leader, 'this Council agrees that amalgamation or merger is not an option for the National Party of Australia in the foreseeable future'.

The council also settled the vexed question of Coalition in Opposition by carrying a motion simply stating that 'this Council endorse the continuance of the Federal Coalition to the next election'. The motion was moved by Sparkes.[2]

It adopted the draft Nixon constitution, with minor amendments, and referred other recommendations to the state parties for co-ordinated action. Specifically, these covered strengthening preselection processes and improving co-operative arrangements, communications and profile building. The new federal constitution clarified the parliamentary party's autonomy, responsibility and relationship with federal council. It streamlined organisational structures, the relationship between state and federal organisations, including financial arrangements, increased the size of federal council and provided for a federal conference to be held once in the life of every federal parliament, or once every three years. It required the parliamentary party to consider the policy decisions of federal conference and federal council in determining its policies. Where the parliamentary party intended taking a position inconsistent with the policy of the organisation, the federal leader was required to advise the federal management committee of the reasons for so doing. The new constitution empowered the parliamentary party to 'enter into, alter the terms of, or terminate, either in Government or Opposition, a coalition or alliance with another Parliamentary political party'. Before doing so, however, the federal leader was required to consult with the management committee and refer its views to the parliamentary party when considering its decision.

There was a new section on candidates for election, which specified that 'no Affiliated Party shall endorse candidates for election to the Australian Parliament in Federal electoral divisions other than those within its State or Territory'.[3] The right of the federal parliamentary party to make its own decisions, albeit with some consultation with the organisation, was, for the first time, constitutionally defined; a Joh-type campaign could not happen again. The role and responsibilities of the federal secretariat were also defined, as were the conditions of affiliation. A new section covering the conditions of association was included. Standing federal campaign and finance committees, each representative of state and federal party interests, were established, thereby improving federal and state party relationships and particularly those between the federal and state secretariats.

All state parties accepted the report and necessary consequential amendments to their constitutions were progressively implemented, giving the party across Australia a greater degree of constitutional uniformity than had previously existed and leading to greatly improved levels of co-operation, information exchange and strategic planning. The report was a landmark in the party's history. Nixon had done his job.

EPILOGUE

> It is my hope that as this Report is considered and debated, personal prejudices and State jealousies will be put aside in the greater interests of the future of the Party in Federal politics.
>
> Peter Nixon, Chairman's Foreword, Nixon report, 6 May 1988, p. 2

The reverberations of the Joh campaign continued, directly and indirectly, for a long time. The post-Joh Queensland government, first under Premier Mike Ahern and then, from 25 September 1989, Russell Cooper, was decimated by Labor at the elections just over two months later, on 2 December. The continued and increased adverse impact of the Fitzgerald inquiry's findings was undeniably central to the defeat, but the strains and uncertainty within the Queensland Nationals caused by the Joh for Canberra campaign, followed by disunity in the government in the lead-up to Joh's resignation, were also significant factors.

The Nationals were reduced from 49 seats after the 1986 election to 26 in 1989; the Liberals were returned with nine; and the Labor Party, led by Wayne Goss, soared from 30 to 54 seats.[1] Partly as a result of the poor election showing, Sparkes resigned as Queensland National Party president early in 1990.[2] There was a short return to a Coalition government under Rob Borbidge from 19 February 1996 to 26 June 1998, after the Goss government resigned in the face of losing a confidence motion in the parliament.[3]

Labor, first under Peter Beattie and later, Anna Bligh, was re-elected from 26 June 1998 and maintained office until an amalgamated non-Labor team, the Liberal National Party of Queensland (LNP), gained a massive majority at the election on 24 March 2012, winning 78 seats and reducing Labor to seven.[4]

Federally, the conservatives emerged from the Joh campaign disoriented, even shell shocked, and disunited. There remained considerable apprehension among Liberals about the reliability of the Nationals, particularly those from Queensland. The Coalition seemed unable to land any meaningful punches on the Hawke administration. Growing backbench dissatisfaction with the leadership of both non-Labor parties, for a variety of reasons, some of which in the National Party had their genesis from the Joh campaign, led to a dramatic double coup on 9 May 1989, with Howard being replaced by Andrew Peacock and Sinclair by Charles Blunt. Sinclair, a man whose political scalp the ALP had been seeking for years, had survived their attacks and the Joh campaign, only to be brought down by his own party room. Both former leaders remained in parliament, and Peacock and Blunt confirmed an ongoing Coalition in Opposition.[5]

The 1990 federal election was a further disaster for the Nationals, with Blunt losing his north coast New South Wales seat of Richmond and the party's House of Representatives numbers falling from 19 to 14 in a House of 148 – the lowest since 1946, when it held 12 seats in a House of 74 members. John Stone, on the encouragement of Sparkes, who was still angling to have him become party leader, had resigned from the Senate to contest the National Party seat of Fairfax, vacated by the retirement of Evan Adermann. The gamble failed. Stone was unable to resist the anti-National mood, with the seat falling to the Liberal Party and his parliamentary career over. The New South Wales Member for Farrer, Tim Fischer, was elected the new party leader.

Epilogue

The Liberals polled strongly, taking their numbers from 43 seats in 1987 to 55 and cutting Labor's majority from 24 at that time to nine. Peacock, however, did not recontest the leadership and the position went to John Hewson, a former executive director of the Macquarie Bank and economic adviser to former treasurers, Phil Lynch and John Howard. The Member for Wentworth in Sydney, Hewson had only been in parliament for three years. Hewson and Fischer renewed the Coalition in Opposition.

There were tensions in the government as well. Hawke was replaced as prime minister by Paul Keating on his second challenge on 20 December 1991. The country had gone through the 'banana republic' of 1986, the 'budget that brings home the bacon' in 1988 and the 'recession Australia had to have' in 1990.[6] Labor's stocks were low. The election on 13 March 1993 was widely billed as being unlosable for the Coalition. But it did lose, prompting Keating to famously remark: 'This is the sweetest victory of all. This is a victory for the true believers.'[7] A key reason for the Coalition's failure was its complex *Fightback!* economic package, the central element of which proposed the abolition of wholesale sales tax, payroll tax and fuel excise, combined with pension increases and income tax cuts for middle-income earners, in exchange for a goods and services tax (GST) of 15 per cent. Keating ruthlessly exploited the complexity of the policy to a hesitant and wary electorate. While the Liberals lost six seats, the Nationals gained two, clawing their numbers up to sixteen. Labor's representation increased by two to eighty.

It was not until the 2 March 1996 election that the Coalition finally triumphed over Labor, with Howard back as Liberal leader and Fischer still leading the Nationals. The Liberals won an impressive 76 seats, including one CLP seat in the Northern Territory – enough to govern in their own right if they wished – and the ALP was reduced to 49 seats. The Nationals won a further two seats taking their House numbers to 18 and returning their representation to reasonable respectability. Howard and Fischer, who had maintained the Coalition in Opposition, agreed to form a Coalition government, the first in 13 years. Finally, it seemed, the shadows and echoes of Joh for Canberra had been put to rest, although Joh would have been deeply suspicious of a government in Canberra that was still being led by a former Fraser government minister.

Perhaps the most significant after-effect of Joh for PM, however, was the speed and relative ease with which the National Party as a whole was able to regroup. Having been torn asunder for most of 1987, to the point where the very existence of the party was under threat, the disparate state organisations, through federal council, came together in October with little, if any acrimony. They agreed to establish the Nixon review and adopted its report just nine months later. This began the process of reuniting the party and protecting against future Joh-like incursions into the rights of the states and the federal parliamentary party. It was a remarkably swift recovery, without which the federal party organisation, the body that gives formal life to the federal parliamentary National Party, may have collapsed. It was a credit to the party's leaders at the time, state and federal, parliamentary and organisational, that this was achieved. It was a fine demonstration of the ultimate philosophy of unity that exists in the National Party, and that is a core reason why it has survived as an influential entity in federal politics for 95 years.

Nonetheless, Sinclair questioned whether the party was ever the same after the Joh campaign: 'The sad part to me of the Joh for Canberra push was that it destroyed what I thought was the ethos of the party and the partnership and the camaraderie and trust that was in the party, and certainly from Joh's day on I don't think the party has really had quite that same level of trust from each other.'[8]

Epilogue

A central question about the Joh campaign is: How was it ever able to reach the stage it did; surely some compromise could have been worked out? The simple answer, in my view, is that compromise could never have been achieved. If the Joh campaign was to have had any realistic chance of success, first and foremost Joh and Sinclair would have had to come to a strategic agreement; namely, that Joh would be the figurehead of the National Party's election campaign and the promoter of its policies, which is to say, Joh policies. Sinclair would never have accepted such an accommodation. He was the elected leader of the federal parliamentary party. His leadership had been re-endorsed by the party room on 28 April 1987. As leader, he was the flag bearer of the National Party's campaign. There were no circumstances under which he would have contemplated relinquishing that responsibility, least of all to someone who was not even a member of the federal parliamentary party. Similarly, Joh would never have agreed to play second fiddle to Sinclair. The impasse was insurmountable.

ACKNOWLEDGEMENTS

Over the years, I have had many conversations, discussions and interviews with people, some now deceased, about the Joh for PM campaign and I gratefully acknowledge those contributions given by, in alphabetical order:

John Anderson, Doug Anthony, Liam Bathgate, Bill Baxter, Florence Bjelke-Petersen, Ron Boswell, Ray Braithwaite, David Brownhill, Ian Cameron, Stan Collard, Bruce Cowan, Ken Crooke, Michael Evans, Tim Fischer, Peter Fisher, Jenny Gardiner, Noel Hicks, Ralph Hunt, Bruce Lloyd, Sandy MacKenzie, Don McDonald, Stuart McDonald, Julian McGauran, Peter McGauran, Shirley McKerrow, Tom McVeigh, Clarrie Millar, Geoff Mort, Paul Neville, Peter Nixon, John Paterson, Ian Robinson, David Russell, Rick Setter, John Sharp, Ian Sinclair, John Stone, Grant Tambling, David Thomson, Warren Truss.

I also acknowledge the assistance of party professional officers and parliamentary staff, Sophie Drew, Ben Franklin, Cathy Heidrich, Brad Henderson, Meg Keating, Douglas Martin, Scott Mitchell, Sue Mitchell, Jen Southwell and Gerrie van Dam, and Don Boadle at The Page Research Centre Library, Wagga Wagga, and Paul O'Donnell at the Charles Sturt University Regional Archives, Wagga Wagga. I particularly thank Cecile Ferguson, a colleague at the National Party federal secretariat throughout my tenure as its director, who took my

Acknowledgements

original draft, bashed out with two fingers on an Olivetti golf-ball typewriter, and brought it into the computer age.

I further thank cartoonist Geoff Pryor for giving me permission to use a selection of his work from *The Canberra Times*.

This story – a significant event in the history of Australian politics – has been brought to fruition thanks to the support of The Page Research Centre, and I express my sincere appreciation to its board of directors for their confidence in the worthiness of the publication.

I thank my publisher, Elspeth Menzies, my editor, Marie-Louise Taylor, and the team at NewSouth Publishing for their enthusiastic advice, design and support – input that is so crucial to bringing a project of this nature to a successful conclusion.

The Page Research Centre Limited was established in 2002 to take over the responsibilities of the Sir Earle Page Memorial Trust, an organisation established to preserve and honour the memory of the founding members of what is today the National Party of Australia.

The Page Research Centre explores issues and develops imaginative and practical measures to promote prosperity and excellence in rural pursuits. It seeks measures that allow all regional Australians to share in the growth and prosperity of the nation. The centre continues to explore issues of prominence in regional Australia. Its findings are used to develop advice on policy that can be delivered to the highest echelons of the Commonwealth Government.

In 2007, the centre embarked on a new line of work – to preserve the history of the National Party at state and federal levels. This was the beginning of The Page Research Centre Library. The library has acquired a range of documents, diaries, memos, newspaper articles, photos and audio and visual tapes, CDs and DVDs. These resources are made available to researchers interested in the party's history. The centre has also supported the publication of books on various aspects of the history of the party.

To learn more about the life of Sir Earle Page and The Page Research Centre visit www.page.org.au

NOTES

Text of documents

The full text of several archived documents, now held by The Page Research Centre Library and referred to in this publication, are available through the library's website at <www.page.org.au>.

The documents are:

1. Coalition Agreement released by the Opposition leader, John Howard, and the National Party leader, Ian Sinclair, 15 April 1987 (chapter 7, page 94).
2. Joint statement by John Howard and the Premier of Queensland, Sir Joh-Bjelke Petersen, Brisbane, 3 June 1987 (chapter 10, page 137).
3. Statement by Sir Joh Bjelke-Petersen, Brisbane, 3 June 1987 (chapter 10, page 138).
4. Explanatory comments by the Queensland National Party president, Sir Robert Sparkes, Brisbane, 3 June 1987 (chapter 10, page 138).
5. Newsletter from the former Queensland Senator, Stan Collard, to Queensland National Party branches, 21 July 1987 (chapter 11, page 153).
6. Letter from the Queensland Member for Dawson, Ray Braithwaite, to Sir Robert Sparkes, 17 July 1987 (chapter 14, page 183).
7. Letter from Sir Robert Sparkes to the National Party federal president, Stuart McDonald, 27 July 1987 (chapter 16, page 190).

8. Letter from the Queensland National Party vice-president, Sir Charles Holm, to Stuart McDonald, 28 July 1987 (chapter 16, page 191).
9. Letter from Stuart McDonald to Sir Robert Sparkes, 28 July 1987 (chapter 16, page 195).
10. Letter from Sir Robert Sparkes to Queensland National Party members, 28 September 1987 (chapter 19, page 219).
11. Explanatory paper by Sir Joh Bjelke-Petersen on the Joh for Canberra campaign, Queensland National Party annual conference, Townsville, 6 November 1987 (chapter 21, page 242).
12. Presidential report by Sir Robert Sparkes to the Queensland National Party annual conference, Townsville, 6 November 1987 (chapter 21, page 243).
13. Letter from Stuart McDonald to Sir Robert Sparkes, 27 November 1987 (chapter 21, page 248).

Prologue

1. *The Courier-Mail*, Brisbane, 20 July 1976, p. 1.

1 Prelude to conflict

1. *Parliamentary Handbook of the Commonwealth of Australia*, 30th edition, Department of Parliamentary Services, Canberra, 2005, p. 601 (hereafter Parliamentary Handbook) – see also online at <www.aph.gov.au/About_Parliament/Parliamentary_Departments/Parliamentary_Library/Parliamentary_handbook>.
2. The policy to ban sand mining on Fraser Island was opposed by the National Party. Information from Ian Sinclair, 22 June 1994, author files.
3. David Russell interviewed by Danielle Miller and Peter Spearitt for *Queensland Speaks*, University of Queensland Centre for the Government of Queensland, 16 December 2011 – see <www.queenslandspeaks.com.au/david-russell> (hereafter Russell, Queensland Speaks).
4. Interview with Doug Anthony, 21 February 2013.
5. Joh Bjelke-Petersen was made a Knights Commander of the Order of St Michael and St George (KCMG) on 23 June 1984 for services as Premier of Queensland – see <www.itsanhonour.gov.au>.
6. *The Canberra Times*, 2 November 1986.
7. *The Australian*, 3 November 1986.
8. Robert Sparkes, report to Queensland National Party annual conference, Gold Coast, 18 July 1986.
9. Bill Hayden, *The Canberra Times*, 28 February 1987.
10. Transcript, Robert Sparkes, ABC Television *7.30 Report*, 2 March 1987.
11. The Brisbane seats, on boundaries existing at the time, were Bowman, Brisbane, Fadden, Forde, Griffith, Lilley, Moreton, Oxley, Petrie, Rankin and Ryan.
12. Hughes, CA, *A Handbook of Australian Government and Politics 1975–1984*, Australian National University Press, Canberra, 1987, p. 181 (hereafter Hughes, Government and Politics 1975–1984).
13. The seats were Ballarat, Burke, Casey, Chisholm, Corangamite, Corio, Dunkley, Flinders, Goldstein, Henty, Higgins, Isaacs, Melbourne Ports and Streeton.
14. Adelaide, Boothby, Hawker, Kingston and Makin.
15. Hughes, Government and Politics 1975–1984, pp. 165, 178.
16. Information from David Brownhill, 14 December 2014.
17. Formed as a federal party on 22 January 1920, the Australian Country Party changed its name to National Country Party of Australia on 2 May 1975 and to National Party of Australia on 16 October 1982. Davey, P, *Ninety Not Out: The Nationals 1920–2010*, UNSW Press, Sydney, 2010, p. 402 (hereafter Davey, Ninety Not Out).
18. Davey, Ninety Not Out, pp. 197–99.
19. National Party of Australia federal constitution, 1987, clauses 10–12. Interestingly, while the CLP had been associated with the federal party for several years, there was at this time no provision in the party constitution for associated organisations – an omission that was rectified in a post–Joh campaign constitutional review.

2 Not always plain sailing

1. *An Introduction to the National Party of Australia*, 1990, p. 4, National Party federal secretariat, Canberra.

2   Ellis, UR, *A History of the Australian Country Party*, Melbourne University Press, 1963, p. 51 (hereafter Ellis, Country Party); *The Argus*, Melbourne, 23 January 1920; Ellis, UR, *Research Notes, Australian Country Party (Federal) 1902–1923*, Office of Rural Research, Canberra, 28 July 1954, p. 5.
3   Commonwealth Parliamentary Debates, 10 March 1920, p. 250 (hereafter CPD).
4   Unless otherwise specified, the following synopsis of federal coalitions is drawn from Davey, Ninety Not Out; Davey, P, *The Country Party Prime Ministers – Their Trials and Tribulations*, Dobson's Printing, Sydney, 2011; Ellis, Country Party; Fadden, AW, *They Called Me Artie: The Memoirs of Sir Arthur Fadden*, The Jacaranda Press, Brisbane, 1969; Golding, P, *Black Jack McEwen: Political Gladiator*, Melbourne University Press, 1996; Jackson, RV, *John McEwen: His Story*, edited text of November 1974 recordings by John McEwen for the National Library of Australia, privately published, 1982, and republished by The Page Research Centre, Canberra, 2014; and Page, E, *Truant Surgeon: The Inside Story of Forty Years of Australian Political Life*, Angus and Robertson, Sydney, 1963.
5   Parliamentary Handbook, Ministries, p. 679.
6   Coalition oppositions in Canberra have been maintained without exception when Labor is in government since the double dissolution election of 11 July 1987.
7   The following summary of attitudes to Coalition among the state Country/National parties is drawn from Davey, P, *The Divisive Issues: Coalition and Amalgamation*, research paper, The Page Research Centre, August 2008.
8   Bruxner returned to the parliamentary leadership, succeeding Buttenshaw in 1932, and held the position until his retirement in 1958. Davey, P, *The Nationals: The Progressive, Country and National Party in New South Wales 1919 to 2006*, The Federation Press, Sydney, p. 496 (hereafter Davey, The Nationals).
9   The VFU was renamed the Country Party in 1926.
10 Layman, L & Duncan, W (eds), *Blood Nose Politics: A Centenary History of the Western Australian National Party 1913–2013*, The National Party of Australia (WA) Inc., Perth, 2014, pp. 6, 122, 135.
11 Hughes, CA, *The Government of Queensland*, University of Queensland Press, Brisbane, 1980, pp. 16–19.
12 Interview with Doug Anthony, 21 February 2013.
13 Agenda, Queensland National Party annual conference, Gold Coast, 16–20 July 1986.
14 *The Canberra Times*, 21 July 1986.
15 Resolutions, New South Wales National Country Party annual general conference, Armidale, 11–14 June 1981.
16 NSW National Party central council minutes, 10 April 1987; Report on 1987 Federal Council Meeting by NSW party chairman, Doug Moppett, 10 April 1987. The Nationals – NSW.
17 *The Herald*, Melbourne, 19 February 1987.
18 Interview with John Anderson, 1 December 2014.
19 Minutes, Victorian National Party annual conference, Wangaratta, 10 April 1987.

3   The Joh campaign hits the road

1   *The Daily Advertiser*, Wagga Wagga, 2 February 1987.
2   Addressing the NSW party's annual conference in Coffs Harbour on 24 June 1977, Anthony called for a flat rate of tax of around 20 per cent. NSW National Party magazine, *National Leader*, September 1985, p. 6.
3   *Queensland's Taxation Reform Package including Single Rate Tax Proposal*, as

presented to the National Taxation Summit in Canberra, 1–4 July, 1985 by the Honourable Sir Joh. Bjelke-Petersen, Premier and Treasurer of Queensland.

4   Bjelke-Petersen's Wagga Wagga speech also included commitments to crack down on trade union power, cut red tape and abolish 'useless commissions' – the Constitutional Commission, Equal Opportunity Tribunal, Human Rights Commission and Anti-Discrimination Board would 'disappear like a morning mist on a hot summer's morning'. *The Daily Advertiser*, Wagga Wagga, 2 February 1987.
5   *The Canberra Times*, 3 February 1987.
6   Transcript, Ian Sinclair news conference, Canberra, 3 February 1987.
7   Doug Moppett media release, 4 February 1987.
8   Transcript, Joh Bjelke-Petersen news conference, Perth, 3 February 1987.
9   Transcript, Joh Bjelke-Petersen ABC Radio *AM*, 5 February 1987.
10 Heatley, A, *The Territory Party: The Northern Territory Country Liberal Party 1974–1998*, Northern Territory University Press, Darwin, 1998, pp. 5, 62 (hereafter Heatley, Territory Party).
11 Minutes, federal management committee, 5 February 1987.
12 Russell, Queensland Speaks.
13 National Party of Australia, federal constitution, 1987, clause 35.
14 Author files.
15 'I've got the support of the party, they very strongly supported me. The whole question of leadership did not arise … .' Transcript, Ian Sinclair, ABC Radio *AM*, 17 February 1987.
16 See transcripts ABC TV *7.30 Report*, 16 February 1987, and ABC Radio *AM*, 17 February 1987, and *The Canberra Times*, 17 February 1987.
17 Information from Ian Sinclair, 22 June 1994.
18 *The Canberra Times*, 14 February 1987.

4   Turning a skirmish into a war

1   *The Canberra Times*, 26 February 1987.
2   Sparkes acknowledged on the ABC TV *7.30 Report* on 2 March 1987 that he had been 'the author of the [Hervey Bay] motion'.
3   Information from Stan Collard, 13 August 2014.
4. *The Canberra Times*, 21 July 1986; Ron Boswell noted that Sparkes had been described as 'the most important non-parliamentary member of any political party in Australia', adjournment speech on the death of Sir Robert Sparkes, CPD, 12 September 2006, p. 95. Sparkes died from Parkinson's disease on 6 August 2006, aged seventy-seven.
5   Davey, The Nationals, p. 286.
6   Hervey Bay resolutions, Queensland National Party magazine, *National Outlook*, March 1987, p. 4.
7   Interviews with Tom McVeigh, 18 and 23 January 2015.
8   Information from Ray Braithwaite, 18 August 2014.
9   Davey, Ninety Not Out, pp. 220, 221.
10 *The Canberra Times*, 1 March 1987.
11 *The Canberra Times*, 2 March 1987.
12 *The Canberra Times*, 3 March 1987.
13 Doug Moppett report to NSW National Party central council, 10 April 1987.
14 Legal advice to Shirley McKerrow, 3 March 1987; Federal Director's Backgrounder – National Party Situation, 14 April 1987.

15 Australian Country Party Association constitution, adopted by a conference of state and federal Country Party delegates, Melbourne, 23–24 March 1926.
16 Doug Moppett report to NSW National Party central council, 18 June 1987.
17 Queensland National Party constitution, 1987, clauses 75(a), 93.

5 Tactics and numbers
1 *The Canberra Times*, 1 and 2 March 1987.
2 Transcript, Robert Sparkes, ABC TV *7.30 Report*, 2 March 1987.
3 Doug Anthony speech, Sydney Rotary Club luncheon, 2 March 1987.
4 Browning, AR (ed), *House of Representatives Practice*, 2nd edition, Australian Government Publishing Service, Canberra, 1989, p. 706.
5 Transcript, Robert Sparkes, ABC Radio *AM*, 4 March 1987.
6 Minutes, NSW National Party central executive, 6 March 1987.
7 Minutes, NSW National Party central executive, 6 March 1987.
8 *The Australian*, 16 March 1987.
9 Transcript, Tom McVeigh, ABC TV *7.30 Report*, 2 March 1987.
10 *The Australian*, 18 March 1987.
11 *Richmond River Express*, Casino, 4 March 1987.
12 Davey, Ninety Not Out, p. 218.
13 Davey, Ninety Not Out, pp. 217, 218.
14 *The Canberra Times*, 22 March 1987.
15 Interview with Tim Fischer, 1 December 2014.
16 National Party of Australia federal constitution 1987, clause 35.
17 The following account of the CLP's relations with the National Party is drawn from records, correspondence and minutes held by The Page Research Centre Library, from Heatley, Territory Party, and from the author's files.
18 Arguably, the CLP could have been entitled to seven delegates, as the party had representation in the Commonwealth Parliament through a senator, Bernie Kilgariff, and the Member for Northern Territory, Paul Everingham. Parliamentary Handbook, pp. 604, 632. While both sat with the Liberal Party, there was no stipulation in the National Party's federal constitution requiring federal parliamentary representation to be with the National Party to entitle an affiliated party to an additional delegate to federal council.
19 Transcript, Joh Bjelke-Petersen, ABC Radio *AM*, 24 March 1987.

6 A Queensland backdown?
1 This and following quotes are from transcripts and minutes of the federal management committee meeting, Canberra, 27 March 1987.
2 *The Age*, Melbourne, 15 April 1987.
3 *National Outlook*, March 1987, p. 3.
4 Minutes, special conference of the Northern Territory Country Liberal Party, Darwin, 3 February 1979.
5 Ian Sinclair speech to federal council, Canberra, 27 March 1987.
6 *The Canberra Times*, 28 March 1987.
7 Joh Bjelke-Petersen speech to federal council, Canberra, 28 March 1987.
8 *The Canberra Times*, editorial, 30 March 1987.
9 This and following motions and debate are from transcripts and minutes of federal council, Canberra, 27–29 March 1987.
10 National Party of Australia federal constitution, 1987, clauses 25–28. The joint meeting provisions were removed in a revised constitution adopted by federal

council at its meeting in Canberra on 29–31 July 1988.
11   Information from Peter Nixon, 26 October 2014; Davey, Ninety Not Out, p. 223.
12   *The Canberra Times*, 30 March 1987.
13   Headlines from *The Australian*, *The Courier-Mail*, Brisbane, *The Sydney Morning Herald*, *The Canberra Times*, *The Age*, Melbourne, 30 March 1987.

7 Confusion
1   *The Sydney Morning Herald*, 3 April 1987.
2   *The Weekend Australian*, 11 April 1987.
3   Transcript, Ian Sinclair media conference, Wangaratta, Victoria, 10 April 1987.
4   *The Canberra Times*, 11 April 1987.
5   Ian Sinclair speech to Victorian National Party annual conference, Wangaratta, 11 April 1987.
6   *The Canberra Times*, 12 April 1987.
7   Bob Katter senior held Kennedy for the National Party from 1966 until retiring in 1990. His son, also Bob Katter, succeeded him in 1993, quitting the National Party in 2001 and sitting as an Independent until forming Katter's Australian Party in the lead-up to the 2013 federal election. Parliamentary Handbook, p. 644.
8   Transcript, Ian Sinclair, Channel 9 *Sunday*, 12 April 1987.
9   Transcript, Joh Bjelke-Petersen, ABC Radio *AM*, 13 April 1987.
10 Parliamentary Handbook, 25th edition, 1991, pp. 43, 176.
11 Transcript, Clarrie Millar, ABC Radio *The World Today*, 15 April 1987.
12 Transcript, Clarrie Millar, ABC Radio *AM*, 23 April 1987.
13 Transcript, Ian Sinclair media conference, Canberra, 23 April 1987.
14 Ian Sinclair media release, 28 April 1987.
15 Transcript, Tom McVeigh, ABC Radio *PM*, 24 April 1987.

8 The Coalition breaks
1   Information from Noel Hicks, 11 January 2015.
2   John Howard media release, Canberra, 28 April 1987.
3   Ian Sinclair media release, Canberra, 28 April 1987.
4   Parliamentary Handbook, Ministries, p. 679.
5   Davey, Ninety Not Out, p. 228.
6   Noel Hicks, Keeping the hounds in the pack, *The Page Review*, vol 4, no 1, June 2008, page 18.
7   Davey, Ninety Not Out, p. 229.
8   *The Sydney Morning Herald*, 30 April 1987.
9   Ian Sinclair media release, 30 April 1987.
10 Malcolm Mackerras article, *The Sydney Morning Herald*, 30 April 1987.
11 CPD, 30 April 1987, p. 2277.
12 National Party of Australia Shadow Committees, Ian Sinclair media release, 30 April 1987.
13 *The Sun*, Sydney, 1 May 1987.
14 Interview with Ian Sinclair, 30 November 2014.
15 *The Daily Telegraph*, Sydney, 4 June 1987; *The Australian*, 6 June 1987
16 Interview with Ian Sinclair, 30 November 2014.
17 *The Courier-Mail*, Brisbane, 2 May 1987.
18 *The Canberra Times*, 3 May 1987.
19 *The Sydney Morning Herald*, 5 May 1987.
20 Ian Sinclair speech to National Press Club, Canberra, 8 May 1987.

9 The indiscretions of Ian Cameron
1. Transcript, Ian Cameron, ABC TV *7.30 Report*, 16 February 1987.
2. The following is from the minutes, Maranoa Divisional Council meeting, St George, Queensland, 16 May 1987.

10 An early election looms
1. *The Australian*, 6 May 1987.
2. *The Sydney Morning Herald*, 11 May 1987.
3. *The Courier-Mail*, Brisbane, 2 May 1987.
4. The first winter election was held on 21 August 1943. Parliamentary Handbook, p. 333.
5. Introduced into the House of Representatives on 22 October 1986, the bill had been rejected by the Senate on 10 December 1986 and again on 2 April 1987. Bills Digest, 159 1986, Australia Card Bill 1986 – see <www.aph.gov.au/Parliamentary_Business/Bills_Legislation>.
6. *The Sun*, Sydney, 28 May 1987.
7. *The Age*, Melbourne, 30 May 1987.
8. *The Age*, Melbourne, 31 May 1987.
9. *The Sun News-Pictorial*, Melbourne, 1 June 1987.
10. *The Sydney Morning Herald*, 1 June 1987.
11. *The Canberra Times*, 29 May 1987.
12. Transcript, Ian McLachlan, ABC Radio *AM*, 2 June 1987.
13. Davey, Ninety Not Out, p. 231.
14. *The Weekend Australian*, 6 June 1987.
15. *The Weekend Australian*, 6 June 1987.
16. Davey, Ninety Not Out, p. 232.
17. Interview with Ian Sinclair, 30 November 2014.
18. *The Canberra Times*, 11 June 1987; *The Sydney Morning Herald*, 11 June 1987.

11 Two memorable events
1. *The Canberra Times* on 13 June 1987 reported: 'No federal National Party MP, including Queensland senators, has seen what is in Sir Joh's policy despite several requests for briefings, and it is understood that most were not even officially advised of the launch.'
2. Minutes, National Party federal council meetings, Canberra, August 1984, October 1985, March 1987.
3. *The Age*, Melbourne, 15 June 1987.
4. CPD, 5 June 1987, page 3689.
5. *Daily Sun*, Brisbane, 16 March 1987.
6. *The Morning Bulletin*, Rockhampton, editorial, 30 April 1987.
7. Extract, Vic Sullivan letter to Shirley McKerrow, 23 March 1987.
8. Stan Collard, doorstop interview, Brisbane, 13 June 1987; *Daily Telegraph*, Sydney, 15 June 1987.
9. John Stone article, *The Sydney Morning Herald*, 17 June 1987.
10. *The Canberra Times*, 15 June 1987; *The Sydney Morning Herald*, 17 June 1987.
11. Transcript, Bob Katter senior, ABC Radio *World Today*, 16 June 1987.
12. *The Australian*, 18 June 1987.
13. *The Australian*, 18 June 1987.

12 Sinclair delivers the policy
1. *The Canberra Times*, 17 June 1987.
2. *The Australian*, 5 June 1987.
3. *The Sydney Morning Herald*, 17 June 1987.
4. Interview with Shirley McKerrow, 10 January 2015.
5. *The Age*, Melbourne, 18 June 1987.
6. *Financial Review*, 19 June 1987.
7. *The Australian*, 19 June 1987.
8. Fred Maybury media statement, 22 June 1987.
9. *The Australian*, 25 May 1987.
10. Jenny Gardiner, general secretary's report to the annual meeting of the New South Wales National Party central council, Dubbo, 16 July 1988.
11. *The Australian*, 22 June 1987.
12. Robert Sparkes media release, 21 June 1987.
13. *The Courier-Mail*, Brisbane, 22 June 1987.
14. *The Australian*, 23 June 1987.
15. *The Age*, Melbourne, 26 June 1987; *The Sydney Morning Herald*, 26 June 1987.
16. *The Australian*, 7 July 1987.

13 The irritation of Joh Independents
1. Davey, The Nationals, p. 298.
2. For the 1987 election, South Australia and Western Australia each had 13 House of Representatives electorates. Hughes, CA, *A Handbook of Australian Government and Politics 1985–1999*, The Federation Press, Sydney, 2002, pp. 227, 229 (hereafter Hughes, Government and Politics 1985–1999).
3. *The Australian*, 5 June 1987. *The Sydney Morning Herald* on 5 June 1987 reported that Joh 'has also offered campaigning assistance to a rebel National Party candidate who is standing against Mr Sinclair ...'
4. *The Canberra Times*, 7 July 1987.
5. *The Canberra Times*, 7 July 1987.
6. Australian Electoral Commission, 1987 federal election results by division – see <www.aec.gov.au>

14 The recriminations fly
1. Parliamentary Handbook, p. 593.
2. Hughes, Government and Politics 1985–1999, pp. 220–234.
3. Davey, Ninety Not Out, p. 238.
4. Transcript, Joh Bjelke-Petersen press conference, Brisbane, 11 July 1987.
5. *The Age*, Melbourne, 13 July 1987.
6. *The Courier-Mail*, Brisbane, 13 July 1987.
7. *The Courier-Mail*, Brisbane, 13 July 1987.
8. *The Courier-Mail*, Brisbane, 13 July 1987.
9. *The Age*, Melbourne, 13 July 1987.
10. *The Australian*, 13 July 1987.
11. Bob Katter senior letter to Robert Sparkes, 14 July 1987.
12. *The Australian*, 16 July 1987.
13. Ralph Hunt press release, 20 July 1987.
14. Ian Sinclair press release, 20 July 1987.

15 Back towards Coalition
1. Davey, Ninety Not Out, pp. 242, 243.
2. Note for file, Liam Bathgate, principal private secretary to Ian Sinclair, 23 July 1987.

16 A Queensland no show
1. This chapter is based on the minutes and correspondence of the meeting of the federal management committee, Sydney, 28 July 1987.
2. Davey, Ninety Not Out, p. 244.

17 The Coalition re-forms
1. *The Canberra Times*, 31 July 1987.
2. Transcript, Robert Sparkes, ABC Radio news, Brisbane, 31 July 1987.
3. Ian Sinclair media release, 2 August 1987; *The Canberra Times*, 3 August 1987.
4. Doug Moppett press release, Quambone, 3 August 1987.
5. Transcript, Tom McVeigh, ABC Radio *AM*, 4 August 1987. Note that Moppett said that Sinclair was the 'undisputed' leader of the party, not that he had been 'unchallenged' for the position.
6. John Howard news release, 6 August 1987.
7. McVeigh met with 164 Groom electorate party branch members on 11 August. The meeting carried by 161 to three a motion reaffirming the local party's objection to Coalition in Opposition, but also acknowledged that the new Coalition was a fact of life and that McVeigh could best serve his electorate by being a part of that arrangement. McVeigh telegrammed Lloyd on 12 August advising that he would be a member of the National Party in Coalition.
8. John Howard, shadow ministry press release, 14 August 1987.
9. *The Canberra Times*, 16 August 1987.

18 Once more unto the breach …
1. The following account of the Western Australian National Party annual conference is drawn from circulated speeches by Hendy Cowan and John Paterson and minutes of the conference, Perth, 14–15 August 1987.

19 Flames flare in Queensland
1. See – <www.abc.net.au/4corners/stories/2011/08/08/3288495.htm>
2. Sparkes later revealed that he had been contacted by Gunn about the *Four Corners* program and had agreed that an inquiry should be instigated: 'I told him (Mr Gunn) that I thought it was essential that we have a full and open inquiry. Sir Joh had a few reservations at the time, not against this inquiry in particular, but because he thinks all inquiries are a bonanza for the legal profession and don't necessarily do anything else.' *The Age*, Melbourne, 30 September 1987.
3. Terry Lewis was removed as commissioner on 19 April 1988. Crime and Misconduct Commission, Queensland, the Fitzgerald Inquiry – see <www.cmc.qld.gov.au>; *Daily Telegraph*, Sydney, 6 October 1987.
4. *Daily Telegraph*, Sydney, 29 September 1987; *The Courier-Mail*, Brisbane, 1 October 1987 and editorial, 6 October 1987.
5. *The Age*, Melbourne, 29 September 1987.
6. *The Canberra Times*, 3 October 1987.
7. *The Age*, Melbourne, 30 September 1987.
8. *The Age*, Melbourne, 1 October 1987.

9   *The Sun News-Pictorial*, Melbourne, 1 October 1987.
10 *The Sydney Morning Herald*, 2 October 1987.
11 ABC TV *7.30 Rep*ort, 1 October 1987; *The Age*, Melbourne, 2 October 1987; *The Australian*, 2 October 1987. Hinze later retreated from his position, saying he had maintained at all times that 'the Premier alone should decide when he will retire' and adding that sections of the media could not be relied on to report accurately. Russ Hinze media release, 2 October 1987.
12 Bjelke-Petersen did not pursue this idea, which originated from a number of party members, reportedly members of the management committee, who were prepared to put up $500 000 for its establishment because they were 'fed up with the organisation's performance', *The Courier-Mail*, Brisbane, 3 October 1987.
13 *The Courier-Mail*, Brisbane, 3 October 1987.
14 *The Australian*, 5 October 1987.
15 *The Australian*, 5 October 1987; *The Canberra Times*, 5 October 1987.
16 *The Age*, Melbourne, 6 October 1987.
17 Joh Bjelke-Petersen media release, 6 October 1987.
18 *The Australian*, 8 October 1987; *The Canberra Times*, 8 October 1987.
19 *Daily Telegraph*, Sydney, 9 October 1987.
20 *The Age*, Melbourne, 9 October 1987.
21 *The Sun News-Pictorial*, Melbourne, 12 October 1987.

20 Let's have a committee!

1   The Hunt Committee reported on 20 November 1987. Its main recommendations were to enhance the working relationship between the federal and state secretariats; establish a standing federal campaign committee, including state party representation; levy the affiliated state parties to meet the costs of meetings of the federal council, federal management committee, women's federal council, the federal Young National Party and any federal conferences; and 'invite' state organisations to make annual contributions towards the operating costs of the federal secretariat. *The Future: A Report by The Committee of Review into the Future Direction of the National Party of Australia*, May 1988 (hereafter Nixon report), p. 22.
2   David Russell was the party's federal vice-president from 1990–95 and 1999–2005. He was president of the Queensland party from 1995–99 and federal president from 2005–06. Warren Truss media statement, 27 January 2012. Russell was made a Member of the Order of Australia (AM) on 26 January 2012 'for service to the National Party of Australia and to politics, to taxation law and legal education, and to the community'. – see <www.itsanhonour.gov.au>
3   Nixon report, p. 4.
4   Correspondence received, federal management committee minutes, Canberra, 16 October 1987.

21 The eye of the storm

1   *The Bulletin*, 10 November 1987.
2   Transcript, Joh Bjelke-Petersen, ABC Radio *AM*, 6 November 1987.
3   Joh Bjelke-Petersen paper, *Joh for Canberra*, November 1987.
4   Robert Sparkes, presidential report to Queensland National Party annual conference, Townsville, 6 November 1987.
5   Motions for closed session, Queensland National Party annual conference, Townsville, 6 November 1987.

6   Transcript, Robert Sparkes, Queensland National Party annual conference, Townsville, 6 November 1987.
7   Transcript, Robert Sparkes press conference, Townsville, 7 November 1987.
8   Stuart McDonald letter to Robert Sparkes, 27 November 1987.
9   Joh Bjelke-Petersen, ABC Radio news, Brisbane, 9 November 1987.
10 Transcript, Robert Sparkes press conference, Townsville, 8 November 1987.
11 *The Canberra Times*, 12 November 1987.

22 Joh's last campaign
1   *The Courier-Mail*, Brisbane, 25 November 1987.
2   Transcript, Mike Ahern news conference, Brisbane, 24 November 1987.
3   *The Canberra Times*, 27 November 1987.
4   *The Courier-Mail*, Brisbane, editorial, 27 November 1987.
5   Transcript, Joh Bjelke-Petersen doorstop interview, Kingaroy, 29 November 1987.
6   In Sinclair media release, Canberra, 29 November 1987.
7   *The Canberra Times*, 1 December 1987.
8   Joh Bjelke-Petersen media statement, Brisbane, 3 June 1987.
9   See also Hughes, Government and Politics 1985–1999, p. 109.
10 *The Sydney Morning Herald*, 2 December 1987.

23 Nixon does his job
1   This and following extracts are from Nixon report.
2   Minutes, federal council, Canberra, 29–31 July 1988.
3   National Party of Australia federal constitution, July 1988, clauses 44–47, 53.

Epilogue
1   Hughes, Government and Politics 1985–1999, pp. 324, 325.
2   *The Sydney Morning Herald*, obituaries, 9 August 2006.
3   Hughes, Government and Politics 1985–1999, pp. 113–19.
4   Minor parties won four seats. The Legislative Assembly at the time comprised 89 seats. Electoral Commission Queensland – see <wwwe.ecq.qld.gov.au>
5   Ian Sinclair was speaker from March to August 1998, when he retired after 34 years and nine months as the Member for New England, the ninth longest serving member of the House of Representatives. 43rd edition, Parliamentary Handbook, 2011 – see online at <www.aph.gov.au>. John Howard returned to the Liberal leadership and was Australia's 25th prime minister from March 1996 until December 2007.
6   Economic and budget comments by the Treasurer, Paul Keating. See also reports on the 1986/87 cabinet papers, *The Australian*, 1 and 2 January 2014.
7   *The Australian*, 15 March 1993.
8   Ian Sinclair, ABC Television, *A Country Road – The Nationals*, 2 December 2014.

SELECT BIBLIOGRAPHY AND FURTHER READING

Party records held at The Page Research Centre Library
PG2717 – Documents from the Federal Secretariat, National Party of Australia:
Box 4, item 20 – agendas, minutes, correspondence, federal council, March 1987, vol 1
Box 4, item 21 – agendas, minutes, correspondence, federal council, 1987, vol 2
Box 7, items 43, 44 – agendas, minutes, correspondence, including Northern Territory affiliation record, federal management committee, 1985–87 and 1985–97
Box 18, item 156 – federal National Party policy objectives, 1987
Box 18, item 157 – National Party of Australia, policy summary, 1987; election, 1987
Box 39, item 357 – Ralph Hunt committee review of role and functions of federal secretariat, 1987–88
Box 48, item 464 – legal advice and opinions, 1987–92
Box 69, item 625 – Queensland National Party conference agenda and minutes, 1987
Box 57, items 600, 601 – Northern Territory, 1987–90
Box 81, item 855 – newspaper cuttings, federal director, Joh for Canberra, Coalition split, 1987
Box 81, items 856, 857 – newspaper cuttings, media transcripts, media releases, correspondence, Joh for Canberra, 1987, vols 1 and 2

Other party records
Agendas, resolutions and minutes of select state party conferences, councils and executive meetings, 1980 to 1988
Australian Country Party Association Constitution, March 1926
Federal parliamentary leaders' speeches to state annual conferences, federal councils and election campaign launch, 1987
Federal party platforms, policies and policy objectives, 1984–87
National Party of Australia Constitution, 1982, 1987, 1988
National Party of Australia – Queensland Constitution, 1987
The Future: A Report by The Committee of Review into the Future Direction of the National Party of Australia, federal secretariat, Canberra, 1988

Select national and regional newspaper clippings and radio and television transcripts as identified in Notes

Secondary sources and further reading
ABC Television, *A Country Road: The Nationals*, 25 November, 2 & 9 December 2014
ABC Television, *Dynasties*, episode 6, 'The Anthonys', 14 December 2004
ABC Television, *The Howard Years*, 2008
Aitkin, DA, *The Country Party in New South Wales: A Study of Organisaton and Survival*, Australian National University Press, Canberra, 1972
Australian Dictionary of Biography online – <www.adb.online.anu.edu.au>
Australian Electoral Commission, *Electoral Pocketbook*, Canberra, 1988, 1991, 1994, 1996, 1999
Botterill, LC & Cockfield, G (eds), *The National Party: Prospects for the Great Survivors*, Allen & Unwin, Sydney, 2009
Browning, AR (ed), *House of Representatives Practice*, 2nd edition, Australian Government Publishing Service, Canberra, 1989
Costar, B & Woodward, D (eds), *Country to National*, Allen & Unwin, Sydney, 1985
Commonwealth Parliamentary Debates, House of Representatives and Senate, Canberra
Davey, P, *Ninety Not Out: The Nationals 1920–2010*, UNSW Press, Sydney, 2010
Davey, P, *Politics in the Blood: The Anthonys of Richmond*, UNSW Press, Sydney, 2008
Davey, P, *The Country Party Prime Ministers: Their Trials and Tribulations*, Dobson's Printing, Sydney, 2011
Davey, P, *The Nationals: The Progressive, Country and National Party in New South Wales 1919 to 2006*, The Federation Press, Sydney, 2006
Davey, P (ed) *The Page Review*, vol 4, no 1, Canberra, June 2008
Department of the Parliamentary Library, *Parliamentary Handbook of the Commonwealth of Australia*, Canberra, 25th edition 1991, 28th edition 1999, 30th edition 2005, and online – see <www.aph.gov.au/library/handbook/>
Ellis, UR, *A History of the Australian Country Party*, Melbourne University Press, 1963
Ellis, UR, *The Country Party: A Political and Social History of the Party in New South Wales*, FW Cheshire, Melbourne, 1958
Fadden, AW, *They Called Me Artie: The Memoirs of Sir Arthur Fadden*, The Jacaranda Press, Brisbane, 1969
Gallagher, P, *Faith & Duty: The John Anderson Story*, Random House Australia, Sydney, 2006
Golding, P, *Black Jack McEwen: Political Gladiator*, Melbourne University Press, 1996
Graham, BD, *The Formation of the Australian Country Parties*, Australian National University Press, Canberra, 1966
Heatley, A, *The Territory Party: The Northern Territory Country Liberal Party 1974–1998*, Charles Darwin University Press, Darwin, 1998
Howard, J, *Lazarus Rising*, HarperCollins Australia, Sydney, 2010
Hughes CA, *A Handbook of Australian Government and Politics 1965–1974*, Australian National University Press, Canberra, 1977
Hughes CA, *A Handbook of Australian Government and Politics 1975–1984*, Australian National University Press, Canberra, Sydney, 1987
Hughes CA, *A Handbook of Australian Government and Politics 1985–1999*, The Federation Press, Sydney, 2002
Hughes CA & Graham BD, *A Handbook of Australian Government and Politics 1890–1964*, Australian National University Press, Canberra, 1968

Select bibliography and further reading

Layman, L & Duncan, W (eds), *Blood Nose Politics: A Centenary History of the Western Australian National Party 1913–2013*, The National Party of Australia (WA) Inc., Perth, 2013

Nixon, P, *An Active Journey: The Peter Nixon Story*, Connor Court Publishing, Melbourne, 2012

Page E, *Truant Surgeon: The Inside Story of Forty Years of Australian Political Life*, Angus and Robertson, Sydney, 1963

Rees P, *The Boy from Boree Creek: The Tim Fischer Story*, Allen & Unwin, Sydney, 2001

INDEX

The National Party at its various levels went through several name changes during the period covered by this book. I have referred to the federal body as the National Party of Australia or NPA throughout, to avoid confusion, and the state parties under the names of the states. Cross-references to the National Party of Australia and the relevant state bodies have been made from the other names. 'JBP' in subheadings refers to Joh Bjelke-Petersen. 'QNP' is Queensland National Party.

7.30 Report, Robert Sparkes on, 54, 58–59

Abbott, Tony, becomes prime minister, 1
Aboriginal lands in Queensland, 9
Adermann, Evan, 275
Agars, Neville, 192
Ahern, Mike
   becomes premier, 264
   cabinet recommendations quashed by JBP, 217
   elected QNP leader, 259–260
   JBP attempts to sack, 251–255
   loses premiership to Russell Cooper, 274
   moves leadership be declared vacant, 259
Ahern NP government in Queensland, 274
Albury rally, 64–65
Allen, Bill, 44, 124
Anderson, John, on early Joh campaign, 29
Anderson, Julian, 18, 183–184, 192
Ansett, Bob, 135
Anthony, Doug
   as Minister for Trade, 97
   becomes deputy PM, 8–9
   becomes party leader, 24
   condemns Joh for PM campaign, 52
   dissolves and re-forms Coalition, 23, 26
   flat tax policy, 32
   in Opposition under Whitlam, 16
   on QNP, 57–58
   resigns from parliament, 10
   retires from politics, 23
Aurukun, federal intervention in, 9
Austin, Brian, 11, 253–254
Australia Card Bill, 129, 246
Australian Capital Territory, candidates for, 166–167, 169, 171–172
Australian Country Party *see* National Party of Australia
Australian Electoral Commission, 238–239
Australian Farmers' Federal Organisation, 19–20
Australian Labor Party
   electoral losses, 266
   improves election chances, 108–109
   Joh campaigns raise support for, 60
   Sinclair attacks policies of, 161–163
   under Rudd and Gillard, 1
   wins third term, 174

Barambah electorate lost to Citizens' Electoral Council, 267
Bathgate, Liam, 50–51
Baume, Peter, 96, 175
Beale, Julian, 96
Beattie Labor government in Queensland, 275–276
Bellino, Vincenzo, 241
Bicentennial celebrations, 174
Bicentennial Road Development Program, 145–146
Bjelke-Petersen, Flo
   as Senate candidate, 131

Index

becomes NPA deputy Senate leader, 215
campaigns for NT Nationals, 43
fails to attend QNP meeting, 98
retains Senate endorsement, 149
view of Joh campaign, 107
votes against policy motion, 115
Bjelke-Petersen, Joh
Albury rally, 64–65
as Premier of Queensland, 134, 226, 251–255, 260–262
author given gift by, 2
background of, 3–4
Canberra move planned by, 127–128
Canberra press conference, 166–167
Dalby Young Nationals meeting, 115–116
electoral popularity, 42–43, 47, 60, 89, 136
federal ambitions, 11–12, 122–123
federal council addressed by, 76, 78–79
goals of, 73
Howard negotiates with, 137–138
interviews with, 34–35, 138–139, 264–265
Japan trip, 57
Joh Independents funded by, 171–172
knighthood granted to, 11
McLachlan meets with, 135
Morgan poll criticised by, 70
Narrabri rally, 91
New Right supports, 13
NPA criticised by, 205
on calls to resign, 216
on early election, 130
on Hawke, 130, 167
on Joh for... campaigns, 242–243, 265
on New National party, 91–93
on policies, 7, 115
on Sinclair, 34, 40, 42, 65, 108, 165
on Southport by-election, 159
opposes Coalition in Opposition, 188
post-election recriminations, 178–179
predicts leadership spill, 158–159
QNP conference speech, 241–242
QNP council meets with, 61–62, 223–224
QNP ordered to quit Coalition by, 89–90
QNP revolts against, 254–259
relations with media, 183
resigns as premier, 263–264
response to federal support for, 41
Sinclair meets with, 44, 116
Sparkes falls out with, 217, 220–221, 224–227, 240–241, 250, 257–259, 265
Stone falls out with, 249
tax policy, 31–33, 142–146
Victorian National Party threatened by, 157–158
Bjelke-Petersen government in Queensland, 217–218, 251, 254–255
see also Bjelke-Petersen, Joh
Black, Philip, 29, 172
Blaxland electorate, Joh National candidate runs in, 169
Bligh Labor government in Queensland, 274–275
Blunt, Charles
at executive meeting, 110
in shadow ministry, 97, 208
loses seat to ALP, 275
moves to block JBP policy initiatives, 114–115
replaces Sinclair as leader, 275
runs for deputy leadership, 186
Borbidge Coalition government in Queensland, 274
Boswell, Ron
absent for policy motion, 115
appeals for NP unity, 51–52
as Senate candidate, 131, 149
doubts over Hervey Bay resolutions, 56
withdraws from Senate leadership race, 214–215
Braithwaite, Ray
at executive meeting, 110
at QNP state conference, 245
critical of QNP resolutions, 51, 56
Howard replaces in shadow cabinet, 96
in shadow ministry, 94, 208–209
runs for leadership, 186–187
Sparkes criticised by, 183
Sparkes fails to contact, 46
tax policy, 88
Brisbane City Council elections, 266
Brown, Neil, 96, 183
Brownhill, David, 15

Bruce, Stanley, 5
Bruce Nationalist government, Coalition in, 21
Bruxner, Mick, 24
Burns, Tom, 8
Buttenshaw, Ernest, 24

Cameron, Archie, 21–22
Cameron, Ian
  at executive meeting, 110
  in shadow ministry, 208–209
  meeting details leaked by, 118–126
  runs for deputy leadership, 186
  supports re-forming Coalition, 188
Cameron, Rod, 89
Campbell, Mendy 86
Campbell, Walter, 253, 259–260, 262
Canberra *see* Australian Capital Territory
Canberra Lakeside International meeting, 71–73
Capricornia federal electorate, 132
Caton, Hiram, 240, 247
Cessnock, NPA policy launched in, 160–164
Chappell, Greg, 135
Chappell, Ray, 159–160
Citizens' Electoral Council, 267
Clifford, John, 157
Coalition of NPA with Liberal Party of Australia *see also* Liberal Party of Australia; National Party of Australia
  break-up of, 15–16, 101–117
  effect of break on election results, 181–182
  history of, 19–30
  in Opposition, 16, 27, 185, 210–214
  leads Hawke government in polls, 18
  moves to re-form, 192–193
  news of QNP break strategy leaked, 119
  Nixon report on, 266–273
  NPA attitudes to, 19–22, 187–188
  QNP abandons, 27–28, 89
  QNP critical of, 50, 200
  QNP moves to leave, 80
  re-formation of, 196–209, 216, 276
  Sinclair–Howard agreement on, 94–95
  tensions within, 14
  wins government, 276
Cobb, Michael, Joh National candidate runs against, 169
Collard, Stan
  as Senate candidate, 131
  as shadow minister, 94
  at executive meeting, 110
  declares support for Coalition, 61
  doubts over Hervey Bay resolutions, 56
  Howard replaces in shadow cabinet, 96
  Katter senior criticises treatment of, 182
  loses Senate endorsement, 142–143, 147–154, 220
  member of federal management committee, 18
  on Hervey Bay resolutions, 46, 52
Colston, Mal, 8
Committee of Review into the Future Direction of the NPA, 228–239, 266–273, 277
Commonwealth Electoral Act, 238
Cooper, Russell, 274
Copeman, Charles, 135
Corbett, Jim, 118
Country and Progressive National Party, 25 *see also* Queensland National Party
Country Liberal Party of NT
  affiliation status of, 68–70, 75–76
  delegates from, 17
  disaffiliation confirmed, 191–192
  links to Joh campaigns, 35–37
  requests reaffiliation talks, 237–238
  Senate seat won by, 177
  senator from made whip, 215
Country Party *see* National Party of Australia
Country Progressive Party, 25 *see also* National Party of Australia; Queensland National Party
Cowan, Bruce, 63, 101, 198
Cowan, George, endorsed for Senate ticket, 149
Cowan, Hendy, 80, 84, 210–211
Crooke, Ken, 77, 137

Dalby Young Nationals meeting, 115–116
Davey, Paul (author)
  at AEC hearing, 239
  comments on JBP, 86–87
  coordinates election campaign, 133
  discussions with, 51

Index

parliamentary duties, 216–217
policy speech printed by, 160–161
reaction to Joh campaign, 2–3
review proposed by, 232–233
Deakin, Alfred, Coalition under, 21
Dempster, Quentin, 58–59
Drake-Brockman, Tom, 17, 66–67

Eggleton, Tony, 216
Election '87 Policy Summary, 134, 161
elections *see* federal elections; Northern Territory elections; NSW elections; Queensland elections
Electoral Act, Joh Independents in contravention of, 172
Everingham, Paul, 36
Ewart, Heather, 41

Fadden, Arthur, 22, 25
Fancher, Wiley, 9
Farmers and Settlers' Association, 24
Farrell, John, 167, 171
federal elections
    1919: first ACP members elected, 19
    1922: ACP holds 14 seats, 21
    1929: ALP wins under Scullin, 21
    1932: UAP wins under Lyons, 21
    1943: ALP wins under Curtin, 22–23
    1949: Coalition wins under Menzies, 23
    1972: Coalition splits following loss, 23
    1974: Coalition restored after, 16, 23
    1975: Coalition wins under Fraser, 9, 23
    1983: ALP wins under Hawke, 10, 23
    1984: NPA fails to win metropolitan seats, 14–15
    1987: ALP wins under Hawke, 175–176
    1987: campaigns for, 127
    1987: disaster for NPA, 174–176
    1987: Maranoa held for NPA, 126
    1987: poor showing by Joh Independents, 172–173
    1990: disaster for NPA, 275
    1990: Maranoa held for NPA, 126
    1993: NPA recovers two seats, 276
    1996: Coalition wins under Howard, 276
    1996: NPA recovers two seats, 276
    2013: Coalition wins under Abbott, 1
Field, Albert, 7–8
Fife, Wal, 31, 169
Fightback! package, 175, 276
Fischer, Tim
    at executive meeting, 110
    becomes NPA leader, 275–276
    in shadow ministry, 97, 208
    on Albury rally, 64–65
    runs for deputy leadership, 186
Fisher, Peter, 101, 169, 172–173
Fisher federal electorate, NPA loses, 176
Fitzgerald, Tony, 217
Fitzgerald inquiry, 217–218, 241, 255
flat tax policy, 31–33
Four Corners program, 217
Fraser, Malcolm, 9–10, 84
Fraser Coalition government, 7–9
Fraser Island, sand mining banned on, 9
Free Trade – Protectionist Coalition, 21
fuel deregulation policy, 144–145
Fuller, George, 24
Future, The (Nixon report), 268–273

Gardiner, Jenny, 160, 163–164, 171, 179–180
Garms, Ann, as Senate candidate, 131, 149–150
Goanna Press Pty Ltd, 160–161
Gorton, John, 3, 5
Goss, Wayne, 274
Goss Labor government in Queensland, 274
Grassroots 2000 movement, 31
Graziers' Association, 24
Greiner coalition Government in NSW, 266
Groom electorate, 134–135, 267
Gunn, Bill
    announces leadership contest, 254
    as deputy premier, 217, 259, 264
    JBP attempts to sack, 251–255
    rift with JBP, 249–250

Hancock, Lang, 4
Hare, John, 69, 76
Hatton, Steve, 36–37, 43
Hawke, Bob
    announces early election, 129–130
    elected prime minister, 10

JBP's relations with, 128
Keating replaces, 276
on Coalition break-up, 109–110
on election timing, 89
returned as prime minister, 174
Hawke Labor government
election timing, 89
failure of Opposition to damage, 275
JBP attacks, 10–12
Opposition under, 10
trails Coalition in polls, 18
Hayden, Bill, 13, 40, 218
Heaslip, Grant, 36, 69, 237–238
Herbert federal electorate, 132
Hewson, John, 175, 276
Hicks, Noel
as party whip, 107
at executive meeting, 110
at special parliamentary meeting, 102–103
notice of meeting given by, 186
runs for deputy leadership, 186
Hinkler federal electorate, 176
Hinze, Russ
announces leadership contest, 254
confronts JBP on premiership, 226
on Queensland election campaign, 180–181
runs for QNP leader, 259
support for JBP's premiership, 221
Holm, Charles
at JBP–Sinclair meeting, 44
at Maranoa meeting, 124
author's contacts with, 174
in Bellino photograph, 241
JBP meets with, 116
knighthood granted to, 165
letter to post-election meeting, 189–191, 194–195
on campaign speech, 127–128
proposed for NPA review committee, 235
qualified support for Sinclair, 202–203
re-elected QNP senior vice-president, 247
runs for federal presidency, 85
strategy meetings with, 84
supports JBP as premier, 221
supports NT Nationals, 39
Holt, Harold, 5

House of Representatives Practice, 59–60
Howard, John
as Liberal leader, 183
at Liberal party meeting, 203–204
Coalition formally ended by, 105–106
Coalition re-established by, 196–201, 205
Coalition supported by, 16
concern over Nationals split, 41–42
JBP challenged by, 33
Joh campaigns condemned by, 52
non-Coalition arrangements, 96, 113–114
NPA clause changes unacceptable to, 104–105
on break-up of Coalition, 101–102
on JBP, 105–106, 264
Peacock replaces as leader, 275
post-election recriminations, 179
post-election shadow ministry, 206–208
reservations about re-forming Coalition, 202
Sinclair's relations with, 23, 77, 189
Sparkes and JBP negotiate with, 137–138
tax policy, 141
tries to save Coalition, 91, 93–96
Hughes, Billy, Page forces resignation of, 5
Hughes, Colin, 172
Hunt, Ralph
as shadow minister for Primary Industry, 97
at executive meeting, 110
at Narrabri rally, 29
backs Lloyd for deputy position, 187
Bicentennial Road Development Program, 146
chairs review into federal secretariat, 232
declines to stand again for deputy leader, 184
Joh National candidate runs against, 169
on NPA management committee, 18
on NPA review committee, 234
primary industry policy, 129
retirement plans, 207–208
Sinclair's discussions with, 50–51

Index

independent Country Party, 25
industrial relations policy, 82, 128–129

Japan, JBP's trip to, 57
Jennings, Doug, 159
Joh for Canberra campaign
  blamed for election defeat, 175
  Collard on, 147–148
  election plans, 130–133
  emphasis of shifts to Senate, 156–157
  JBP's reflections on, 242–243
  Joh for PM campaign switched to, 63–64
  reasons for failure, 278
  review of called for, 244
  'termination' of, 138
Joh for PM campaign, 45–56, 63–64, 265
  see also Joh for Canberra campaign
Joh Independent candidates, 168–173

Katter, Bob senior
  critical of Joh campaign, 91, 93
  declines to run for deputy leader, 186
  fails to attend party meeting, 198
  joins NPA executive, 111
  on Collard losing endorsement, 150
  on confusion, 88
  on Sinclair's unpopularity in Queensland, 202–203
  post-election recriminations, 181
  supports re-formed Coalition, 206
Keating, Paul, 29, 276
Kelly, Paul, 138–139
Kennett, Jeff, 90
Khemlani loans affair, 8–9
Kilgariff, Bernie, 36
Kippin, Vicki, endorsed for Senate ticket, 149
Knox, William, 251

Lambie, Jacqui, quits PUP, 2
Laming, Bruce, 131, 150
Lane, Don, 11
Lazarus, Glenn, quits PUP, 2
Leard, John, 135
Lehmann, Neil, 172
Leichhardt federal electorate, 132
Lewis, Terry, 218, 255
Lexcen, Ben, 135, 170
Liberal National Party of Queensland, 275

Liberal Party of Australia *see also* Coalition of NPA with Liberal Party of Australia
  election campaign, 175
  Joh campaign takes votes from, 136
  leadership changes, 275–276
  loses seats in Queensland, 11, 177
  tax policies, 32, 141
  votes to re-form Coalition, 203–204
Liberal–Country Party of Victoria, 25
Lingard, Kevin, 255
Lloyd, Bruce
  at executive meeting, 110
  in shadow ministry, 97, 208
  Joh National candidate runs against, 169
  promotes re-forming of Coalition, 205
  runs for deputy leader, 186–187
Lyons, Joe, 5, 21

MacDonald, James, 212–213
MacDonald, Peter, 131–132, 170
Mackerras, Malcolm, 108–109
Macphee, Ian, 96
management committees, 45–46
Maranoa electorate, 122–125, 135
Martin, Ray, 135
Maybury, Fred
  author's contacts with, 143, 146
  co-ordinates Joh campaigns, 89, 127–128
  on Southport by-election, 159
  refuses federal election aid, 133–134
McCarthy, Thelma and Bill, 160
McDonald, Stuart
  as federal NPA president, 133
  at AEC hearing, 239
  at QNP state conference, 246
  author reprimanded by, 87
  letter to Sparkes, 240
  post-election meeting managed by, 189, 191, 194
  proposed for NPA review committee, 235
  reconciliation talks with NT parties, 238
  response to Holm and Sparkes, 194–195, 248
  runs for federal president, 85
  supports review proposal, 233–234
McEwen, John

as Minister for Trade, 97
becomes ACP leader, 22
brinkmanship tactics, 5
establishes NPA in NT, 36
expelled from Victorian UCP, 24–25
grooms Sinclair, 16
proposes federal secretariat, 3
McGauran, Julian
  as Senate candidate, 157
  at party meeting, 198
  elected to Senate, 169, 176, 185
McGauran, Peter, 111, 157–158, 186
McIntyre, Jean, 18, 86–87, 192
McKechnie, Peter, 253–254
McKerrow, Shirley
  as federal NPA president, 17, 71
  discussions with, 50
  on legal status of resolutions, 53
  on NT Nationals, 74–75
  on Peter Ross-Edwards, 158
  Peter Nixon approached by, 83–84
  press conference, 37–38
  strategy meetings, 84
  voting rights checked by, 66–70
McLachlan, Ian, 135–136, 219
McLean, Allen, 21
McMahon, William, 5, 23
McVeigh, Tom
  appointed agent-general to London, 266–267
  corrects Sinclair vote report, 200
  Moppett critical of, 203
  on approach to McLachlan, 136
  on full meeting clause, 104
  on Hervey Bay resolutions, 51
  on Joh campaigns, 178
  on possibility of sitting as Independent, 205–206
  on Sinclair leadership, 99–100, 127, 134–135
  withdraws from Coalition, 62–63
McWilliams, William, 20
Menzies, Robert, 5, 21–22
Menzies governments, 21–23
Millar, Clarrie, 97–98, 115, 145, 206
Milliner, Bertie, 7–8
Moppett, Doug
  at federal council meeting, 73–74
  condemns Hervey Bay resolutions, 54
  condemns Joh for PM campaign, 52

JBP criticised by, 33
QNP criticised by, 203
supports co-operation with Liberals, 113–114
Morgan Gallup polls, 60, 70, 182
Morning Bulletin, The, 148
Mort, Geoff, 50–51
Moses, John, JBP interview, 264–265
Muntz, Geoff, 253–254
Murray, Wal, 113

Narrabri rally, 29, 91
National Country Party *see* National Party of Australia
National Joh for PM Committee, 48
National Outlook, Sparkes article, 74
National Party of Australia – Northern Territory *see* NT National Party
National Party of Australia (NPA) *see also* Coalition of NPA with Liberal Party of Australia; NSW National Party; Queensland National Party; South Australian National Party; Victorian National Party; Western Australian National Party
  1987 election results, 172–173
  attitudes to Coalition, 19
  author's role in, 2–3
  brinkmanship tactics, 5–6
  camaraderie in, 2
  Coalition re-established by, 196–209
  Committee of Review into the Future Direction of the NPA, 228–239, 266–273
  discussion paper on goals, 77
  election preparations, 129–130, 132–134
  electoral support for, 177
  federal autonomy confirmed, 193
  federal constitution, 26–27, 82–83, 271–272
  federal council meetings, 57–58, 72–73
  federal management committee, 17–18, 37–38, 189–194
  federal secretariat, 3
  formation of, 20
  implements review recommendations, 277
  Joh campaigns opposed by, 6
  Joh Independents run against, 168–173

non-Coalition arrangements, 110–111
parliamentary wing of, 88, 102–103, 106–107, 114–115
policies, 32, 97–98
regroups after Joh campaign, 276
senators from, 151, 153
Sinclair not supported by, 40–41
state party affiliations, 45–46, 53–55
National Press Club, Sinclair addresses, 116–117
New National party, 91–92
New Right movement, 13
Newman LNP government, Queensland, 4
Newspoll, on support for Joh campaign, 42–43
Nicklin, Francis, 25
Nixon, Peter
  agreement drawn up with, 168–169
  as negotiator, 83–84
  moves to re-form Coalition, 192–193
  NPA review chaired by, 233–234, 237
  report delivered by, 266–274
Nixon report, 268–273
Northern Tablelands by-election, 159–160
Northern Territory Country Liberal Party *see* Country Liberal Party of NT
Northern Territory elections, 1987: NT Nationals win one seat, 36–37, 43
Northern Territory electorate, 176–177
NPA *see* National Party of Australia
NSW elections, 24, 28
NSW National Party
  amends motions at federal council, 79–80
  asks for draft NPA review committee report, 268
  Coalition supported by, 28–29, 61
  electoral support for, 177
  federal council proposals from, 230
  history of, 24
  JBP challenged by, 33
  Joh campaigns opposed by, 6, 158
  Liberals co-operate with, 113–114
  response to Hervey Bay resolutions, 54
  Sinclair supported by, 28–29, 61
  urban seats not contested by, 14–15
NT National Party
  applies for affiliation with NPA, 67–68, 74–75, 189, 191–192

applies to register as political party, 238–239
JBP campaigns for, 172
links to Joh campaigns, 35–39
QNP reduces support for, 247
wins one seat in NT elections, 43

O'Regan, Bevan, 29, 168, 171–172
O'Sullivan, Larry, 171

Page, Earle
  as caretaker PM, 21
  as Country Party leader, 20–21
  brinkmanship tactics, 5
  enters Coalition with Lyons, 21
Palmer, Clive, 1, 3–4
Palmer United Party, formation of, 2
Paterson, John
  joins NPA review committee, 234
  motion on meeting dates, 194
  on NT Nationals, 192
  opposed to Coalition in Opposition, 185, 188, 211–212
Peacock, Andrew
  as deputy Liberal leader, 183
  as Liberal leader, 10, 23, 275
  as shadow Treasurer, 196
  does not recontest leadership, 276
  replaced by Neil Brown, 96
  rumours of Howard challenge by, 175
  sacked as foreign affairs spokesman, 90
Pendarvis, Jay, 135
pensioner assets test, 144
Petrich, James, 38–39
Premiers' Conference, 128
Progressive Party, 24 *see also* NSW National Party
Protectionist – Free Trade – Tariff Reform Coalition, 21
Pullar, Phillip, Joh National candidate runs against, 169
Punch, Leon, 28

Queensland elections
  1956: Coalition improves position, 25
  1957: Coalition victory, 25
  1983: QNP forms majority government, 11
  1986: QNP increases majority, 11
  1989: ALP victory, 274

1996: Coalition victory, 274
1998: ALP victory, 274
2012: LNP victory, 275
Queensland National Party (QNP) *see also* Bjelke-Petersen, Joh; Joh for Canberra campaign; Joh for PM campaign; Sparkes, Robert
  ALP wins government from, 274
  annual conferences, 12–13, 19, 240–251
  anti-Coalition motions passed by, 80, 82
  Coalition abandoned by, 27–28, 89
  coalitions in state government, 25
  constitution of, 55–56
  details of meeting leaked, 118–126
  electoral support for, 177–178, 266–267
  federal aspirations of, 66
  federal council proposals, 229–232
  federal election aid refused by, 133–134
  Hervey Bay meeting, 43, 45–56
  Howard unpopular with, 10
  industrial relations policy, 82
  JBP's relations with, 61–62, 221–222, 262
  leadership contest, 254–262
  moves to disaffiliate, 52–54
  non-attendance at post-election meeting, 189–191
  non-attendance at Sinclair press conference, 165–166
  NT Nationals supported by, 39
  plans to run candidates against NPA, 168
  post-election meeting, 200
  pressures Sinclair to accept tax policy, 150–152
  Senate candidates, 131
  sense of disaster in, 218
  Sinclair unpopular with, 10, 98–99, 140, 202
  suspect donations alleged, 241
  tax policies, 33, 56, 82, 142–146
  wins majority government, 10
Queensland Speaks project, 10

Rabuka, Colonel, 218
Reid, George, 21
road funding policy, 145–146

Robinson, Ian, 63, 101, 115, 186
Rogers, Hugh, 17
Ross-Edwards, Peter, 157–158
Russell, David
  as federal NPA president, 10
  in *Queensland Speaks*, 37–38
  joins NPA review committee, 234
  Liberals win seat from, 267
  Sinclair meets with, 44

Scullin, Jim, 21
Senate
  attendance of NPA Senators, 151, 153
  campaign plans for, 156–157
  Joh National candidates for, 169–170
  NPA leadership positions, 187, 214–215
Sharp, John, 106, 114–115, 186, 208
Sheil, Glen
  as minister for two days, 256
  as NPA Senate whip, 215
  as Senate candidate, 131
  votes against policy motion, 115
  wins Senate seat, 185
Simpson, Gordon, 255–256
Sinclair, Ian
  Ahern supported by, 261
  as deputy leader of the Opposition, 10
  as parliamentary party leader, 15–17, 23, 39–42, 102–105, 108, 186–187
  at Dalby Young Nationals meeting, 115–116
  at executive meeting, 110
  at National Press Club, 116–117
  at post-election meetings, 185–186, 190, 192–193
  at QNP state conference, 246–247
  at WA NP meeting, 212
  briefed on NPA review committee report, 268
  campaigns in Queensland, 133–134
  Coalition formally ended by, 106
  Coalition re-established by, 197–200, 202, 205
  considers approaching Privileges Committee, 60
  election policy speech, 155, 161
  electoral support for, 89
  federal council meetings, 50–51, 73, 76–78

Index

forgery allegations, 17
Howard negotiates with, 91, 93–96, 104, 196–198
in shadow ministry, 96–97, 208
JBP blamed for election defeat by, 174
JBP meets with, 44, 116
Joh National candidate runs against, 169
Lloyd backed for deputy by, 187
McDonald supported by, 85
member of federal management committee, 17
no confidence motion in, 222–223
non-Coalition arrangements, 113–114
Northern Tablelands by-election campaign, 160
on Collard losing endorsement, 150, 152
on Hunt, 184
on JBP's resignation as premier, 264
on Joh campaigns, 33–34, 60–61, 277–278
on NPA in Coalition, 82
on NT Nationals, 74–75, 191–192
on post-election issues, 109
on QNP resolutions, 52
on QNP split from Coalition, 89–91
on QNP tax policy, 146, 150–153
over-optimism of, 86
post-election recriminations by, 178–179
press conferences, 37–38
QNP blamed for loss of influence by, 98
QNP hostile to, 50, 140
QNP leaders meet with, 165–166
reaction to Howard negotiations with JBP, 140
replaced by Blunt, 275
review proposal backed by, 233
strategy meetings, 84
Slipper, Peter, on Joh for Canberra campaign, 148
Smith, Dick, 135
Smith, Ewart, 246
Snedden, Billy, 16, 23, 26
Solomons, Adrian, 69
South Australian National Party
fails to pay affiliation fees, 67
motion on Coalition, 77
opposes Coalition in Opposition, 30, 80, 206–207, 210
poor showing in 1987 election, 177
proposals to federal council, 231
splits over coalitions, 25
urban seat candidates lose deposits, 14
Southport by-election, 159
Sparkes, Robert
anti-Coalition motion defeated by, 28
appears on *7.30 Report*, 54
attacks Hawke government, 12–13
author's contacts with, 2
changes tack of campaign, 63–64
concerned over QNP split, 37–38
election result defended by, 219–220
extraordinary QNP meeting called by, 254–256
federal council meetings, 72–73, 79–80
Howard negotiates with, 137–138
intimidatory tactics, 57–60
JBP falls out with, 217–221, 224–227, 240–241, 250, 257–259
JBP meets with, 76, 116
launches QNP election slogan, 141
McLachlan meets, 135
moves for special meeting of federal council, 193–194
NPA members critical of, 182–183
on alternate candidates, 71, 73–74
on campaign donations, 13
on election timing, 128
on goals of QNP, 155–156
on New National party, 92–94
on NT Nationals, 74–75
on pensioner assets test, 144
on QNP running candidates against NPA, 168
on threat to withdraw from Coalition, 86
proposes members for NPA review committee, 234
QNP meets with, 61–62
QNP members ordered to quit Coalition by, 89–90
QNP post-election meeting, 189–191, 194–195, 200
QNP re-elects as president, 247
QNP state conference, 243–250
reaction to Cameron leak, 119–120, 123–125

reaction to Sinclair speech, 164–165
Sinclair attacked by, 140, 151
Stone put forward for leadership by, 179
strategy meetings with, 84
view of federal council, 18
State and Territory National/Country parties, 190, 272 *see also under names of states and territories*
Stone, John
as candidate for NPA leader, 158–159, 179
at QNP state conference, 249
becomes NPA Senate leader, 215
fails to win Fairfax, 275
hired to develop tax policy, 131
in shadow ministry, 208–209
popularity with QNP, 245–246
runs for deputy leader, 186–187
tax policy released by, 141, 142–146
Sullivan, Vic, letter to McKerrow, 148–149
Sunday program, 91–92
superannuation tax policy, 145

Tambling, Grant, 36, 177, 191, 215
Tasmanian National Party, attempts to revive, 67
tax policy
election platform, 140–141
in campaign launch speech, 161
Liberal confusion over, 175
QNP calls for change in, 82
QNP reaction to Sinclair speech, 164–165
released by QNP, 142–146
state parties pressured to accept, 157–158
Territory Nationals *see* NT National Party
The Future (Nixon report), 268–273
The Morning Bulletin, 148
Thomson, David, 17

Torres Strait Islands, federal intervention in, 9
Trade portfolio, 96–97
Truss, Warren, 1, 226
Tuxworth, Ian, 36–37

Uebergang, John, 29
United Australia Party, relations with Country Party, 5

Victorian Farmers' Union *see* Victorian National Party
Victorian National Party
1987 state conference, 29–30, 89–91
attitudes to coalitions, 24–25
Coalition supported by, 29–30
electoral support for, 177
JBP threatens, 157–158
urban seat candidates lose deposits, 14

Wagga Wagga rally, 31–33
Waley, Jim, 91–92
Walker, Frank, 17
Warburton, Neville, 251
West, Katherine, 135
Western Australian National Party
electoral support for, 177
moves anti-Coalition motion, 80–81
opposed to Coalition in Opposition, 30, 185, 188–189, 210–214
proposals to federal council, 230–231
splits in, 25, 66–67
Whitlam Labor government, 7–8, 16
Whykes, Les, 247
Willesee program, 64
Willis, Ralph, 128–129
Wilson, Alexander, 22
World Today, 155
Wran Labor government, NSW, raises Sinclair allegations, 17

Young National Party, 29, 115–116, 183–184